The Great Recession

Profit cycles, economic crisis
A Marxist view

by

Michael Roberts

ISBN 978-1-4452-4408-2

Contents

My thanks go to Ian Ilett and Mick Brooks for their encouragement and constructive criticism. I also must thank the pioneering work of Alan Freeman and Andrew Kliman whose incisive contributions to Marxist economics inspired me to do this book.

There are many others in flesh and spirit who made contributions to this book. I want to thank them too and have made every effort to credit or reference those who gave me an idea or an approach in various places.

Of course, all the stupidities, errors and mistakes must be laid at my door.

'Prediction can be very difficult, especially if it is about the future'
Neils Bohr

The Great Recession

The Great Recession started at the beginning of 2008 and finished in the middle of 2009. At least, that is what the US National Bureau Of Economic Research (NBER) reckons. The NBER has taken on the responsibility of pronouncing and measuring the start and end of each economic slump in the US economy.

On its measure, the Great Recession was the longest in duration and deepest in contraction that the global capitalist economy has seen since 1929-32. Indeed, it was probably worse than the Great Depression in that it had even greater global impact than the long slump of the 1930s. Capitalism has spread its tentacles to all parts of the earth in the last 80 years.

From the peak of the previous boom in capitalist growth in 2007 to the trough of the Great Recession in mid-2009, the world economy contracted by 6%. In the 30 most advanced capitalist economies that are members of the Organisation of Economic Cooperation and Development, the drop in output and income was 6.5%. If you compare global output in 2009 to where the world economy should have reached without a slump, then the loss of income is even greater, at 8% (see graphic).

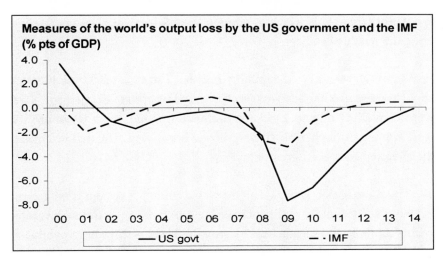

Measures of the world's output loss by the US government and the IMF (% pts of GDP)

INTRODUCTION

The Great Recession was even more damaging in its global impact. World trade during the slump fell by 25-30%, truly staggering. And the wealth of the world, as expressed in the value of businesses, real estate and financial assets, like bonds and stocks and shares, plummeted by $11trn.

The Great Recession has confirmed what those with a Marxist view of the world economy already knew. Capitalism, as a mode of production and human organisation based on profit, is subject to periodic convulsions of boom and slump. This is as much a fact of the capitalist system as evolution is a fact of nature.

The Great Recession was not an Act of God; it was not a bolt from the blue; an unpredictable tsunami. It was not a random chance event in human development. It was not a momentary blip of instability. It was not caused by some outside shock to the stable and smooth path of capitalist production, like plague, wars or climate change may have been to previous systems of human organisation.

No, the Great Recession was a product of the dynamics of the capitalist system and, as such, was subject to the laws of motion of capitalist production. Capitalist production depends on the private appropriation of value generated from human labour. Production will not be sustained if it is not profitable. This is an exceedingly wasteful and unjust way of delivering the needs of society.

Profitability is the key to capitalist health. The Great Recession came about because profitability weakened in the years prior to the slump. There were unavailing attempts to keep production going, even when profits were waning through excessive credit and borrowing. But that just made the eventual bust even greater.

The Great Recession is over. But the world capitalist system is not out of the woods. Profitability will not have been restored to sufficient levels to enable capitalism to sustain healthy growth. There is still a huge overhang of dead capital weighing down the system and profitability is still in a cycle of downturn. That will have to be liquidated in another slump, probably in the next five years.

This book aims to explain why the Great Recession happened, in what form it took and what will happen next. As such, it is divided into three parts: before, during and after the Great Recession. It takes the form of a collection of essays, some of which have been published elsewhere and some unpublished. Many of these essays were written as early as 2005-6 and were already starting to forecast the oncoming slump, eventually with a reasonable degree of accuracy. At the end of each chapter, the date when they were written is identified. I have not updated the graphics as they appear in each chapter, so the reader can see how accurate the forecasts are as the years move towards 2009. In the latest chapters, some of the key graphics are brought up to date to show their progress.

The theoretical foundation of the book is based on the analysis of capitalist production developed by Karl Marx over 150 years ago. In particular, it is argued that Marx's most important law of capitalist motion — the tendency of the rate of profit to fall as capitalists accumulate capital — is the most powerful cause of booms and slumps in capitalist economies.

But the book also tries to outline that there are other laws of motion connected with capitalism, driven by the underlying movement of profit, but nevertheless with their own cycles of development, that play a role in generating economic crises, particularly in their timing, duration and depth. Indeed, the Great Recession was so severe precisely because the troughs in all these cycles of motion coincided, a fairly rare event.

This book argues that a Marxist view can provide a scientific analysis of capitalist production, scientific in the best sense, in that it can provide a causal explanation with some predictive power on what will happen next and when. As Friedrich Engels, Marx's long-time colleague, often said, the proof of the pudding will be in the eating.

November 2009

The Great Recession

— before

"There are known knowns. These are things we know that we know. There are known unknowns. That is to say, there are things that we know we don't know. But there are also unknown unknowns. These are things we don't know that we don't know."
Donald Rumsfeld

"We are ready for any unforeseen event that may or may not occur"
George W. Bush

"The profit motive, we are constantly being told, is as old as man himself. But it is not. The profit motive as we know it is only as old as modern man".
Robert Heilbroner

Profits: the life blood

Let's keep it simple. Profits are the lifeblood of capitalism. If a capitalist investor or owner of a business cannot make a profit, he or she soon stops investing capital or employing workers to produce things or provide services. It's the law of the market, say the economists of capital.

Marxists agree with the economists. Profits are the fuel of capitalist production — without them there would be no production. But the apologists of capital make two other propositions. First, they say there is no other system of human social organisation that works. So a profit-based system will continue forever. Second, a profit-based system of production and social organisation works for the benefit of all, maybe to differing degrees, but nevertheless for all.

It is here that Marxists disagree. Marxists reckon that there are other systems of social organisation that have worked (in a fashion) before capitalism where production for profit played no role. Moreover, in the future, human beings can develop a social organisation that will work without profit-making being necessary.

And the profit system of production and organisation, far from working for all, leads to huge inequalities between rich and poor, both within nations and between nations on the globe. Moreover, the capitalist profit system actually breeds periodic crises that generate massive unemployment, poverty and war.

If profits are the lifeblood of capitalism, their size and growth must be an excellent guide to health of the capitalist system. The bigger the profit for capitalists, the more likely is the capitalist system of investment and production to thrive, at least for a while.

If that's right, what does that tell us about the current state of the world capitalist economy? Well, we can get the best figures on profits from the

PROFITS — THE LIFE BLOOD OF CAPITALISM

data provided in the US, the world's largest economy. And what do the figures show? We can most easily measure profits as share of annual national output (GDP).

This is not the correct or Marxist definition of profits in a capitalist economy. Marxists would define profits as the surplus value produced by an economy's labour force. That surplus value is the value of annual production sold in an economy minus the cost to the owners of all the businesses of paying its workers. Also, Marxists would measure profitability against the cost of investing in machinery and raw materials as well as employing workers. The US government measure of profitability merely takes profits against sales, not costs.

Even so, the official government data can still show trends in the size and growth of profits. That's helpful to judge the health of US capitalism. And what do the figures reveal? They show that US corporate profits as a share of GDP have moved up from lows in 2001 to reach near record

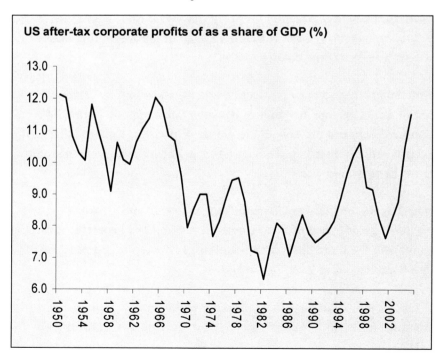

US after-tax corporate profits of as a share of GDP (%)

levels in 2005. But if you look over the much longer term, US profits are still below the levels achieved in the 'golden years' of capitalism back in the 1960s.[1]

The profits of US companies (excluding the banks and after paying tax) are about 8% of total sales this year. That's much higher than the low of around 4% achieved in November 2001, nearly equalling the low of the 1980-82 economic recession. The figure is now just below the peak of 1997 which reached 9% of sales. That peak was the highest level of profitability reached since the 1960s, when it was common for US profits to be 10-12% of sales. That was truly the 'golden age' of US (and world) capitalism).

The steady decline of the ability of capitalists to extract profits from their workforces is revealed even better when we look at the profit figures before tax.

In the 1960s, US corporations achieved annual profits of 15-20% of sales. Then came the first post-war economic slump or crisis of 1969-70, quickly followed by the worldwide economic crisis of 1974-5, which signalled the end of the 'golden age'. In 1974, profits before tax fell to just 9% of sales, half the levels achieved in the golden age. Economic recovery up to 1978 took the profit rate back to 14% but then the 'double-dip' recession of 1980-82 saw profitability fall back to an even lower level of 8%.

Capitalists in the advanced capitalist economies then launched a major offensive against the working-class to remove all the gains achieved by the labour movement during the golden age. The 1980s saw the Thatcherite battles in the UK and Reaganite ones in the US. Trade unions were shackled and crushed. The welfare state was mutilated through spending cuts and privatisation of state industries.

Even so, the profit rate only crawled up to a peak 10% in 1989 before the next recession drove it back down to 8% again. Further attacks on the wages and conditions of the labour force followed with 'downsizing' (i.e.

PROFITS — THE LIFE BLOOD OF CAPITALISM

cutting back on the labour force and driving up unemployment). This helped to take profit share back up. In the late 1990s, the hi-tech revolution also added to profitability. By 1997, before tax profits reached 13% — still way below the golden age, but a lot better than in 1980s.

But the very 'mild' economic recession of 2001 was not mild for US capitalism. Profits slumped to 6% of sales before tax. The boom since then has taken them back to nearly 12%.

But again this new peak reached this year is still below the peak of the 1990s, just in line with that of the 1980s and still below that of 1970s. And of course, it is way below the golden age levels of the 1960s.

What does this history of US profits since the 1950s tell you? It shows that the long-term health of capitalism is deteriorating. US capitalism, the rising economic power of the early 20th century, the strongest economic power of the post-war period, is now getting old. Whatever, US corporations do: cut the workforce, employ casual and temporary labour, use the latest hi-tech equipment, relocate to cheaper places around the globe, try to protect their profits with tariffs and trade restrictions, it seems that they cannot restore the great days of the 1960s.

And the secular decline in US corporate profitability is mirrored in the figures for profits in the UK, Europe, Japan and Australia. Modern capitalism is weakening.

Marx's great economic law of the tendency of the rate of profit to decline is visible in these figures. Sure, there are periods when the use of new technology and the ability to weaken the ability of the workforce globally to obtain decent wages and conditions allow capitalists to restore somewhat their profitability.

But that is achieved only after destructive periods of economic recession or slump when millions lose their jobs, small businesses collapse in their hundreds of thousands, or even worse capitalists engender wars to enable them to get labour or resources cheaper.

The post-war period of secular decline in profitability has been accompanied by the powerful American state overthrowing progressive anti-capitalist governments in Latin America, conducting a horrifically damaging war in Vietnam, installing an agent provocateur state, Israel, in the midst of oil-rich but 'unstable' Middle East, and, of course, now occupying a major oil state directly with US troops.

The huge cost, not just in lives and livelihoods for the masses, but also in productive resources and profits made by capitalism, was necessary — for capitalism. It was needed in order to try and reverse or slow the inevitable decline in the economic health of the system.

Now 60 years after US capitalism became the dominant economic, political and military power on the globe, it has been unable to restore the profitability of its capitalist companies. With the next recession, profitability will plunge even lower depths and will require even more destruction and struggle to rise again.

If profits are the lifeblood of capitalism, then the blood of US and the top capitalist nations keeps seeping away. Capitalists desperately suck harder on the labour power of the working-class globally to get more blood. And for a while, they succeed. The latest upturn in profitability has now lasted four years. But eventually, profitability will start to fall back again.

The two great propositions of the apologists of capitalism: that is the only system of human social organisation that works and that it brings with it prosperity for all, are thus exposed.

1. Data are from US Bureau of Economic Analysis.

The property time bomb

The world economy is being sustained by US consumer spending and Chinese manufacturing. US consumer spending is based on the illusion of growing property values, but these cannot keep going up forever. The property bubble in the US will burst and when it does it will have devastating effects on the whole of the world economy.

The world capitalist economy is being held up like Atlas by just two forces: US household spending and Chinese manufacturing production. If either or both of these should die, then world capitalism will slip into slump.

US household spending is probably the more important of these two factors. What is driving this 4-5% annual growth in spending? It's not rising wage rates. Indeed, for the average American household, income from work is falling. No, what's been keeping Americans spending has been partly tax cuts, as Bush cuts back on social spending programmes to make handouts, mainly to the rich, through cuts in big business taxes, but also to middle-class Americans in personal tax rebates.

But the main reason has been very low interest rates, driven down by the policy decisions of the US Federal Reserve Bank under Alan Greenspan. This has led to historically-low mortgage rates across America. As a result, there has been a property boom that has reached breakneck proportions, particularly in the 'hot spots' of California, Las Vegas, Florida and New England.

National house prices are now rising at a 15% annual rate, unheard of in all previous US housing booms. This unprecedented rise in housing wealth has enabled Americans to refinance their debt at low rates and then use the cash they've borrowed to spend, confident in the belief that when they sell their properties they will have risen so much in value that they can pay off the debt comfortably. This is a house of cards.

THE PROPERTY TIME BOMB

World capitalist growth now depends on US household spending and US spending depends on house prices in the US rising indefinitely. This is a pyramid scheme that will topple over eventually.

As the *Economist* pointed out in its June 2005 issue: "Never before have real house prices risen so fast for so long in so many countries". The total value of residential property in the OECD has more than doubled from $30bn to $70bn in the last five years and is now equivalent to over 100% of these countries' annual output.

Yet this value is not represented by any new production and it is a global phenomenon. House values (if measured against the rents that can be got from property) have never been higher in America, Britain, Australia, New Zealand, France, Spain, Holland and Ireland[1].

This is purely a speculative bubble — a bubble bigger than the stock market boom of the late 1990s that collapsed in 2000 or the great boom of

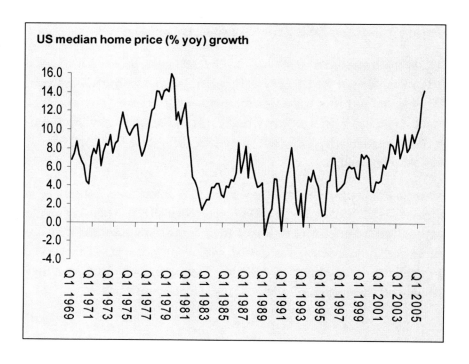

US median home price (% yoy) growth

the 1920s that ended in the Great Depression of 1929-33. The *Economist* reckons it is the biggest bubble in history!

That's proven when the US estate agent association revealed that around one in every four properties bought in 2004 were for investment not occupation and another 15% were bought as second homes. In Florida, as many as half the buyers of property resell their purchases immediately! And they are financing this binge from mortgage lenders that offer 100% mortgages or even higher, with reduced interest payments (60% of mortgages in California were like this in 2004).

But the US housing bubble is now set to burst. According to another expert, average US house price rises were about 25% over trend, but in hot spots the level of over-valuation was more like 50%. In Los Angeles, the real estate association has calculated that only the top 17% of all wage earners can now afford the price of an average home! It does not matter that mortgage rates are still low. The level of prices in many areas is so high that hardly anybody can buy.

The indicators of a future bust are already there from the collapse of other housing bubbles in Australia and more recently, the UK. The price levels reached in the UK and Australia coupled with rising interest rates finally broke the back of the housing market there. In the last 12 months, Australia has seen falling prices and the UK is flat at best.

Now the US Federal Reserve is raising interest rates. Eventually that will seep through to mortgage rates. Then, my own calculations suggest that affordable housing will only be restored in the US if house prices drop at least 15-20% from current levels[2]. That spells bust!

If that turns out to be right, then the US economy will drop like a stone, as many Americans face bankruptcy when they cannot make their mortgage payments, while others will have to pull in their spending horns to make ends meet.

And have no doubt that the US economy depends on this low interest-rate housing boom like no other. The big US banks have made huge profits in the last few years from lending on real estate. Now 45% of all the profits made by the top 500 companies in the US come from the financial sector. If the housing market collapses, that will make a huge hit on the profits of big business.

Even more serious, most US mortgages are sold on by the banks to semi-government agencies, called Fannie Mae and Freddie Mac. Because they are backed by the US government, it is assumed they cannot go bankrupt. And these agencies have been engaged in many financial con-tracts; using the mortgages they hold as collateral.

If these Americans start defaulting on their mortgages in a big way, it could mean that government agencies will be in trouble and require tax-payers to bail them out. That will slow the economy even more. Worse, the trouble could spread through the financial sector like a disease, bring-ing down a swathe of banks.

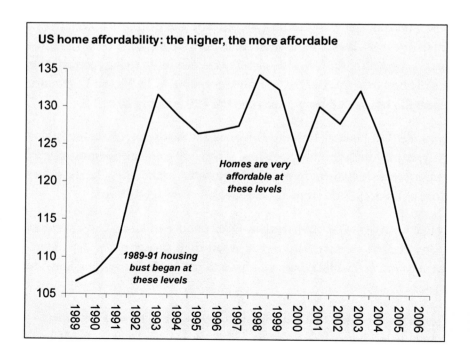

US home affordability: the higher, the more affordable

Homes are very affordable at these levels

1989-91 housing bust began at these levels

Indeed, in Britain, there are already some signs of how the US housing market might pan out. The number of people declaring bankruptcy in the UK reached record levels in the first quarter of 2005, up 28% on a year ago. And there are record numbers of mortgage repossessions already.

Personal bankruptcies are one-fifth higher than they were during their peak in the early 1990s, when the UK economy was in recession and almost one million households were in 'negative equity' (their mortgages were bigger than the sale of their property could cover).

According to John Butler, economist at Britain's biggest bank, HSBC, "the vulnerability of the household sector is acting like a time-bomb, which will ultimately cast a shadow over the UK economy".

Of course, the US authorities are not stupid. They are aware of the risk. But for the moment, they seem blithely confident that nothing will go amiss. Federal Reserve chairman and financial guru, Alan Greenspan, recently said he thought there "was some froth" in the housing market and some risky forms of financing, but he was sure that "the US housing market was not a bubble that was going to burst".

Perhaps his serenity is due to the fact that for the richest people in the world, a housing bust may have little effect on their wealth. After all, it is the middle class, and even the working class to some extent, in the US, the UK and Europe, who invest any savings or credit they have into their house. For the very rich, property is a much smaller proportion of their overall wealth. Financial wealth — company shares, government bonds and just cash in the bank — is just as big.

Indeed, the world's wealth is more concentrated than ever. The difference between what the 'average' man or woman is worth and what the super-rich are worth has never been so great. A new Merrill Lynch study shows that 8.3 million people around the world now have a million or more dollars in 'investable assets' and this does not include their homes[3]. In contrast, for the average person, the main asset is the home.

THE PROPERTY TIME BOMB

With $30.8 trillion at their command, the "really rich" control one quarter of the world's financial wealth. This translates into the following: the super-rich, who comprise just 0.13% of the world's population, own 25% of the world's wealth!

But very few of the super-rich made their money investing in stocks (Warren Buffett is one great exception and even he buys companies more than stocks). Most made it through inheritance, or building a business, or in investment banking. That means they got rich on the back of other people's investments. So the super-rich may not be worried by any housing crisis. But it's an issue for the rest of us.

The US economy is currently motoring on at about a 3.5% real growth rate. Last year, the UK was nearly achieving that on the back of rocketing house prices and big spending by British households as they used up the cash borrowed on their houses. Australia was growing at over 5%.

But this year, the UK and Australian housing markets have slumped. With that, economic growth has slowed to under 2% a year. Spending in the shops has stopped growing altogether.

The UK and Australian economies are not decisive in driving global capitalism. But the US economy is. If it suffers a similar fate to the UK and Australia in the next year, the world will too. Japan's recovery is still stuttering, while Europe is growing painfully slowly. If the US stops spending, then China and the rest of Asia will feel the cold draught of slowing export sales too. The world will go into recession.

1. OECD Economic Outlook, April 2005
2. US National Association of Realtors Affordability Index
3. Merrill Lynch World Wealth Report, 2005

The time bomb is now ticking

One of the key elements in holding up consumer spending — and there-fore sales and profits — in the US has been growing house prices. The growing nominal value of housing has led to a widespread phenomenon of remortgaging, i.e. borrowing more to keep up annual family incomes. This cannot continue for much longer. The signs are already there that we are close to the limit.

There is a property time bomb that threatens to drive the advanced capi-talist economies of North America and Europe into economic recession. There are two strong forces that were keeping world capitalism motoring along: US household spending and Chinese manufacturing production. If one of these should falter, then world capitalism would slip into slump.

The capitalist economists remain very optimistic that neither of these things will happen or that they will not make any difference. And the latest economic data coming out of the US would suggest that all is well.

As one American economist put it: "January was not only hot in the sta-tistical sense, but it was literally the hottest January on record insofar as US climatic conditions are concerned". US house builders increased their number of new housing starts by nearly 7% in one month. Sales in American shops and malls jumped 30% in January relative to December.

As a result, the economists are now forecasting the US economy will grow at a 5% annual rate in the three months to the end of March. That compares to a very poor expansion of just 1.5% in the last quarter of 2005.

But, as one sceptical American economist put it[1]: "Which outcome is closer to the true state of the US economy — the energy-shocked, con-sumer-led slowdown of late 2005 or the apparent heat-seeking burst of activity in early 2006? Financial markets have voted for the latter. My advice is don't play with statistical fire. There may have been more truth to the weakness of the economy in late 2005 than most are willing to accept. The case for a post-housing-bubble capitulation of the American consumer remains a very real threat in 2006."

National house prices are now rising at a 12% annual rate, unheard of in all previous US housing booms. This unprecedented rise in housing wealth has enabled Americans to refinance their debt at low rates and then use the cash they've borrowed to spend, confident in the belief that when they sell their properties they will have risen so much in value that they can pay off the debt comfortably.

Recent data on US property transactions and prices show that the downturn in the US housing market has now started. Existing house sales (roughly 80% of the market) have been edging down since last June. The number of unsold homes is now at its highest level since spring 1986.

House builders are scaling back forecasts for next year. Toll Brothers, the largest builder of luxury homes in America, recently reduced its sales projections for 2006 by 4-7%. The National Association of Home Builders index portends a further deterioration in new home starts. Mortgage applications have also drifted south since the summer.

Housing affordability, particularly in the coastal cities, is stretched to its limits. America's households are leveraged up to their eyeballs and now rely on rising house prices to supplement their incomes. Home equity withdrawal (cash generated from the rising value of homes) accounts for a record share of their disposable income.

So even just a slowdown in house price rises would hit consumption. A recent survey of homeowners in 13 areas of sharpest home price rises found that one in four would have to curb spending if house prices simply stopped rising. Now home price increases are beginning to slow from previously breakneck levels. Indeed, prices of new homes just built are falling.

All this will sound familiar to British homeowners. The collapse of the house price boom in the UK (and in Australia) last year is the future for

US homeowners. House prices don't have to fall; the increase in prices just has to slow to cause a big headache for many households.

Even though the UK and Australia did not experience outright nominal house price falls; in *real* terms, they did. The fall in real house prices deducted something like 2-3% points from real spending growth in those economies.

UK retail sales are now growing at their weakest rate for 20 years and recorded the worst figures for the January sales since 1945! The Chancellor, Gordon Brown, has been forced to halve his economic growth projections for 2006. In Australia, real retail sales are growing just 1% a year and business confidence is at a three-year low. For the first time since New Labour came into office, unemployment is steadily rising.

America has a new chairman of its central bank, the Federal Reserve. Ben Bernanke's first statement to the US Congress was to raise the question of a housing bust. Naturally, he was not too worried when he argued that "a levelling out or a modest softening in housing activity seems more likely than a sharp contraction." But a so-called soft landing in housing could still translate into a hard landing for the economy.

The house price boom in the UK, Australia and the US has been driven by an accumulation of debt. At the end of 1999, UK, Australian and US household debt levels were similar at 69-73% of GDP. Over the previous ten years, debt had risen just over 1% of GDP a year. But in the last five years, these countries accumulated debt more than five times faster.

On many measures, Americans would suffer more from a housing bust than Australians or Brits. Household debt to GDP may be higher in Australia and the UK, but only 30% of Australian homeowners have any mortgage at all, while 45% of Americans do. And when mortgage debt is measured against assets, Australians have only 21% of the home value mortgaged, while Americans have double that. As a result, it costs Americans around 18% of their household disposable income to service their housing debt, but just 12% for Australians and 10% in the UK.

TIME BOMB NOW TICKING

Moreover, the US financial system has become heavily linked to property. Commercial banks have more than half their assets in real estate. While property prices rose, households felt confident to borrow even more at favourable interest rates. And banks were happy to provide credit since the risk was spread against the consumer's main asset, which was rising in value.

At their peak, UK and Australian citizens sucked out the equivalent of 8% of household disposable income in borrowing on the rising value of their homes. In a recent report, erstwhile Fed Chairman Alan Greenspan calculated that US households had extracted much the same amount from their homes in 2004. This extra boost to incomes was key in driving the consumer-led boom in the UK, Australia and the US.

The end of the UK and Australian housing boom occurred when the Bank of England and the Reserve Bank of Australia raised interest rates. That caused house prices to stop rising and there was an abrupt drop in equity extraction. This provided a big shock to consumer income in those countries. While mortgage rates in the UK and Australia are directly linked to the movement of short-term rates set by their central banks, this is not the case in the US. They do not determine mortgage rates. Indeed, only one-third of all US mortgages are financed on variable rates, while over 70% are in the UK and Australia. Even so, in the last few months there have been signs of an upturn in mortgage rates.

It won't take much of a rise in mortgage rates to kill off the current US house price boom. That's because, according to the National Association of Realtors, US house prices are at their highest relative to average income for 15 years. So just a small rise in mortgage rates would make most US homes 'unaffordable' and home prices would have to fall. As US mortgage rates rise, mortgage equity withdrawal in the US will fall, just as it did in the UK and Australia.

In the last two years, the US property bubble has meant that housing and related sectors have contributed 1.5% points to average real GDP growth of 3.75%. Similarly, housing-related job growth has been twice as fast as other sectors of the economy and has contributed nearly one-quarter of all net new jobs in the last two years. If annual house prices only slow to half the current rate of 12%, housing's contribution to private consumption growth will disappear. So the US real growth rate would fall towards recession levels.

Most important, unlike the other 'Anglo-Saxon' economies, a property bust in the States would have a significant impact on the world capitalist economy. Should the current US house price growth of 12% year on year in the third quarter of 2005 halve in 2006, that would cut global output growth by 1% point at least.

The dynamic impact of a housing slowdown on the US economy is likely to be much worse. Foreign investors won't recycle their capital into the US fixed income assets at current yields if US growth slumps. This will force up US interest rates. Rising mortgage rates will then compound the misery for households and encourage them to save more and spend less.

So, by the end of this year, one of the legs holding up the world capitalist economy may have well and truly buckled.

1. Stephen Roach, Morgan Stanley Global Economic Forum, February 2006

The perfect circle of success

It works like this. The economies of the advanced world, as represented by what are called the G7 countries (the US, Japan, Germany, the UK, France, Italy and Canada — in that order), no longer need to make things. Increasingly, they just need to invent, design and market things. They can leave the making of things to the less developed world — in particular, China and other parts of Asia, Mexico and Brazil.

Also the G7 countries (and other smaller advanced economies like Switzerland) can concentrate on financing the investment in the making of things in the less developed world. The banks and financial institutions based in New York, London and Geneva, along with Paris and Frankfurt can suck up the huge savings generated in China, Japan, Korea and the oil-rich economies of the Middle East and Russia. These savings, in the hands of the global financial sector, are used to buy the bonds of the G7 governments, the bonds of the big corporations and mortgage banks and the shares of the major G7 corporations.

Looking down the telescope from the other end, this means that the G7 governments and the big corporations and the average households on the G7 countries can borrow huge amounts of money to finance their purchases of houses, pay for government spending on arms, education etc and finance the building of factories in the so-called Third World.

It's perfect. The US now runs a huge trade deficit equivalent to 6% of its annual national income. It also has built up net debts with the rest of the world equivalent to 25% of its annual output and rising. But no problem — it has this deficit because it is buying containerloads of 'things' from China at very cheap prices to fill its shops.

It does not need to make these things at home any more when they are so cheap from China, Mexico or the rest of Asia. And these things are being made in China by American, Japanese and European corporations who have transferred their factories to China and other cheap-wage, plentiful labour locations.

It all works because the export revenues generated by Chinese sales to the US and the rest of the G7 are put in the Chinese banks by the foreign-owned corporations, which promptly use the money to buy US bonds and other financial assets. Indeed, in 2005, the US ran up a trade deficit of nearly $700bn, but it received back over $900bn in credit as foreigners bought US government bonds, corporation bonds and mortgage bonds.

As a result, the US financial system is flush with cash. It can lend money at historically very low rates of interest to Americans to buy ever more expensive houses or purchase ever more quantities of Chinese goods, or ever more clever hi-tech services from India and techno gadgets from Korea, Taiwan and Japan.

Such is the perfect circle of success. So perfect is it that some strategists of capital are now convinced that this has guaranteed a prosperous capitalist world for some time ahead. They have called it Our Brave New World[1].

In this world, G7 capitalist companies are 'platform companies'. They won't make anything. "The new business model is to produce nowhere, but sell everywhere... platform companies then simply organise the ordering by the clients and delivery by the producers...they keep the high value-added parts of the research, development and marketing in-house and farm out all the rest to external producers".

Think of this Brave New World as a new stage of capitalism. First, there was the development of agricultural capitalism in the 17th and 18th centuries in Europe and in the 19th century in the US and Japan. Then came industrial capitalism, pioneered by the UK at first and then adopted by the US, Europe and later Japan. The rest of the world was reduced to providing the raw materials and food that enabled industrial capitalist countries to make the things everybody wanted.

PERFECT CIRCLE OF SUCCESS

But now has come finance capitalism (more broadly defined to include what Marx called the unproductive sectors of capitalism, namely, finance, marketing, legal services, property 'development' etc). This is how the G7 economies increase their wealth. They take the savings of the newly industrialised world and invest or spend it for them!

Indeed, if you take the argument further, China would have no market to sell its TVs, toys, textiles, bras and every other item you can think of, if American households did not have the money or credit to buy them. What is important in this view of capitalism is not production, but consumption.

It is a repeat of the ironic story first raised by the great Dutch economist, Bernard Mandeville way back in 1705 of the *Fable of the Bees*[2]. As he explained in his brilliant doggerel verse, it is not the bees (workers) that are important. Without the drones (the do-nothing members of the community who just consume the honey), there would be no point to the worker bees.

Without somebody ready to eat you out of house and home, there would be no need to make any food or the shopping — it's logical, isn't it? So without Americans spending like there was no tomorrow, China would not be able to sell and it would have no place to lend its money. The US spender/debtor keeps the capitalist world going round, not the Chinese saver/lender.

There must be something wrong with this! And there is. This whole view of capitalism assumes that profits are irrelevant. What is important is that the price of stocks and shares keep rising, the price of property keeps rising and that interest rates keep low, not making profits. If the value of your house keeps going up, you can borrow more to spend more; if the value of shares keeps rising, you can borrow more to invest in factories in China and design new things for the Chinese to make. If interest rates stay low, the government and others can borrow more to build more armaments while keeping taxes relatively low.

PERFECT CIRCLE OF SUCCESS

This is a view of capitalism as seen by the banker or the rich consumer. It is not the reality of capitalism. That's because the prices of property, shares and government debt won't go up forever because they depend on something else: profits of capitalists. This is the life blood of capitalism. If the profits of the big corporations start to wane, then all bets are off. Investment into China will fall off, share prices will fall and fewer goods will be purchased. G7 economies will slow and move into slump.

Profits do not come from bankers lending money, rich people buying luxury goods, governments selling arms or people buying houses. The profits have already been made. These economic actors are merely redistributing profit made by others, namely the producers of things in the US and China. This is one of the fundamental discoveries of Marxist economics.

Profits are the unpaid labour of the working class, but also they only arise from the sale of things made that people want. The marketing, advertising and distribution of goods add nothing to profit; but are just a necessary (under capitalism) cost of making a profit for individual capitalists in competition with each other.

Similarly, workers in public services are necessary to capitalism to keep the workforce healthy, educated and functioning. But they don't produce profits for capitalists. In that sense, they are 'unproductive' for capitalism. Bankers, mortgage and insurance brokers, real estate agents and financial analysts may get paid huge sums but they do not make profits for the capitalist system, even if they do for the companies they work for. In that sense too, they are unproductive.

Yet the Brave New World of capitalism now suggests that it is precisely these unproductive sectors of capitalism that keep the whole system going. Buying a house in America keeps the whole world going round. What will prove this wrong is when the profitability of the capitalist system starts to fall. At present, US profitability in the whole economy is around 8.5% of annual output. That's very near the historic peak of the last 25 years of 9%. But it is now beginning to decline.

There are three indicators of whether the Brave New World will end in tears. First, are US housing prices falling? If they start to do so, then the profit of investing US mortgage bonds for foreigners will decline and they will stop buying them. That will force up interest rates in the US and make it more difficult to finance the huge trade deficit. As of now, US house prices are shooting along at near 15% a year. But they have just started to slow.

The second indicator will be how much the US and other G7 companies keep investing in China to boost profitability. If that starts to decline, then it means that G7 corporations have less to spend or they are worried about not getting enough profit out of the workers in China. In 2005, foreign capitalists invested $58bn in China. That's very high, but it is slightly less than in 2004. Just the first signs.

Finally, there are the figures for Chinese exports to the rest of the world. If they start to decline, it means that G7 consumers have less money to spend on goods in the shops and/or foreign manufacturers are experiencing a slowdown or fall in the profits they are making from their exports. In 2005, exports from China were at record levels.

So far then, the Brave New World of capitalism is still holding together. It still seems that the bankers, property developers and arms manufacturers of the G7 economies are successful and profitable. But there are signs of fraying at the edges.

Let's go back to Mandeville's fable. In the natural world, of course, the drones do have a role. They may do nothing and do not even guard the Queen bee. But they are the only males of the bee community and so they mate with the queen, thus providing a role in procreation. The worker bees are all female. Once mating is over, the drones are driven out of the hive by the worker bees and left to die. In the human world, worker bees are both male and female and do their own mating. So they have no need of drones at all!

PERFECT CIRCLE OF SUCCESS

1. A Kaletsky, Charles and Louis-Vincent Gave, Our Brave New World, *2005*

2. B. *Mandeville,* The Fable of the Bees, *1705*

Marx's law of profitability

Nobody argues that the world capitalist economy moves in a straight upward path. Everybody recognises that it is subject to 'turbulence', booms and slumps, even crises. In these periods of slump or crises, people's lives are disrupted, jobs are lost, businesses go bust, families are made homeless etc.

Can we say why these crises come about? The orthodox bourgeois economists say they are the result of interference in the market economy by the state, by monopoly power (mainly trade unions) or as the result of 'bad' policies that do not allow capitalists the freedom to make profits (too high taxes or interest rates etc). There is no inherent fault in the capitalist mode of production that generates periodic crises in the economy.

Followers of the Marxist economic tradition would disagree. For us, the capitalist system is not only unjust, unequal and barbarous. It is also shot through with periodic failure.

The primary reason is that the productive forces that provide prosperity and a better life are only unleashed under capitalism if there is a profit for the owners of capital. In other words, the productive forces are privately owned and turned into 'capital', so society only benefits if that capital is invested in production. If the profit is not there, things and services that people need are not produced. So profits and the profitability of capital are key to the health of the capitalist mode of production.

Marx argued that capitalism will suffer periodic crises precisely because the owners of capital will not be able to generate sufficient profits indefinitely to sustain an untrammelled growth in production and living standards. For that reason, capitalism may be the most expansive mode of production seen on the earth so far, but it is also most wasteful, unequal and crisis-ridden. Human beings can do better.

MARX'S LAW OF PROFITABILITY

Why cannot capitalists generate sufficient profits indefinitely so that the world's productive forces can expand smoothly forever? Marx argued that the most important law of the motion of capitalism that explained periodic crises was the law of the tendency of the rate of profit to fall[1].

Of course, each capitalist business, large or small, earns a different amount of profits. And each earns a different rate of profit, as measured by the amount of profits produced in, say a year, against the amount of money capital that the capitalist owner had to put into the business.

Marx argued that the only way to understand the forces at work in a whole economy was to aggregate all the profits and capital in all the businesses and come up with an average rate of profit. He then said that, if this average rate of profit dropped so low as to cause the capitalists to stop investing further in production, the economy would go into crisis. There would be what modern economists call a 'recession' or 'slump', with all that entails for jobs and living standards for the mass of working people and their dependents.

What could make the average rate of profit in the capitalist economy fall to such a low level, and for that matter what would make it rise? Marx starts from the fundamental fact that nothing is created without human beings spending time making or delivering it. Under capitalism, however, that labour time has been appropriated by the owners of capital (namely those that own and control the plant and equipment, raw materials and the money to buy them). Production depends on workers, but production does not happen without the say-so of the owners of capital. They own the means of production.

Thus, the labour time of the workers is turned into a certain *value* that the owners of capital measure against the costs of employing their workers and the cost of setting up the businesses and supplying the necessary raw materials and services.

Only if the workers expend labour time is there any production and any profit. The workers get paid a certain amount for their time. The capitalists own and control the product of their labour and sell it in the market. The difference between the revenues of those sales and cost of employing the workforce is what Marx called the *surplus-value* that the owners of capital had appropriated over and above the value of the production paid to the workers for their time.

From the capitalists' point of view, the capital invested in paying the workers is variable, in that the workers add more value. Marx called that *variable capital*. But the capitalists also have the costs of setting up and running the businesses. Factories, offices and supplies cannot add any production value in themselves. But they still have to be paid for. From the capitalist viewpoint, this is *constant capital*.

In any one period, the capitalists put up money for variable capital (workforce) and constant capital (plant and machinery etc). At the end of the production period, they sell the production in the market and receive revenues to cover their original money capital and more. The rate of profit is thus the surplus value (s) created by the workers divided by the sum of the cost of variable (v) and constant capital (c), or (s/c+v).

Marx argued that over a whole economy, there was tendency for that rate of profit to fall. And indeed, after a period of time, it would fall, causing an economic crisis.

Why is there a tendency for the rate of profit to fall? The reason is inherent in the capitalist mode of production. Capitalism is a system of production where individual owners of capital (or limited companies with lots of small owners or shareholders) compete in the market place to sell their goods at a profit. So there is an inherent drive to keep costs down relative to likely sales revenues.

Assuming, for the moment, that the price that a business is going to get for its product or service is fixed by the market, then each business can raise (or just maintain) profits either by lowering the costs of employing the workforce or by lowering the costs of raw materials and offices etc.

The latter costs are usually fixed or out of the control of the individual capitalist, so the big drive is to lower labour costs.

Capitalists can do this by reducing the workforce to the minimum required to make the business function. Or they can make an existing workforce work harder or longer. These measures will either raise the *absolute* size of surplus value created by the workforce or its *relative* value compared to the costs of employing the workforce (the *rate of surplus value*), or both.

In the modern capitalist world, the most effective way of raising the rate of surplus value is to introduce new technology that can either reduce the number of workers needed or increase how much they produce in the same period of time, or both. The rate of surplus value will rise and, other things being equal, so will profits and the rate of profit.

But other things are not equal. New technology means more money capital must be invested in machinery. Most important, Marx said, the amount of capital devoted to machinery and technology will rise relative to the amount of capital invested in the workforce. So there will be a tendency for the value of constant capital (c) to rise relative to variable capital (v). Marx called this ratio: the *organic composition of capital, or c/v*.

If the organic composition of capital (c/v) rises, then, unless the rate of surplus value (s/v) rises as fast or faster, the rate of profit (s/c+v) will fall. Marx argued that under capitalism, the forces of competition and the drive for profit will mean that the organic composition of capital will rise. If it is rising, it is because capitalists are cutting back on labour and substituting machinery. More technology may well raise the productivity of the workforce, but a smaller workforce will reduce the amount of value produced, as only workers expending labour time can add value. Thus relatively more spent on technology and relatively less on labour will tend to reduce the amount of value produced for each unit of money capital invested. There is a *tendency* for the rate of profit to fall.

However, Marx identified a whole number of 'countervailing tendencies' that could mean either the organic composition of capital would not rise or the rate of profit would still rise even if it did — for a while[2]. And that last point is key. The countervailing tendencies were just that. The tendency for the organic composition of capital would exert itself and so would the tendency for the rate of profit to fall. Eventually, such would be the effect on the average rate of profit and the mass of profits in the economy, that it would push many capitalists into bankruptcy and others to stop producing (as much). There would be an economic crisis.

Of course, this is where it all gets controversial, especially among Marxist economists themselves! The first big argument is that many economists who consider themselves Marxists reckon that Marx made such important theoretical errors in his explanation of the law of the tendency of the rate of profit to fall that it just does not hold up.

The second big argument against Marx's rate of profit theory is that it is just not empirically correct. The average rate of profit has not fallen over time and, even more significant, the organic composition of capital has not risen to explain it. Marx is just plain wrong, they say.

So with Marx wrong both theoretically and empirically, his explanation of economic crisis falls to the ground. The critics say we should look elsewhere for an explanation of economic crisis. Many fall back on the inadequate theories of the orthodox bourgeois economists or alternatively try to work out a bastardised Marxist version that does not rely on Marx's rate of profit theory.

I hope to try and answer these critics and defend Marx's theory of profitability and crisis both theoretically and empirically. The aim is not just to defend Marx, but also to show that his profit theory is both relevant and crucial to understanding through what stage world capitalism is currently passing.

MARX'S LAW OF PROFITABILITY

The graph in the next chapter shows the movement in the average rate of profit and the organic composition of capital in the US since 1945. The US is the biggest and most important capitalist economy. As such, it provides the best indicator of the laws of motion of capitalism, just as Marx found Britain was in the 19th century.

And this graph provides strong empirical confirmation of Marx's analysis of the capitalist economy and his explanation of the nature of capitalist crises. From it, we can draw some startling conclusions, as the next chapter will try to show.

1. K Marx, Capital *Vol III, Part III, Chapter 13*
2. K. Marx, Capital *Vol III, Part III, Chapter 14.*

Marx and the profit cycle

Marx's law of the tendency of the rate of profit to fall is revealed in a graphic showing the movement of the average rate of profit in the US economy between 1946 and 2005[1]. The graphic also shows the movement of the organic composition of capital over the same period.

I indicated that the graphic shows several interesting things. First, the average rate of profit does fall under capitalism. Second, when it falls, the organic composition of capital rises, and vice versa, as Marx argued. Third, the average rate of profit was generally much higher in the period (the golden age) 1948-65 than it is now. Fourth, it appears that the rate of profit moves in waves of about 16-18 years, up, then down. Fifth, if that is right, we are now in a wave where the average rate of profit will fall and by around 2015 it will be as low, if not lower than, it was in 1982. Sixth, that means capitalism is now in an era where economic crisis will

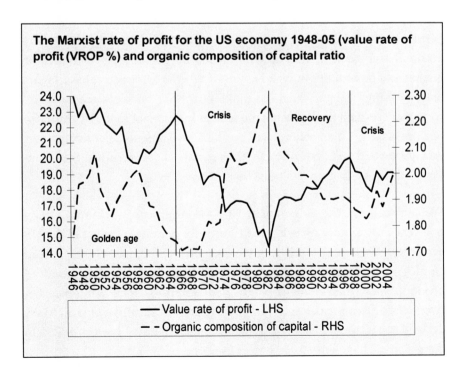

The Marxist rate of profit for the US economy 1948-05 (value rate of profit (VROP %) and organic composition of capital ratio

be more frequent and more severe and the political repercussions much greater.

Before I start to draw out some of the conclusions from these observations, let me explain how the data in this graph are worked out. We are trying to measure the rate of profit and the organic composition of capital by the Marxist definition. The Marxist rate of profit is defined as surplus-value divided by the sum of constant capital and variable capital (s/c+v). The organic composition of capital is defined as the ratio of constant capital to variable capital (c/v).

Can we measure these value concepts in the hard-headed world of capitalist economics and statistics? We sure can. There is nothing mysterious and or metaphysical about Marxist economic categories measured in value terms.

At the level of aggregates (the whole economy), the necessary data for the US have been compiled by the US government's Bureau of Economic Analysis. We can measure constant capital as the value of the accumulated stock of fixed assets owned by businesses. We exclude houses and government-owned assets. Only the 'productive' assets that are committed by capitalists to make profits in business are relevant. Note that constant capital is not the annual investment made by capitalist businesses. It is the accumulated stock of investments over many years that are owned and controlled by the capitalists. It is against this accumulated capital that profits must be measured.

We can measure the value created by the American workforce in any one year very simply by using the figures for national product of the US economy. We can also measure the variable capital, namely the cost of employing that workforce to make that value, as the total 'compensation' of employees (that includes wages and benefits). The difference between these two measures gives you the annual surplus-value as Marx defined it. All these data are available for the US going back to 1925. In the graphic I have only gone back to the end of WWII.

Thus the annual rate of profit is the surplus-value (GDP less employee compensation) divided by the sum of constant capital (fixed asset stock) plus variable capital (employee compensation). The organic composition of capital ratio is constant capital (stock of fixed assets) divided by variable capital (employee compensation). When you run the average rate of profit and the organic composition of capital data as a time series together, you get the graphic[2].

Now those of you who follow these things closely will know that these measures of the value rate of profit have some problems. The problem with using GDP, for example, is that the capitalist statisticians include what they call 'depreciation' in GDP. Depreciation is a measure of how much of the fixed assets have been used up in any one year. That is not part of the new value created by the workforce and ought to be deducted.

You can use net product instead of gross product for that or it could be balanced by using a measure of *gross* fixed asset stock for constant capital. Then both the top and bottom lines of the formula of the rate of profit (s/c+v) would include depreciation. However, for the US economy we only have data for *net* fixed asset stock, i.e. after deducting depreciation. Fortunately, whether you use net or gross measures, it does not really change the trends and turning-points shown in graphic[3].

The orthodox bourgeois economists do not use the Marxist definition. They measure profits more or less as accountants do for a company. They take total revenues, deduct the cost of producing things or services that are being sold (including advertising and marketing etc), then make estimates of the 'depreciation' of machinery and plant being used; etc. That produces a very different measure of profit compared with the Marxist surplus-value.

Also, the economists do not identify the cost of employing the workforce in their measure of profitability. Their measure of the 'return on assets' is really profit (as defined above) divided by the stock of fixed assets. In this way, the role of labour in creating value and surplus-value is hidden and lost.

For the capitalist economists, profit is purely a return on the accumulated money capital invested by capitalists of things that they own (land, plant, machinery, stocks of raw materials). Thus it would seem that money invested in dead things, not living labour, produces profit. Profits go to the capitalists because they invested the money — it is nothing to do with the labour of the workforce.

But here is the interesting thing. When you make up a graphic of the rate of profit defined in the way capitalist economists do, it shows very much the same trends over the last 20 years as the Marxist value rate of profit graphic and would also do if I took the data further back. That suggests the underlying validity of the Marxist definitions.

So what does the graphic on the *value rate of profit* tell us? The most important message is that, on the whole, when the organic composition of capital ratio rises (right-hand scale), the rate of profit falls — and vice versa.

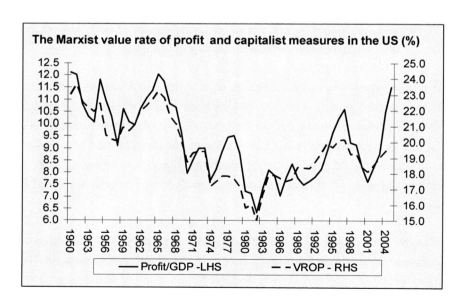

The Marxist value rate of profit and capitalist measures in the US (%)

That is not always the case. But remember Marx's law was of the *tendency* of the rate of profit to fall. There would be periods when 'countervailing' forces would work to overcome the downward pressure on the rate of profit from a rising organic composition of capital.

But you would have to say that there is a strong *inverse* relationship between the organic composition of capital and the rate of profit in the US from 1946-2005. The turning points in the direction of the organic composition of capital ratio match very closely the opposite turning points of the rate of profit.

So it would appear that Marx's causal explanation of the movement in the rate of profit is proven: it depends primarily on the movement in the organic composition of capital[4]. That offers powerful support to Marx's argument that what generates profit under capitalism is the value created by living labour (working people), not some mystical role for private owners of capital.

And it also supports Marx's view that, if the amount of living labour is reduced relative to the amount of money invested in dead capital (machinery and plant), then profitability will fall. Thus capitalism has an inherent tendency to go into economic crisis, wasting resources and destroying people's lives.

What the graphic also highlights is that there appears to be a profit (and an organic composition of capital) cycle. Over the last 60 years, that profit cycle has had two upwaves and two downwaves, each of about 15-17 years. In the first wave, which I have called the Golden Age, profitability was very high throughout. And after falling back in the 1950s, it rose to reach a peak in 1965.

From then, the organic composition of capital rose and the rate of profit fell to reach a low in the economic recession of 1982. The rate fell sharply in the first great post-war economic recession of 1974-5. But the seeds had been set for these falls by the steady decline in the rate of profitability from 1966.

By 1982 after two big economic recessions, such was the reduction in the organic composition of capital, the rate of profit steadily rose, apart from the merest of pauses in the recession of 1990-2, up to a new peak in 1997. This was the great period of disinflation (slowing price rises), low interest rates and, above all, new technological inputs from computerisation and the internet. Thus the value of constant capital was kept down and employment was maximised to deliver rising rates of profit.

But under capitalism all good things come to an end, at least for working people. After 1997, the rate of profit declined, at first even though the organic composition of capital continued to slide. This was probably because full employment allowed the workers to pull back some of the new value that was being appropriated by the capitalists as profits previously.

However, since the mild economic recession of 2001, the organic composition of capital has started to turn up ever so slightly. Profitability continued to rise for a while, however, just as it did for a while after the recession of 1974-5. But the value profit rate may now have peaked. So the graphic still suggests that we are now in the downwave of the profit cycle similar to the period 1965-82[5].

Nothing in life goes in a straight line and both the long upwave and downwave of the profit cycle are interspersed with smaller turns (of about 4-5 years) that go in the opposite direction to the more secular wave. The period of 2001-5 is one such short upturn. I shall return to these shorter cycles on another occasion.

If this is all valid, then the profit cycle is telling us that capitalism will suffer from a falling profit rate that could go down to a low last experienced in 1982, or even lower. That would happen about 2013-15. So the next seven to eight years are going to be tough for capitalism, with extreme competitive pressures and with at least one, maybe two, economic recessions over that period of a severity not seen since 1974 and 1982[6].

1. The graphic has been updated to 2008.
2. See Appendix A on page 305 for a full account of the methodology for measuring the rate of profit.
3. See Appendix A op cit.
4. See Alan Freeman, What makes the US rate of profit fall, *for a similar analysis in 2009.*
5. The most recent data have confirmed this prognosis.

Secular decline in profitability

In this chapter I continue my discussion of the graphic of the previous chapter that shows the movement of the average rate of profit in the US economy between 1946 and 2005. The graphic also shows the movement of the organic composition of capital over the same period.

As I have indicated before, the graphic shows several interesting things. First, the average rate of profit does fall under capitalism, as Marx predicted. Second, when it falls, the organic composition of capital rises, and vice versa, as Marx argued. Third, the average rate of profit was generally much higher in the period (the golden age) 1948-66 than it is now. Fourth, it appears that the rate of profit moves in cycles with up and down waves of about 16-18 years. Fifth, if that is right, we are now in a downwave, where the average rate of profit has a tendency to fall and by around 2015 it will be as low, if not lower than, it was in 1982. Sixth, that means capitalism is now in an era where economic crisis will be more frequent and more severe and the political repercussions much greater.

I have dealt with items one, two and four in the previous two chapters. In this chapter, I am going to consider item three, namely that it appears the rate of profit was high in the period 1948-66, the Golden Age, when capitalist economic growth was exceptionally fast, and inflation and unemployment were generally low. In that period, the value rate of profit averaged around 22%.

But subsequent to 1996, the rate of profit has generally been lower. Even in what I call the 'recovery period' between 1982 and 1997, the value rate of profit averaged about 18%, or about 15% lower than in the Golden Age (see the trend line for profitability in the graphic below). If I am right about the current profit downwave that began in 1997, then the average rate of profit through to 2015 or so is likely to be even lower and the trend fall over the 70 years since 1945 will be even more.

SECULAR DECLINE IN PROFITABILITY

There seems to be a secular decline in the rate of profit around which the profit cycle revolves. The cause does not seem to be due to a secular rise in the organic composition of capital, at least over the last 60 years. At around 1.9, the organic composition of capital is little different than it was in the Golden Age. However, as we are now in a downwave for the rate of profit and thus an upwave of the organic composition of capital, I expect the ratio to finish higher (perhaps around 2.2) by 2015[1].

So what can be the cause of this secular decline? I think the answer may lie in the development of modern capitalism from a primarily industrial and manufacturing economy to one that increasingly is turning into one based on services, finance and property — what we can call a *rentier* economy or finance capitalism.

If that is right, it expresses the view that Marxists argue: namely that capitalism is no longer a progressive force that is developing the world's productive forces. Increasingly, in order to appropriate surplus-value, it is

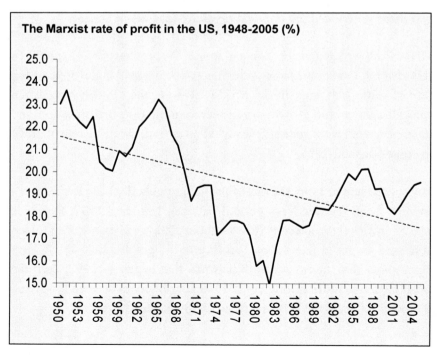

The Marxist rate of profit in the US, 1948-2005 (%)

forced to divert profits from the 'productive' sectors of the capitalist economy into 'unproductive' sectors.

By productive, I mean those sectors of the economy that employ labour that generates surplus-value, namely manufacturing, transport and communications. The unproductive sectors would be finance, real estate, marketing, advertising, government and public services like health and education.

These unproductive sectors are still very necessary to keep capitalism going, so that it can appropriate surplus-value. Simply put, businesses need banks to lend them money and capitalism needs healthy and skilled workers to generate surplus-value, and it needs an army and police force to keep 'law and order'. But all these sectors do not create surplus-value and indeed are a cost to the 'productive' sectors of the economy. These unproductive sectors (and the labour force that works in them) are necessary, but 'unproductive'.

Over the last century, these unproductive sectors have grown in size relative to the productive sectors. Capitalism has become imperialism and advanced capitalism has become more and more parasitic (bankers and landlords) on the less advanced capitalist world, like China and India, which increasingly produces a bigger share of surplus-value around the world. Capitalism is getting older and more degenerate. It has passed its sell-by date.

If this is right, it should be reflected in a secular decline in the rate of profit, particularly in advanced capitalist economies like the US. Indeed, we can look for proof of this by measuring the growth in the size of the unproductive sectors relative to the productive sectors of the economy.

In this calculation, I take the period from 1950 to 2005. Between those two dates, the rate of profit for the whole economy has declined by 15%. We can measure whether this secular decline is due to the surplus-value created by the productive sectors of the economy has been increasingly

SECULAR DECLINE IN PROFITABILITY

'siphoned off' or redistributed through the circulation of capital into the unproductive sectors.

Using the data provided by the US agency, the Bureau of Economic Analysis, we can look at the wages or compensation paid to workers in the unproductive sectors compared to the productive sectors during the Golden Age of 1948-66 and compare it with the ratio in 1997-2005[2]. We find that there has been a sharp rise. Whereas in 1948, 60% of employee compensation went to productive workers, by 2005 that ratio had fallen to 50%!

If you add back the amount of profit that the unproductive sector has 'siphoned off' from the productive sector in wages in 2005, it would raise the overall rate of profit from just under 20% to 23%. Indeed, the increase in unproductive labour can explain much of the secular decline in the rate of profit between 1950 and 2005. Around 70% of that fall can be attributed to the rise in unproductive labour.

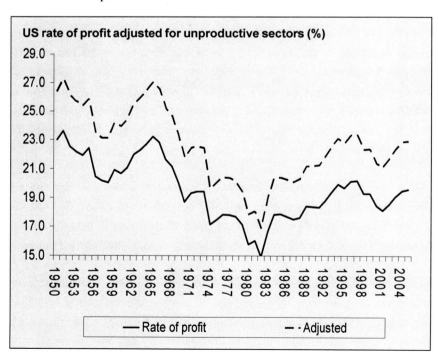

This method of measuring the effect of unproductive labour is a bit of a simplification and other Marxist economists have subtracted all the value produced by the unproductive sectors, not just the wages of unproductive workers[3]. But the resulting trends are not altered by my simplification, so my measure will suffice.

I conclude from the results that there are two factors that change the profitability of capitalism. The first is the movement of the organic composition of capital, as we have seen. This seems to act cyclically. A rise or fall in the organic composition drives down or up the rate of profit over a 15-16 year period. This causes periodic economic recessions when the rate of profit falls so low that it leads to a lowering of the mass of profit and/or stops capitalist accumulation. There is a strong inverse correlation between the organic composition of capital and the rate of profit.

The second is more secular than even 15-16 years. Probably over the last century, unproductive labour has grown compared to productive labour. But since 1945 it has really accelerated. Capitalism has become more unproductive in its own terms. And this can be measured in the secular decline in the rate of profit.

In effect, the cycles of profitability are caused more by the organic composition of capital but the trend decline in profitability is more a result of the growth of unproductive labour under capitalism.

However, there is a risk here of misinterpreting the development of capitalism with the actual cycle of boom or slump that it is passing through. Yes, capitalism is past its sell-by date, but it is still usable. It can still experience booms where economic growth and prosperity can rise for a generation.

Some Marxists have latched onto the secular decline in the rate of profit over the last 60 years as a sign that capitalism is entering a period of permanent economic depression[4]. They cite the different rate of economic growth seen before 1975 and then afterwards. From 1948-74, the average rate of real economic growth (after inflation) in the US economy was 3.85%. After 1975 to 2005, that rate was only 3.1%, about 20% slower.

However, this estimate is misleading. If we look at economic growth in each of the four economic periods of upwave and downwave of profitability from our value rate of profit graphic, we find that real economic growth averaged 4% a year between 1948-65, then it fell back to 2.9% a year up to 1982 (a real bad period for US capitalism). Between 1982-00, real growth averaged 3.6%, nearly matching the 1948-74 period that many economists concentrate on as the Golden Age. In the current wave from 2001, growth has slowed to just 2.6% a year and it will get slower still[5].

So it's incorrect to view the advanced capitalist economy as sliding into permanent depression. On the other hand, we are seemingly into a downwave of profitability that started in 1997. That is already being reflected in a lower economic growth rate than in the upwave of 1982-00. As this downwave is likely to last until 2015 (interspersed as we have seen already with upswings like 2002-05), capitalism is going to have a very rough time, at least as bad as 1966-82 and probably worse.

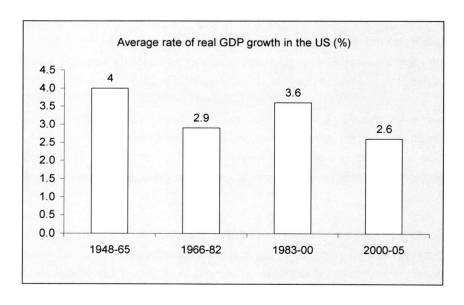

Average rate of real GDP growth in the US (%)

In the next chapter, I shall again look at the cycle of profit and how it closely connected to the cycle of the stock market — or more accurately how the stock cycle follows the profit cycle.

1. It had reached 2.1 by 2008.
2. See the Bureau of Economic Analysis website.
3. See Fred Moseley , The decline in the rate of profit in the post-war US economy, 2000.
4. See Anwar Shaikh, Explaining the global economic crisis, 1999
5. It has — growth since 2001 has been 2.1% a year in the OECD countries up to 2008.

The profit cycle and the stock market

In previous chapters, I have attempted to show that the average rate of profit does fall under capitalism, as Marx predicted. And when it falls, the organic composition of capital rises, and vice versa, as Marx argued. Most important, it appears that the rate of profit moves in cycles with up and down waves of about 16 or so years each.

If that is right, we are now in a downwave, where the average rate of profit has a tendency to fall and by around 2015 it will be as low, if not lower than, it was in 1982. That means capitalism is now in an era where economic crisis will be more frequent and more severe and the political repercussions much greater.

What helps support this argument is that it appears that the prices of the shares of capitalist companies, in aggregate, also appear to move in cycles, with up and downwaves of about 16 years, very similar to the profit cycle. The capitalists call the upwave in stock market prices a bull market and the downwave a bear market. These are very long periods for broadly one direction for stock prices to go. So such waves can be called *secular* bull or bear markets.

Modern capitalist companies do not on the whole raise the funds they need to invest in their businesses from their own profits. That would take too long to build up when they need to expand or need to purchase expensive new equipment or plant that will last years or even decades, or when they want to buy up another company that might help build their business. They need much larger amounts of capital than one or even several years of profit might provide.

So capitalist companies raise extra funds really in two ways: they either borrow or they offer shares in the company to investors. The former method was the first used in capitalism and still remains the largest way that capitalists raise funds. Back in the early days of capitalism, people set themselves up to accumulate money capital and then lend it onto other capitalists — finance capital was born. Lending money at a rate of interest was banking.

Later, companies and even governments adopted another form of borrowing. They issued bonds. The purchaser of the bond paid a lump sum over. In return, he or she got an annual payment of interest and, when the term of the bond ran out, the company bought back the bond. In the meantime, the owner of the bond could sell that bond onto somebody else, perhaps at a profit. Thus the bond market was born.

The stock market is different from bank loans or bonds. The company issues shares that entitle the owner to part ownership of the company and thus a share of the profits. Shareholders do not automatically receive an annual interest payment like bondholders. They must hope that the company annual meeting agrees to pay a dividend (a portion of the profits) to shareholders. There may be no payment at all.

Worse, if the company goes bust, they do not get the money for their shares back because they are last in the queue behind the bank with its loan and the bondholders. But if the company makes lots of money, then profits will be higher than anything the bondholder might get. And of course, shareholders can sell their shares onto others and perhaps make a profit. Thus the stock market is born.

When there is a bull market and share prices generally keep on rising, most shareholders can make more money by buying and selling shares than by any dividends they might get from holding onto shares. Thus speculation in the stock market is a way of making money and also of stimulating people to buy company shares and boost the value of any company. If the share price of a company rises, then it can expect to be able to borrow more money at better rates of interest. Indeed, it becomes more important what the share price is rather than what the profits are. Therein lie the seeds of a stock market crash.

PROFIT CYCLE AND THE STOCK MARKET

Companies do not survive unless they make profits or at least avoid making losses for any length of time. So the share price of a company will always bear some relation to the profits made or the profits likely to be made over a period of time. Indeed, the stock market is much more dependent on company profitability than bank loans or bonds. The latter's value is set by the bankers and in the case of bonds fixed in advance.

Finance capitalists indeed measure the value of a company by the share price divided by annual profits. If you add up all the shares issued by a company and multiply it by the share price, you get the 'market capitalisation' of the company — in other words what the market thinks the company is worth.

This 'market cap' can be ten, 20, 30 or even more times annual earnings. Another way of looking at it is to say that if a company's market cap is 20 times earnings and you bought its shares, you would have to wait 20 years of profits to get your money back!

If profits drive the share prices of companies, then we would expect that when the rate of profit in capitalism rises, so would stock prices. To measure that, we can get a sort of average price of all the company shares on a stock market by using a basket of share prices from a range of companies and index it. That gives us a stock market index.

So does the stock market price index move up and down with the rate of profit under capitalism? The answer is that it does, over the longer term — namely over the length of the profit cycle, although the stock market cycle does not coincide exactly with the profit cycle.

As we know, the rate of profit peaked in 1965, then fell to a low in 1982. Then we entered a rising wave until 1997, after which we appear to be in a downwave. The US stock market cycle follows a similar pattern.

That close relationship can be established by measuring the market capitalisation of companies in an economy against the accumulated assets

PROFIT CYCLE AND THE STOCK MARKET

that all companies have. The latter measures the real value of the capitalist economy to its owners.

We do this for the value of the US stock market by using what is called Tobin's Q. The leftist bourgeois economist, James Tobin developed the measure[1]. It takes the 'market capitalisation' of the companies in the stock market (in this case the top 500 companies in what is called the S&P-500 index) and divides that by the replacement value of tangible assets accumulated by those companies (these figures are provided again by the US Bureau of Economic Analysis and by the S&P's data on company accounts). The replacement value is the price that companies would have to pay to replace all the physical assets that they own (plant, equipment etc).

So Tobin's Q measures the value that speculators on the stock exchange can get over or below the actual real value of the company's assets. As we can see from the graphic below for the period 1948-05, Tobin's Q starts at about 0.33 in 1948. So the value of stock market shares was approximately only one-third of the real value of the assets owned by the companies — very cheap. It rose to nearly 1.04 in 1968. That was the peak of the Tobin Q then. Afterwards it fell back to just 0.19 in 1981.

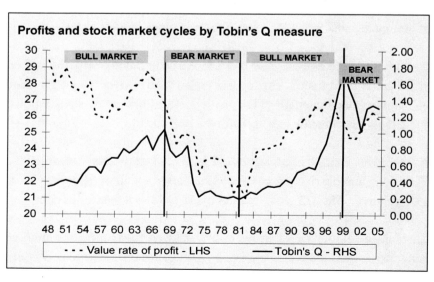

PROFIT CYCLE AND THE STOCK MARKET

That was the trough. From 1982, it rose to reach 1.75 in 1999. So the stock market value was 75% over the real value of the company's assets. From 1999, it fell back to 1.02 in 2002, but then rallied somewhat to 1.30 last year.

The graphic confirms that there was a secular bull market from 1948 to 1968, followed by a bear market until 1981 and then another bull market until 1999. So the stock market cycle appears to be about 32 years in length, pretty much the same as the profit cycle, although slightly different in its turning points. Indeed, the stock market seems to peak in value a couple of years after the rate of profit does.

This is really what we would expect, because the stock market is closely connected to the profitability of companies, much more than bank loans or bonds. When the rate of profit enters its downwave, the stock market soon follows, if with a short lag. This all suggests that we now appear to be in a secular bear market that could last until 2015, pretty similar to the profit downwave.

Of course, the bull and bear markets do not move in a straight line. There are shorter periods of about four years when, in a secular bear market, stock prices can rally. That is what has been happening since early 2003. And, of course, in a bull market, prices can fall for a few years. But at the end of the 16-year period, prices will be lower or at least no higher in a bear market and will be much higher in a bull market.

In a bear market, the value of the stock market will be much lower than at the peak of the last upwave. Indeed, the trough could even be lower than the previous trough. If this is right, the US stock market is likely to fall by at least another 50% over the period up to 2015[3].

Apart from the stock cycle, there are other economic cycles that can help us calculate through what stage capitalism is moving. There is a long-term commodity prices cycle (first discovered by the Russian economist, Kondratiev). There are shorter business cycles of about four years that relate to the movement of raw materials and inventories (named after the bourgeois economist, Kitchin) and there is an increasingly important cycle in modern capitalism for real estate and construction (named after the bourgeois economist, Kuznets). In the next chapters, I shall try to show how each of these cycles work with the all-important Marxist profit cycle.

1. James Tobin, A general equilibrium approach to monetary theory, *Journal of Money, Credit and Banking 1969*
3. The Great Recession has seen that forecast confirmed.

The profit cycle and Kondratiev

In previous chapters of this series on the profit cycle, I have argued that profitability is key to the economic health of capitalism. Marx's explanation of the causes of the movement of profitability under capitalism is compelling. Simply put, he says that when the organic composition of capital rises (i.e. the amount of capital invested in plant, machinery and equipment relative to wages and benefits to the workforce), then the rate of profit for the capitalists will eventually fall.

The drive for getting profit (surplus-value) out of the workforce and the forces of competition between capitalists will lead to a rising organic composition of capital. Thus the rate of profit has a tendency to fall and eventually it will. When it falls sufficiently low, many capitalists start to go bust and others stop investing and thus there is an economic crisis. Capitalism wastes resources, people lose their jobs and poverty ensues for the many.

What the empirical evidence of the period 1946-2006 shows is that the organic composition of capital and the rate of profit move in cycles of about 16-18 years. This is confirmed for earlier periods of industrial and financial capitalism[1].

Also, the evidence shows that the rate of profit has declined on average over the last 60 years. This appears to be an indicator of the steady decline in capitalism's ability to develop the productive forces. Increasingly, in order to drive up profitability, capitalists have been forced to spend more on 'unproductive' activities like education and health for the workforce; and they continually expand their military and police forces to maintain the grip of the capitalist system, both nationally and globally.

Most important, the financial sector of capitalism (banking, investment, insurance etc) has grown mightily as capitalism circulates more capital to try and extract more profit. All of these sectors have become ever more necessary to capitalism, but they are 'unproductive' because they create no surplus-value. In a previous chapter, I showed that the relative increase in unproductive labour versus productive labour in the US economy explained the bulk of this secular decline in profitability.

In the last chapter, we looked at how the profit cycle bore a close relation to the stock market cycle. Indeed, the current downwave in the profit cycle (which I believe we entered in 1997) was followed by a peaking of the stock market in 2000 and a subsequent downwave, or secular bear market, that could last until 2016-18.

Indeed, the value of the US stock market, despite a huge rally since 2003, is still below the levels reached in 2000[2]. And, when measured against the value of the physical means of production owned by the companies on the stock exchange (a measure called Tobin's Q), it is still lower. So the movement of the Marxist profit cycle and the capitalist stock market cycle tells us that capitalism has now entered a long period of economic weakness.

In this chapter, I want to consider whether there are other economic cycles at play under capitalism that confirm this conclusion. In particular, it appears that capitalism has exhibited a long-term cycle or movement in prices of production. Just as the capitalist profit cycle appears to be spread over approximately 32-36 years and so does the stock market cycle, there also appears to be a cycle in prices that is about double that size, or around 64-72 years.

This cycle was first identified properly by Nicolai Kondratiev, a Russian economist, in the 1920s. He noticed that there appeared to be a period when prices and interest rates moved up for about 27 years and then a period when the opposite occurred. At that time, this Kondratiev cycle appeared to last about 54 years[3].

There is some evidence to suggest that this cycle existed before capitalism became the dominant mode of production in society. In agricultural economies, prices seemed to move up when population grew faster. Eventually, when the population pressure was too great for food production, there was famine etc and the population increase slowed or even fell back. Then prices would enter a downwave[4].

Under capitalism, the Kondratiev cycle also seemed to operate as budding national capitalist economies started to compete for world market share in trade. Thus prices rose in the 16th and 17th centuries in periods of new discoveries and battles for control, just as debt for waging war rose. When these battles and debt subsided, so did prices. Thus the Kondratiev cycle operated on money supply rather than just on population pressure. What seems similar in both forms of the cycle is that the up and downwaves in prices and interest rates were about 27 years.

Under modern industrial capitalism, this cycle continued, which was when it was identified by Kondratiev. But now it was much more closely linked to the levels of investment in new technology (and thus the underlying profit cycle) as capitalist companies competed to raise the rate of surplus value and sustain profitability[5]. It seems that the Kondratiev cycle of the movement in the prices of capitalist production is now in line with the profit cycle and the stock market cycle.

Interest rates are a very good proxy for the Kondratiev prices cycle. If we look at the period from 1946 again, the graphic shows that the level of the US short-term interest rate (the Fed Funds rate, it is called, as set by the Federal Reserve Bank, America's central bank), rose from 1946 to a peak in 1981 and then fell back after that.

And 1981 is exactly the point when both the profit and stock market cycles turned from its downwave or bear market into an upwave or bull market. So, as interest rates (and prices) fell back, profitability started to rise and so did share prices.

And here is the interesting thing. Many supporters of the Kondratiev cycle in capitalist economies argue that the peak in the cycle was in

PROFIT CYCLE AND KONDRATIEV

1974-5, about 27 years after the trough of 1946 in prices. On that basis, the Kondratiev downwave began in 1974 and ended 27 years later in 2001. So we are now in an upwave for capitalist prices and growth that could last until 2028. That would be good news for capitalism.

However, this argument does not hold up well with the evidence. The Kondratiev cycle now appears to be much longer[6]. The last peak in prices (interest rates) in the cycle before this one was 1920. The last trough was in 1946, in line with the traditional Kondratiev downwave. However, the latest peak was 35 years later in 1981.

I reckon the profit cycle is now the dominant force in all economic cycles. The evidence of the post-war period is that the Kondratiev cycle is now aligning with the turns of the profit cycle. As we are in a period where the rate of profit is falling and the stock market is in a bear market, then the Kondratiev cycle is still in a downward wave and the prices trough won't come until around 70 years after the last trough in 1946, or 2018. That spells bad news for capitalism over the next decade.

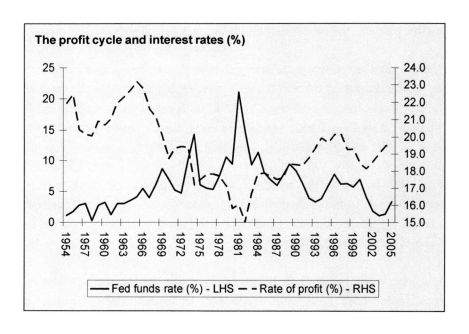

The profit cycle and interest rates (%)

Fed funds rate (%) - LHS — Rate of profit (%) - RHS

There are two other capitalist economic cycles that add support to that conclusion. The most important under modern capitalism is the innovation cycle. The Austrian bourgeois economist, Joseph Schumpeter, a close reader of Marx's ideas, reckoned that the volatility of capitalism depended on investment in new technology.

Marx had explained that capitalists try to boost their profits by investing more in new technology to save labour costs. Schumpeter reckoned that when capitalism went into crisis or slump, it made obsolete much of the old equipment and plant. Other capitalists then began to turn to new technology to gain advantage. So capitalist slumps eventually led to innovations. Schumpeter called this process 'creative destruction'[7].

So a cycle of new technology would start after a major slump, but the new technology would not be developed until the profit cycle moved into an upwave. Then there would be a take-off of the new technology. The next downwave would mean a setback to the new technology cycle and an even worse situation for capitalists depending on the old technology. Finally, in another new upwave for profits, the new technology would take over as the dominant force. In the next downwave, the new technology would become mature and capitalists would look for new systems and the whole process would start again.

The change from innovation, take-off, maturity and decline could take 70 years — not dissimilar to the length of the whole Kondratiev cycle and, of course, to two profit and stock market cycles.

Take the post-war period. In 1946, the dominant technology that made the most profits for the biggest companies was the auto and electronics industries. These industries were in mass production in the upwave of capitalism from 1948-66. The downward profit wave from 1966-82 led to crisis for the auto-electronic industries, while there were the early beginnings of innovation for a new technology: computers and the internet. In the subsequent upwave of the profit cycle from 1982-97 and the bull market in the stock cycle 1982-00, the new technology took off, while the old industries went into serious decline. In essence, General Motors gave way to Microsoft.

We are in another downwave for profitability. This coincides with a mature phase for the former new technology of computers and the internet. In each crisis or slump in this downwave, these dominant industries will struggle and capitalists will search for new technologies of which we cannot yet know (perhaps nano technology and genetics). Eventually, in the next upwave of profitability, due to start about 2015-18, these new technologies will start to take off, while the 'old technology' of computers and digitalisation will start to decline relatively.

So the whole cycle for the new technology of PCs and the internet would have lasted about 70 years, from 1966 to 2036. Of course, this assumes that capitalism is still with us after 2018.

1. *See Chapter 13.*
2. *See Chapter 9.*
3. *See N Kondratiev,* The long waves in economic life, *1926.*
4. *See David Hackett-Fisher,* The Great Wave, *1996.*
5. *M Alexander,* The Kondratiev cycle, *2002.*
6. *The Great Recession has confirmed that the 54-year cycle has now lengthened to align itself with two profit cycles of 34-36 years.*
7. *J Schumpeter,* Business cycles, *1939*

Profit cycle and business cycles

"All of you know that, from reasons I have not now to explain, capitalistic production moves through certain periodical cycles", Karl Marx to Friedrich Engels, 1865

In a previous chapter, we looked at how the profit cycle bore a close relation to the stock market cycle. Indeed, the current downwave in the profit cycle (which I believe we entered in 1997) was followed by a peaking of the stock market in 2000 and a subsequent downwave or secular bear market in stocks that should last until 2016-18.

In the last chapter, we considered two other important economic cycles under capitalism: the cyclical movement of prices and interest rates as discovered by the Russian economist Kondratiev and the cycles of innovatory technology as highlighted by the Austrian economist, Schumpeter. This added support to the argument that capitalism is now in a downwave that will mean more *frequent* and more *severe* economic recessions or crises than it has experienced since the 1930s or the volatile economic period of the 1880s.

There are three more cycles of motion that operate under modern capitalism: the cycle in real estate prices and construction, the cycle of economic boom and slump; and the relatively short business cycle.

The real estate cycle seems to last about 18 years from trough to trough. The growth cycle seems to last half that, about nine years from trough to trough and finally there is a shorter business cycle that seems to have a life of about half that of the growth cycle, of around four years or so.

There appears to be a cycle of about 18 years based on the movement of real estate prices. The American economist Simon Kuznets discovered the existence of this cycle back in the 1930s[1]. We can measure the cycle in the US by looking at house prices. The first peak after 1945 was in 1951. The prices fell back to a trough in 1958. Prices then rose to a new peak in 1969 before slumping back to another trough in 1971. The next peak was in 1979-80 and the next trough was in 1991. The spacing between peak to peak to trough to trough varies considerably. It can be as little as 11 years or as much as 26 years. But if you go far enough back (into the19th century), the average seems to be about 18 years.

As the graphic shows, the last peak in US real estate prices was in 1979-80. Assuming an average cycle of 18 years, then house prices should have peaked in 1998. Instead, on the contrary, they continued to rocket upwards with extra vigour. Only towards the end of last year did a peak seem to have been reached. That would mean a cycle of 25 years — within range, but on the long side.

There seems to be less variability when comparing troughs. The last trough was in 1991. Assuming an 18-year cycle, then the next trough in US house prices should be around 2009-10[2]. If the US house price bubble finally burst in 2005, we can expect US house price rises to slip back and fall, at least relative to overall inflation, over the next four years.

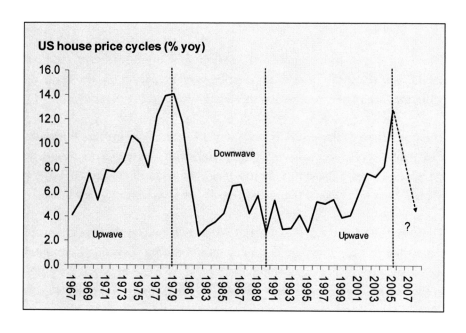

PROFIT CYCLE AND BUSINESS CYCLES

The real estate cycle is clearly not in line with the Marxist profit cycle, the stock market cycle or the Kondratiev prices/money cycle. These latter cycles are products of the laws of motion of capitalist accumulation. They operate in the productive sector of the economy (and by that, I mean 'productive' in the capitalist sense, namely contributing to the production of value).

In contrast, the real estate cycle operates in the unproductive sector of the capitalist economy. New value created and surplus-value appropriated in the productive sectors of the capitalist economy are siphoned off by the unproductive sectors as the owners of capital spend their profits and workers spend their wages. Housing is a big user of consumer income. So the cycle in house prices reflects the spending behaviour of capitalists and workers, not the profitability of capital.

For these reasons, the real estate cycle has different timings in its turns than the profit cycle. As we saw in previous chapters, the profit cycle reached a trough in 1982 before rising for 15-16 years to peak in 1997. The stock market cycle also troughed in 1982 and than ran up to a peak in 2000, 18 years later. In contrast, the US real estate cycle troughed some nine years later in 1991 and only reached its peak in 2005. The next trough is due no earlier than 2009.

Clement Juglar[3] was the first bourgeois economist to notice a business cycle of about ten years although Marx and Engels had spotted it about the same time (see quote above) in the 1860s[4]. This cycle of economic growth and recession now seems to be about 9-10 years. That is the average time between trough and trough (or recession and recession) in the recent period.

Capitalist economists define a recession as two consecutive quarters of a fall in GDP, or annual output, after taking out inflation. On that basis, there have been eleven such cycles since 1933[5].

PROFIT CYCLE AND BUSINESS CYCLES

If we use the real GDP growth of the US economy since 1948, the graphic shows that there have been seven economic recessions over the last 60 years, with varying degrees of severity and length (columns of grey).

In the Golden Age of post-war capitalism, there were three downturns in 1949, 1954 and 1958, but they were very short-lived. But then this was the period of high or rising profitability for capitalism.

In the period of the profit downwave from 1966-82, there was a mild downturn in 1970. But then followed the first worldwide simultaneous recession in 1974-5 and then the double-dip recession of 1980-2. Both recessions were severe.

In the renewed profit upwave of 1982-97, the next economic recession was in 1991, nine years later than the last. It was milder than the previous two.

In the current downwave of the profit cycle, there has been one recession so far, in 2001. This was so mild that there was no absolute fall in GDP.

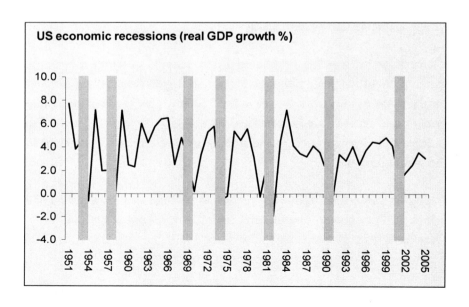

US economic recessions (real GDP growth %)

PROFIT CYCLE AND BUSINESS CYCLES

It bears a close similarity to the mild recession of 1970 that began the profit downwave period of 1966-82.

Juglar's business cycle thus seems to operate on about a 9-10 year cycle, with recessions in 1959, 1970, 1980-82, 1991 and 2001. The worldwide recession of 1974-5 breaks up that pattern and seems to have been engendered by the Middle East oil crisis. If the Juglar cycle is still holding, the next recession should be around 2010[6] and will be much more severe than 1991 or 2001, because capitalism is in a profit downwave.

If we use US unemployment data to measure the cycles of growth and slump, we get a similar picture. The graphic shows the grey columns that highlight the peaks in the US unemployment rate (equivalent to an economic recession or trough in GDP growth).

The peak in unemployment in the Golden Age was in 1958. Once we entered the downturn wave of profitability after 1966, there was a peak in 1971, followed by a much bigger peak in unemployment in 1975 and an even bigger peak in 1982. Once the upwave in profitability began again from 1982, the unemployment peaks or recessions were fewer and milder.

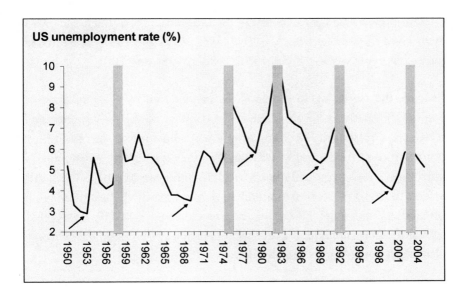

PROFIT CYCLE AND BUSINESS CYCLES

The next one was in 1992 and the last one was the very mild peak of 2002, of about the same degree as the 1971 peak, the first in the profit downwave of 1966-82.

The US unemployment rate in the Golden Age remained very low — culminating in a trough in 1969. In the profit downwave period from 1966-82, the next real low in unemployment was ten years later in 1979 (although there was one briefly in 1973). Once back in the profit upwave period, unemployment hit a new low in 1989 and again in 2000.

So the cycle of unemployment seems to be about ten years, especially if you look at the periods from trough to trough in unemployment. The last low in the unemployment rate was in 2000. That suggests the next low will be around 2009[7]. Then we could expect the unemployment rate to double over a period of about 2-3 years in an economic recession with a new peak in about 2011-12.

The Juglar cycle has different turning points from the Marxist profit cycle, for two reasons. First, the cycle is of the whole economy, the productive and unproductive sectors, including the government sector. Thus the movements in the profit cycle and the productive sectors of capitalism feed through with a lag to the rest of the economy. The turns in the profit cycle since the war have been in 1948, 1965, 1981 and 1997. The turns in the Juglar cycle were in 1958, 1971, 1980-2, 1991 and 2001.

Second, the Juglar cycle seems to be engendered by the decisions of capitalists to invest in constant and variable capital (machinery and workers). Profitability rises and after a while businesses start to employ more workers. As the cycle picks up, then they decided to invest more in machinery. This eventually leads to a fall in the rate of profit. Once this affects the mass of profit for capitalists across the board, they start laying off labour, making machinery idle or even closing down. This crisis takes some time to ensure after the profitability turning point. And the recovery also lags the recovery in profitability.

PROFIT CYCLE AND BUSINESS CYCLES

Finally, there is an even shorter business cycle of about 4-5 years. Joseph Kitchin discovered this in the 1930s[8]. This cycle seems to be the product of even more short-term decisions by capitalists on how much stock to keep to sell. It seems that capitalists cannot see further ahead than about 2-4 years. They expand production and maximise the utilisation of existing production capacity. In the struggle to compete, capitalist producers end up with more stock than they can sell. So production is slowed until stocks are run down.

In the next chapter, I intend to explain how all these cycles or motions of capitalism are linked with the Marxist profit cycle based on the law of the tendency of the rate of profit to fall as the lynchpin of the others. From the evidence I hope to draw some conclusions about what is going to happen to the world capitalist economy over the next ten to 15 years.

1. *Simon Kuznets*, Secular movements in production and prices, *1930.*
2. *The house price trough was duly reached in 2009, with a peak to trough decline in prices of about 30%.*
3. *Clement Juglar,* Commercial crises, *1889.*
4. *Karl Marx,* Value, Price and profit, *Chapter XII.*
5. *See the National Bureau of Economic Research website.*
6. *We now know that it came earlier than 2010.*
7. *The low in unemployment came earlier.*
8. *Joseph Kitchin,* Cycles and Trends in Economic Factors, Review of economic and statistics, *1923.*

Profit cycle and economic recessions

In the last chapter, I explained how there were more cycles in capitalist economic development than just the profit cycle, or for that matter the bear and bull stock market cycle. Russian economist Kondratiev had found that prices of commodities under capitalism appeared to have a cycle of over 50 years divided into an upwave of half that followed by a downwave of similar length. This has probably lengthened to about 64-72 years.

I also showed that there was a real estate or construction cycle that lasts about 18 years from trough to trough and an economic growth cycle that delivers periodic recessions or slumps about every 9-10 years. This is accompanied,with a short lag, by a similar cycle in unemployment.

Two questions: are there any connections between these various cycles? And how do they pan out to provide a forecast for what will happen to the world capitalist economy over the next decade or so?

To answer the latter question, I use the data provided for the US economy yet again. This is the most comprehensive and also deals with the most important capitalist economy in the world. In my view, therefore, it offers the best indication of the future.

The answer to the first question is that the profit cycle is the key cycle that links the others together. Profits drive investment under capitalism. And investment drives growth, employment and this consumer spending. The motion of capitalist production starts and ends with profit.

And when you analyse the movements of the various cycles under capitalism: prices, construction, output and employment, and the shorter business cycle of about four years, it is the profit cycle that links them.

PROFIT CYCLE AND ECONOMIC RECESSIONS

Take a look at the graphic below. That graphic merges all the cycles under capitalism since the second world war. The Kondratiev cycle is the longest, spanning a probable 72 years since the trough of 1946 to the likely next trough in 2018. The next longest is the profit cycle based on Marx's value rate of profit explanation of capitalism. As we have shown in previous chapters, this spans about 32-36 years from trough to trough.

The last trough in profitability was in 1982 and so the next one will be around 2014-18. And the trough in the profit cycle of 1982 coincided with the peak of Kondratiev cycle in prices.

The stock market cycle almost matches the profit cycle in its length if not in its timing; not surprisingly, as stock market investments depend so closely on the rise and fall of profits. So in the graphic it is merged with the profit cycle.

The next stage down in the matrix of cycles is the real estate/construction cycle first identified by Kuznets. That cycle is about 18 years from trough

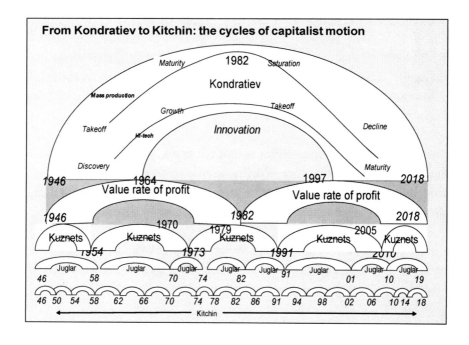

to trough, about half that of the profit cycle and one-quarter of the Kondratiev cycle. There have been three post-war troughs in the construction cycle: 1954, 1973 and 1991. The next one is due in 2009. In other words, the current downturn in the US housing market, after its peak in 2005, should reach a bottom in 2009.

The next stage down is the output and employment cycle first highlighted by Juglar. This appears to be nine years in length from trough to trough. The last trough in the post-war period was the very mild recession of 2001. The next trough should be around 2010, with a peak in growth about now (2006)[1].

Finally, there is the much shorter Kitchin inventory or trade cycle of about 4-5 years from trough to trough. The last trough was in 2002 and so we can expect a 'pause' in economic growth this year, with another trough in 2010[2].

Several things emerge form this description of the various cycles. First, it would seem that the length of the various cycles is divisible. In other words, the long Kondratiev cycle of 64-72 years can be divided downwards to the short Kitchin cycle of 4-5 years. Thus, there are two profit cycles in the Kondratiev cycle, four Kuznets cycles, eight Juglar cycles and 18 Kitchin cycles.[3]

The profit cycle is key though. The upwave in the profit cycle from 1946-65 coincided with the upwave in the Kondratiev cycle. Thus the troughs in the Juglar and Kuznets cycles in the mid-1950s did not produce a very deep recession or downturn in economic growth and employment. Because the Kitchin cycle troughed also in 1958, the 'pause' was longer than in 1954. But high and rising profitability in an environment of a Kondratiev upwave was generally good news for capitalism.

From 1965-82, the rate of profit fell. The Kondratiev cycle was still in an upwave of prices though. So what we got was successively worse economic slumps (1970, 1974 and 1980-2) alongside rising prices — in other words 'stagflation'. In 1974, the Kuznets, Juglar and Kitchin cycles troughed together. In an environment of falling profitability, world capitalism suffered its first post-war simultaneous economic slump.

The 1980-2 recession was so deep and long-lasting because it was when profitability reached lows and the Kondratiev prices cycle peaked. But the real estate Kuznets cycle was also at a peak, so output and employment fell while prices stayed up — the ultimate stagflation crisis.

The next upwave of profitability (1982-97) coincided with the downwave in the Kondratiev prices cycle, which we are still in. Thus rising profitability was accompanied by falling inflation, from 15% in 1982 to just 2-3% by the late 1990s. Rising and high profitability (by 1997) also meant that the Juglar growth troughs of 1991 and 2001 were not nearly as deep or severe as 1974 and 1980-82. The Kuznets cycle troughed again in 1991, making the 1991 economic recession much more severe than the 2001 recession when the housing market in the US and elsewhere was booming.

We are now in another profit downwave that should not bottom until around 2015. So output and employment slumps should be as severe and long-lasting as they were in 1974-5 and 1980-2. This profit downwave now coincides with the downwave in the Kondratriev prices cycle that started in 1982 and won't reach its bottom until 2018. So it is likely that future economic slumps will not be stagflationary but deflationary. Prices could fall absolutely as they did in the 1930s[4], the last time the profit downwave coincided with the Kondratiev downwave, and as they did in Japan in the 1990s (again in the international Kondratiev downwave).

The next troughs in the Kuznets construction cycle, the Juglar growth cycle and the Kitchin inventory cycle are due in 2010. There has not been such a coincidence of cycles since 1991. And this time (unlike 1991), it will be accompanied by the downwave in profitability within the downwave in Kondratiev prices cycle. It is all at the bottom of the hill in 2009-2010[5]!

PROFIT CYCLE AND ECONOMIC RECESSIONS

That suggests we can expect a very severe economic slump of a degree not seen since 1980-2 or more likely since 1929-32, the last time all these cycles troughed or were in downwaves.

And we can expect a similarly severe one about 2014-16, when profitability will have troughed and so will the Kondratiev downwave. That would be similar to 1884 (in the dim past) or 1946.

The war of 1939-45 was a product of the continued failure of capitalism to restore its health. In my view, the fact that the largest capitalist economic powers of the 1930s (the US and the UK) were in a period of Kondratiev and profitability downwaves explains why capitalism did not seem to be able to recover. Its failure bred an arms race and eventually a war through the whipping up of nationalist fervour among the masses by the ruling classes of each capitalist state. The war, in turn, led to a massive physical destruction of capital that restored profitability.

There is another aspect of the graphic: the innovation cycle first described by Schumpeter. Once a new discovery is made in technology, there are four phases in the cycle of innovations that set the structure of the techniques of production in any era: growth, takeoff, maturity and decline. This innovation cycle seems to last about the same time as the Kondratiev cycle, but its phases are best analysed as two parallel cycles.

Let me explain. The auto and electronics industries were innovations of pre-1914. They began small growth between the great wars. After 1945 up to 1964, mass production of autos, electrical goods and other household consumer items took off, while the older, heavy industries of steel, shipbuilding and mining matured, growing slowly.

From 1964-82, the mass production electrical goods and autos sectors entered their mature phase. They dominated markets but no longer grew very fast. The older heavy industries went into catastrophic decline. And in this profits downwave phase, they increasingly did not produce the huge profits of the past, while the heavy industries made serious losses.

PROFIT CYCLE AND ECONOMIC RECESSIONS

Alongside these dominant technological sectors were new, small, but now growing industries around computers (big macroframes) and hi-tech innovations that were just in the early growth stage, having been in the discovery innovation stage in the 1950s.

From 1982-00, profitability recovered, but the mass production sectors were saturated and started to decline: on the whole consumers in the advanced capitalist economies did not need more than two cars, five TVs or microwaves etc. Manufacturers of these faced fierce competition as consumers increasingly decided only on price for these commodities. This was now in the Kondratiev downwave too. Alongside, the new hi-tech sector began to take off and in this profits upwave, the returns on these new products (PCs, the internet, Microsoft, ecommerce) were spectacular.

From 2000, the old mass production sectors will be in serious decline — at least in the top capitalist economies. And the new hi-tech sectors will now enter a period of maturity, where growth and profits will be low (especially as this coincides with the Kondratiev and profit downwaves).

Beneath the surface, the discovery innovations of the period 1982-97 (as yet unclear, but probably nanotechnology, gene technology etc) will begin to grow into commercial sectors. But this will be in a multi-cycle downwave period, unlike any other previous period since the second world war. The 1930s downwaves delayed the real takeoff of the mass production sectors until afterwards. These new technologies could be similarly stunted.

Our graphic shows that capitalism (at least the G7 economies) is now heading for a combination of troughs in all its economic cycles (the motion of capitalism) that will coincide about 2010. The profits cycle is in a downwave alongside the Kondratiev cycle. Capitalism is in its 'winter' period — making it very vulnerable to crisis[6].

1. The peak in growth globally was in 2007.
2. Not much of a pause in 2006, but the trough is about right.
3. The idea of linking all the cycles with the motion of capitalism

was first mooted by Robert Bronson of Bronson Capital Markets Research in 1997. Bronson identified the stock market cycle, but did not link this to a profit cycle, which is key in his Stock Market and Economic Cycle Template (SMECT). See Robert Bronson, A forecasting model that integrates multiple business and stock market cycles, *2002.*

4. Consumer prices are now falling in Germany, the UK and some other OECD economies.

5. The Great Recession was early!

6. The idea of spring, summer, autumn and winter phases in the Kondratiev cycle was developed by PJ Wall — see David Knox-Barker, The K-wave, *1995. These seasons of the K-cycle can be integrated with the profit cycle: a spring phase with rising profitability and rising prices (1946-64); the summer phase with falling profitability and rising prices (1964-82); and then autumns with rising profitability and falling prices (1982-2000); and finally the winter phase with falling profitability and falling prices (2000-2018).*

Profit cycles elsewhere

In earlier chapters, I described how the post-war US economy exhibited cycles of profitability of around 32-36 years, divided into two waves, one showing a rise in profitability (1946-64 and 1982-97) and one showing a downwave (1964-82 and 1997 onwards).

Also, each profitability downwave was accompanied by a rise in the organic composition of capital (as defined by Marx as a rise in the value of the stock of capital equipment and plant owned by capitalists relative to the cost of employing the workforce). Conversely, when profitability was in its upwave, the organic composition of capital fell. Thus, Marx's basic law of the tendency of the rate of profit to fall appears to be confirmed empirically for the US economy.

I used the data from the US economy for two reasons. First, the US economy is the most developed and largest capitalist economy in the world. Just as Marx used the British economy in the 19th century to draw out the laws of motion of capitalism, so the US economy now provides the best evidence for the current forces driving capitalism. Second, there was a very mundane reason. The data available to draw conclusions from are so much better than for any other economy.

But obviously, the question arises: does Marx's law of the tendency for the rate of profit to fall apply to other capitalist economies? In this chapter, I try to draw the evidence together to answer that question.

Let's start with the last great capitalist economy of the 19th century, the UK. The UK economy is also still the fourth-largest by GDP (unless you count the Chinese economy as capitalist). What do the data on profits show?

Accurate data only go back to 1955, but it looks as though the Marx's law holds for the UK too[1]. It would appear that the downwave in profitability started earlier than in the US, in about 1959 to 1975, a period of 16 years. During that period, the organic composition of capital rose.

Then there was an upwave in the rate of profit lasting to 1997, as in the US. This upwave seems to be about 22 years long, again accompanied by a fall in the organic composition of capital. The whole cycle from peak in 1959 to peak in 1997 is 38 years.

That's a slight difference from the length of the US profit cycle peak to peak (1964-97) of 33 years. But that is not the only difference. The turning points in the UK profit cycle, particularly the switch from downwave to upwave do appear be different.

In the UK it was in 1975; in the US 1982, although you could argue UK profitability had a new trough in 1980. And since 1997, although UK profitability has broadly followed the same trend as in the US (a slump to 2001 and then recovery), interestingly the organic composition of capital has continued its decline.

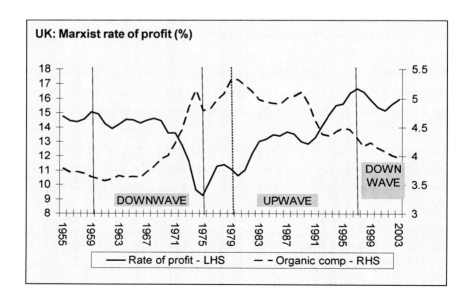

This may be because the UK economy has sustained relatively low un-employment, while UK capitalists have refused to invest more, at least domestically. So profitability has been falling because UK capitalists are being squeezed by a rising share of labour in national income, not because of a rising organic composition of capital.

In other words, the rate of surplus-value in the UK must be falling even more than the organic composition of capital. The most likely reason is the very poor growth in productivity engendered by UK capitalism.

However, unemployment in the UK is now starting to rise. The closures and redundancies in the ailing UK auto industry are one sign. So soon, we can expect the organic composition of capital to rise too[2].

Overall then, the Marxist law of the tendency for the rate of profit to fall appears to operate in UK capitalism but with certain national differences to the US.

What about the world's second-largest capitalist economy, Japan? Here the evidence is much inconclusive, partly because the data are also much

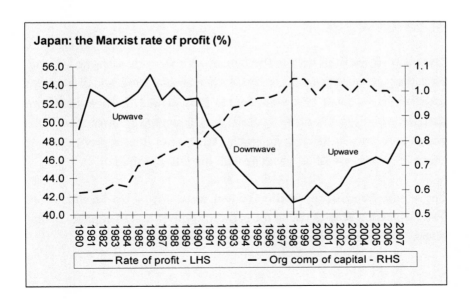

less reliable. For a start, data are available only back to 1969 for measuring profits. Also, that data are not entirely in line with Marxist definitions[3].

With those caveats in mind, what the graphic on Japan shows is that there was a clear downwave from a very high level of profitability prior to 1975. From 1975 to 1988, there was what could be described as an upwave, with profitability being higher at the end of the period. From 1988 there was a clear downwave in profitability to 1998. After that, the data appears to show that Japanese capitalism is now in a profit upwave[4].

Marx's law of profitability seems to hold for the downwave before 1975, with the organic composition of capital rising. In the subsequent upwave, it is less clear, with the organic composition rising, while profitability rose very slightly. In the downwave from 1988 to 1998, the organic composition of capital rose, as per Marx. In the current upwave, the organic composition of capital has been flat..

The current period in Japan has been characterised by increased investment by Japanese companies, but accompanied by sharp falls in employment. Employment is now picking up, so expect the organic composition of capital to stop rising soon. Then we shall see if Marx's law is causal for Japan since 1998[5].

There are clear differences in the Japanese profit cycle with the US one. First, the post-war downwave started earlier, around 1962. and the upwave ended earlier in about 1990 compared to 1997 in the US. Now there is an upwave while the US profit cycle is in a downwave. Also, the profit waves in Japan are different in length. We appear to have profit cycle of about 25 years, not 32-36 years as with the UK and the US.

The *secular* trend in profitability is down, matched as it is with what could be considered a secular rise in the organic composition of capital. In that sense, Marx's law holds.

PROFIT CYCLES ELSEWHERE

Now let's look at Germany, the world's third-largest capitalist economy and the largest in Europe. Here the story gets even more opaque. The graphic on Germany shows that profitability rose sharply from 1967 to 1990. After that, the rise has been minimal.

Again, the data are not nearly as reliable and accurate as the US data. But for what they are worth, the data show that Germany's organic composition of capital fell from 1967 to 1990. So, as a result, German profitability has risen.

Huge investment in plant and equipment in the immediate post-war period and high levels of unemployment drove up the organic composition to huge levels. But as German capitalists started to employ more workers, the organic composition steadily fell and the rate of surplus-value rose. Profitability flattened.

The pace of the rise in profitability also slackened after 1990. That coincided with a slight rise in the organic composition of capital, again confirming Marx's law to some extent.

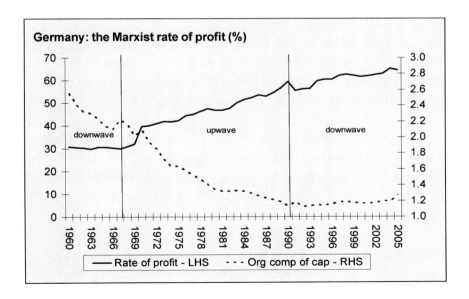

PROFIT CYCLES ELSEWHERE

It is difficult to talk about a profit cycle for German capitalism. But if we try, it would appear that there was an upwave from 1967-90, or 23 years. Since then there has been downwave of sorts, which could last as long as the previous one from 1946-67. So that could come to an end in about 2013. But these are very tendentious conclusions to reach.

The most significant conclusions are the sharp differences in the trends in German capitalist profitability and that of the US and the UK. The first post-war profit downwave was in the period of Golden Age when profitability was rising for the war's victors, Britain and America.

The upwave from 1967 to 1990 does not match the upwave in the US (1982-97). The current downwave started much earlier than in the US or the UK, but it may finish about the same time as German cycle seems longer at about 42-46 years.

Finally, there is China. It is very tendentious to call China a capitalist economy that follows the law of value. Certainly, the law of value was not dominant in that state-owned economy up to 1992. It may still not be dominant, but it is increasingly so. So I've tried to see if Marx's profitability law is beginning to operate there.

If getting good data is difficult for Japan and Germany, it is almost impossible for China, given the crooked nature of the government statistics, apart from their rarity. So I've had to cheat again and not use accurate Marxist definitions to come up with some trends.

If we dismiss the period before 1992 as still in the age of the 'planned economy', then the post-1992 period suggests the law of value is beginning to operate with a rise in the organic composition of capital starting to drive down profitability, at least up to 1999. After that, the rate of profit starts to rise and has picked up pace towards 2004[6].

Since 2002, there has been a sharp rise in the organic composition of capital. This reflects the massive investment in fixed capital that China has been engaging in. This ought to drive down the rate of profit eventually unless there is reversal in the organic composition[7].

Either way, it does appear that since the law of value in China became more dominant after 1992, that Marx's law on profitability has begun to operate with a rising organic composition of capital and a falling rate of profit. The decline in the rate has been about 10% while the organic composition has nearly doubled.

There are some important general lessons to be drawn from this analysis, which I emphasise again is based on some pretty dodgy stats. The first is that profit cycles do appear to exist in other capitalist economies and they do appear to be related to or caused by Marx's law. But these cycles are not in the same time sequence as in the US or even have the same length.

What are the reasons for that? One must be that, despite 'globalisation', world capitalism does not provide a fully 'free market' for the movement of capital and labour. So if a national economy has a higher rate of profit than another, it is not yet possible (and probably never will be) for capital

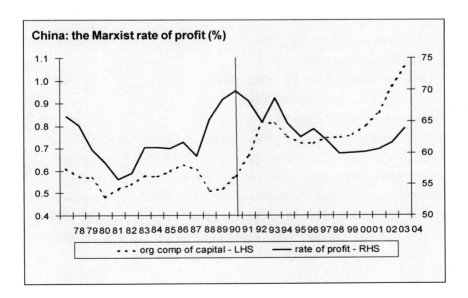

China: the Marxist rate of profit (%)

- - - org comp of capital - LHS ——— rate of profit - RHS

to flow freely into that economy and drive down profitability to a 'world average'.

A world economy with a world average rate of profit does not exist because there are so many barriers still to the movement of capital, engendered by monopolies in various industries, protectionist tariffs and government legislation.

Also there are many sectors of capitalist economies that do not compete in world markets, like building and construction, retail outlets, professional services etc. There is not a global market place.

Finally, the history of economic recovery after 1945 is different for the imperialist US economy or the ageing UK economy, than it was for the reviving German and Japanese economies. Thus the cycle of accumulation and profit is different in length and timing.

That means over the next decade, while US and UK capitalism could be in difficulty, Japan and China may be able to take advantage. In that sense, it may be true that Asia will rule the economic world over the next generation and further.

1. UK national statistics office.
2. The latest data show this.
3. Japan's Ministry of Economy data.
4. Updated results confirm this.
5. Updated results confirm this.
6. My results on China were confirmed by Zhang Yu and Zhao Feng in a paper delivered in Beijing in September 2006 to the International Forum on Comparative Political Economy of Globalisation, entitled "The rate of surplus value, the composition of capital and the rate of profit in Chinese manufacturing industry, 1978-2005", *although Yu and Feng conclude that the organic composi-*

tion of capital was the not the driver of profitability .

7. The latest data would suggest that the rate of profit has started to fall again, which might confirm a downphase in the profit cycle of about 17-18 years.

Marx's law of profitability and 19th century Britain

By the beginning of the second half of the 19th century, Britain was the leading capitalist power by some way. It had the largest share of world trade, particularly in manufacturing, where it was the global leader in industrial innovation and expansion. It had a large colonial empire and military might to maintain it under pax Britannia. The Great Exhibition of 1851 marked the pinnacle of British capitalism's superiority.

Through the second half of the 19th century, it remained the leading economic, financial, military and political power. But it began to decline relative to the US, in particular, but also to Europe (France and Germany) in each succeeding decade up to the First World War.

In that sense Britain between 1850 and 1914 was in a similar position to the US between 1945 and now. It was the most important and advanced capitalist state, but its relative superiority was declining.

Marx's analysis of the laws of motion of capital was based primarily on Britain. He lived there and he used its economic data and events to understand capitalism. So the UK was the right economy to analyse the validity of Marx's theory of capitalist accumulation and crisis in the late 19th century.

Unfortunately for Marx and fortunately for us, we now have much better data about the production of value and surplus value, constant and variable capital for the UK between 1855 and 1914 than Marx did. He had none and could not test any of his laws against empirical evidence, even when he had fully worked them out.

Now we have the data[1]. If we use that data for the period from 1855 to 1914, we can plot the rate of profit in Marxist value terms and other Marxist categories like the organic composition of capital to see if Marx's law of the tendency of the rate of profit to fall holds for the most advanced capitalist economy of the 19th century — as it does for the US in the second half of the 20th century.

When we do that we come up with several startling results. First, the Marxist rate of profit for the UK economy between 1855 and 1914 moves in a cycle of about 30-plus years from trough to trough, with an up phase from 1855 to 1871[2]. This was a boom period for British capitalism and capitalism globally, with very few recessions and weak ones at that. It represents an 'autumn' season in the Kondratiev cycle similar to that of 1982-97.

Marx and Engels complained in their writings about just such a long boom, unlike the period from 1830 to 1848 which had been one of intense class struggle culminating in the revolutions of 1848 — similar to period of the 1970s, or the 'summer' season of the K-cycle.

The up phase of 1885 to 1871 was followed by a down phase from 1871 to 1884, a period noted for frequent and deep recessions — indeed the

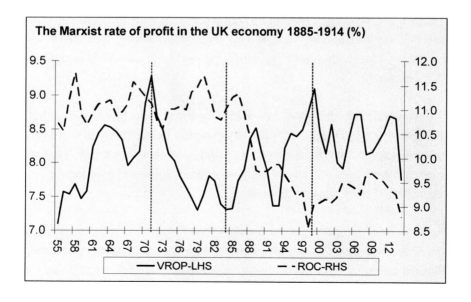

The Marxist rate of profit in the UK economy 1885-1914 (%)

VROP-LHS   — - ROC-RHS

1880s was considered a Great Depression like the 1930s, or the winter phase of the K-cycle.

After 1884, we get another up phase in the rate of profit until 1899 (although it is volatile through to the mid-1890s). This was a period similar to the up phase in profitability seen in the advanced capitalist countries from 1948-73 (a spring season in the K-cycle), with economic recovery being accompanied by a revival of strength in the labour movement in the UK after the depression decade. Marx's daughter, Eleanor was heavily involved in the rise of the new unskilled trade unions and the beginning of the Labour party during this period.

Finally, there was a fall back in profitability from 1900 up to the start of the 1914 war, in a period in which class struggle intensified, with major industrial struggles and rising political movements in Britain and also in Germany, France and America, similar to the period 1964-82 — a summer season in the K-cycle. Then the war cut across the class struggle and allowed capitalism to devalue its overhang of dead capital that had led to low profitability.

The data also show that the main reason for the cycle of profitability under British capitalism between 1855 and 1914 was the movement in the organic composition of capital. There is a significant inverse relationship between the organic composition and the rate of profit of about 0.4[3]. In other words, when the former goes up (over a period of years), the latter eventually goes down.

That would seem to confirm the conclusions reached with the evidence of US profitability between 1948 and 2009. Marx's law holds again.

1. See AJ Arnold and S McCartney, "National income and sectoral rates of return on UK risk-bearing capital 1855-1914", 2002.
2. We cannot ascertain when the up phase commenced as the data only go back to 1855.
3. See data in Arnold and McCartney.

The profit cycle and politics

"Men make their own history, but they do not make it just as they please; they do not make it under circumstances chosen by them-selves, but under circumstances directly encountered, given and trans-mitted from the past." Karl Marx, Economic and Philosophical Manu-scripts.

In previous chapters, I showed that there was upwave and downwave in the rate of profit that alternated at about 16-18 year intervals. This cycle applied most clearly to the US and the UK, but the cycle also operated (in a different time sequence and duration) in Germany and Japan.

In this chapter, I want to argue that there is a relationship between this profit cycle and political developments, namely in the intensity of the class struggle between the owners of capital and the working-class, those who have to sell their labour power to the owners in order to live.

In a period when the rate of profit is high or rising, you would expect the intensity of the class struggle to be less and vice versa when profitability is falling. Why? Because when profits are high or rising, the capitalist class feels more comfortable and confident. The owners of capital can make some concessions to the working-class to keep the profits rolling.

In a rising profit environment, employment is also likely to be rising (par-ticularly when the economic upwave is well under way) and economic recessions will be fewer and shorter. The opposite is likely to be the case when profitability is falling: more recessions and higher unemployment as capitalists try to stem the fall in profitability by laying off workers or cut-ting their benefits.

In the period after 1945, there was an upwave in profitability until 1964, then a downwave until 1982, followed by a recovery until 1997. Now we are in a new downwave that should last until around 2015.

PROFIT CYCLE AND POLITICS

Anecdotally, we can build a political scenario in the US and the UK that matches that cycle. In the period of the 'golden age', once the immediate revolutionary upsurge in Europe, Japan and the UK (Labour government) subsided around 1948, politics in the US and the UK became conservative.

From 1948 under Truman and then the Republican ex-general Eisenhower, the US had a right-wing administration obsessed with the 'cold war' with Russia and the 'reds under the beds' scares. In the UK, the conservatives under Churchill, Eden and Macmillan ruled the roost, culminating in Macmillan's 'you've never had it so good' boast in the landslide election victory of 1959. Germany had a right-wing leader in Adenhauer, while Gaullism triumphed in France by 1958. In Italy, the corrupt right-wing Christian Democrats dominated and in Japan, the similarly right-wing Liberal Democrats began an interminable period of rule..

But once the upwave in profitability came to an end around 1964, the political atmosphere changed and soon became more volatile. In the US, there was the election of Kennedy in 1960 but he followed a basically conservative policy like his predecessor.

His assassination in 1963 led to the Johnson administration. Ironically, he was regarded as a reactionary redneck from Texas and yet his policies were the most 'liberal' in government spending, although he pursued the war in Vietnam began by Kennedy with a vengeance. During the late 1960s and into the 1970s, America became a cauldron of opposition to the war, the civil rights movement erupted and trade union action reared its head.

The Democrats were led by leftist leaders like Senator McGovern. The Republican administration of Nixon from 1968-73 may have been one of the most crooked and awful in US history, but it was not the most reactionary. Nixon did not attack the labour movement (instead he bribed the Teamsters); he even eventually ended the war in Vietnam; while taking the dollar off the gold standard (the ultimate Keynesian economic policy move). He was followed by a very 'wet' administration under Democrat Carter.

In the UK, the mid-1960s saw the return of the Labour government under Wilson, increased trade union action and a move to the left in the labour movement. The return of the Tories under a very mild conservative leader, Edward Heath, was enough to provoke a major miners strike and the quick return of Labour during the 1970s. Political action intensified along with more economic recessions, rising unemployment and inflation.

This period of political crisis and struggle came to an end with the end of the profitability downwave. Capitalist profitability rose as the severe economic slump of 1980-2 weakened the labour movements of the US and the UK so that corporations could draw on cheaper labour and reduce production costs. That coincided with the arrival of more reactionary and conservative governments.

In the UK, after Wilson resigned in 1976, the Labour government under Callaghan and Healey moved to the right as UK profitability headed for lows. Callaghan renounced Keynesianism in a famous speech to the Labour conference and imposed heavy public spending cuts. He paved the way for the return of the Tories in 1979.

The Tories were led by Thatcher from 1979-90, followed by Major up to 1997. I don't need to tell British readers what Thatcherism meant for the working-class. Suffice it to say that the defeat of the miners in 1984-5 was as much a *political* turning point leading to a long period of reaction as the 1982 *economic* recession was the beginning of new era of rising profitability for the capitalist system.

It was Reagan in the US from 1980 to 1988 (with his huge spending on weaponry and his crushing of the labour movement starting with the air traffic control workers), followed by George Bush senior, who took the country into another war, this time against Iraq. The Clinton era was little different despite the label of a Democrat administration, engaging in more wars than any previous US administration.

Just as in an era of falling profitability the Republican Nixon administration was quite 'Keynesian' in its spending and labour movement policies and protectionist in trade, so in the era of rising profitability, the Democrat Clinton was conservative in government spending, anti-labour and 'free trade'. Similarly, the Blair Labour government was 'new' and very anti-trade union, pro-US and war-mongering in the Balkans and Iraq at the same time.

The upwave in profitability appears to have come to an end in 1997 in both the US and the UK. Since then, the rate of profit (at least expressed in Marxist terms) has not got back to the level of 1997, despite a rally since 2002. If we are now in a downwave of profitability, then it seems likely that the years of political reaction are over.

From here, the level of the class struggle should heighten and there will be governments elected that will be unable to follow outright pro-business policies. The labour movement should revive and move increasingly to the left over the next decade as economic recessions of the severity of 1974-5 and 1980-2 are repeated. The days of Bush and Blair are numbered.

The thesis is that when profitability is rising (and particularly when it is high and reaching its peak), capitalism has openly right-wing governments (Churchill 1953 to Macmillan 1964 or Truman 1948 to Eisenhower 1960; or in the second upwave: Reagan in 1980 to Bush Jnr in 2004 or Thatcher in 1979 to Blair in 2005). Bourgeois politicians and commentators become boastful and confident about capitalism as the only successful system of human organisation (free trade, privatisation, anti-Keynes). The labour movement becomes relatively passive and the ideas of Marxism and socialism weaken.

Alternatively, when profitability is declining and particularly when it is reaching its low, then capitalist governments are shamefaced or 'liberal' or 'reformist', even anti-big business (Wilson 1964 to 1976 for the UK or Johnson in 1964 to Carter in 1980 in the US). At the same time, the labour movement becomes very active and socialist and revolutionary ideas become much stronger, while capitalist ideology is watered down and lacks confidence (the ideas of Keynesianism and the mixed economy and public services strengthen).

Of course, this is a generalised account and approximate. Clearly, the turning points and periods of the profit cycle do not match exactly the politics of capitalism and the class struggle. One obvious example is that both Bush Jnr and Blair are still in office, nearly ten years since the profit cycle turned into its downwave. That is because the political cycle and minds of people often lag the economic reality.

Also, we are still early into the downwave, which should have at least another decade to run. Just as there was only a mild economic downturn in 1970, six years into the profitability downturn and the first big recession did not come until 1974, so we have had only a mild downturn in 2001 and

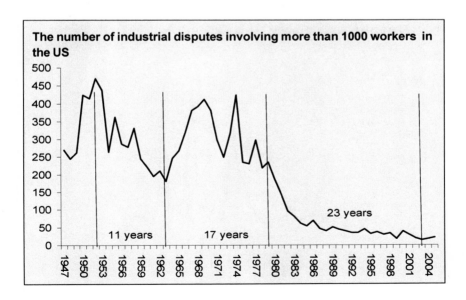

The number of industrial disputes involving more than 1000 workers in the US

next big recession is still brewing up (2009-10?). Politics will follow the economics as well as vice versa.

It is difficult to get the timing of these political turning points right. But we can try to put some facts together to see if there are any signs of political turnings to match the change in the profit cycle.

One of the best measures of the intensity of the class struggle is the level of strikes and industrial disputes, for which there are very good historical data. The graphic below shows the number of work stoppages in the US since 1947.

What the graphic reveals is that in the periods of upwave in profitability (1948-64 and 1980-1997), work stoppages declined to new lows. In the periods of declining profitability (1964-1979), the number of work stoppages rose and stayed at a high level. But this argument must be tempered by the length of the decline in stoppages, over 23 years since 1980. There is just a sign of a pickup in industrial action in the last two years.

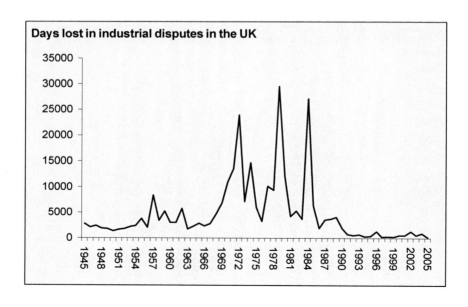

Days lost in industrial disputes in the UK

PROFIT CYCLE AND POLITICS

It is a similar story in the UK, where the period 1966-84 saw an unprecedented level of industrial action. However, since the defeat of the miners in 1985, days lost in industrial action have fallen to record lows.

When the working-class becomes more active in struggle, it forces the governments of the capitalist system to 'reform' or to concessions. Thus, as capitalist profitability moved into a downwave after 1964 and the American labour movement and working class became more antagonistic to the capitalist system, successive administrations tried to accommodate them by allowing public spending to rise, as the graphic below shows.

Of course, much of this extra spending was on arms in wars against Vietnam and in the arms race against the USSR. But it was also the period of the Great Society programme of Johnson 1964-68. Even under Nixon and Carter later, the spending was increased. Eventually, capitalist politicians came to power determined to reverse 'Keynesianism' and the labour movement, which they saw as destroying profitability.

After a deep recession in 1980-2 that weakened the working class, Reagan and the first George Bush after him attacked the labour movement and

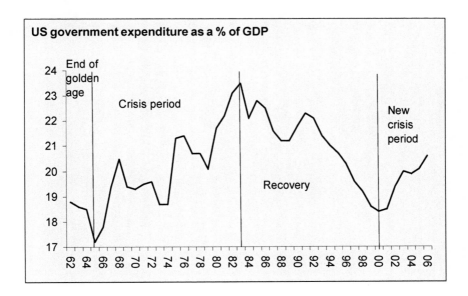

then began heavy cuts in social spending, designed to switch resources to productive sectors of capitalism.

Under the new downwave of capitalism since 1997, the two-term Bush administration has again reversed that 'small government' policy. Sure, much of the increased spending is for arms and wars in the War Against Terror, but Bush has also not tried any longer to hold back on certain social spending like Medicare as he steadily loses popularity. The process of rising government expenditure will continue[1].

So the political cycle of labour movement struggle and capitalist government spending in countries like the US and the UK broadly matches the movement of the profit cycle. If that is right, then, as profitability falls over the next decade and we experience more economic recessions, expect rising labour movement action and more spending by governments to placate the working class.

1. Under Obama in the US and Brown in the UK, public spending has rocketed to deal with the Great Recession in a Keynesian way.

Summing it up

This chapter tries to sum up all that has been said so far.

I started from the premise expressed by Marx that the tendency of the rate of profit to fall was the most important law of the motion of capitalism. Marx argued that capitalism is still the most dynamic mode of production that human beings have yet lived under. But capitalism does not move in a straight line. Economic growth leaps forward at some times, along with employment and prices. At other times, production slows or even falls back absolutely and prices rocket or fall along with employment.

How do we know where capitalism is going? The law of the tendency of the rate of profit to fall under capitalism is the most important in explaining and predicting the motion of capitalism.

As I explained in an earlier chapter, Marx's law is as follows. If the organic composition of capital rises on a sustained basis, then the rate of profit will eventually fall. The organic composition of capital is defined as the amount spent by capitalists on plant, equipment and raw materials relative to that spent on the labour force. The rate of profit is defined as the amount of surplus-value produced by the workforce employed by the capitalists divided by the total cost of production for the capitalists in plant, equipment and the workforce. In other words, a rising organic composition of capital means that constant capital is increasing faster than variable capital.

I wanted to find out if Marx's law holds. I measured the organic composition of capital and the rate of profit under Marx's definition using the statistics from the US at first. Later I looked at other capitalist economies. I found that if the organic composition of capital rose, then, on the whole, the rate of profit fell. Marx's law is confirmed.

SUMMING IT UP

But more than that, I found that there was a profit cycle, under which the organic composition of capital would fall for about 16-18 years before reversing and rising for about 16-18 years. The rate of profit moved inversely to the movement of the organic composition of capital.

I reproduce the graphic for the US (yet again!).

But the evidence also showed that over the whole post-war period, the rate of profit fell. Each peak in the profit rate in the cycle was lower than the previous one. There appeared to be a secular decline in the rate of profit as well as a cyclical law of motion[1]. The best explanation for this was that increasingly mature, late, imperialist capitalism was becoming more 'unproductive' in its own terms. In other words, more and more labour was being employed in sectors of the economy that did not generate surplus-value, but merely either circulated it or helped to make sure that productive sectors functioned[2].

Thus, the finance and property sectors, the government sector, the armed forces, the layers of advertising, marketing, and promotional employees: all these seemed 'necessary' to capitalism working, but were unproduc-

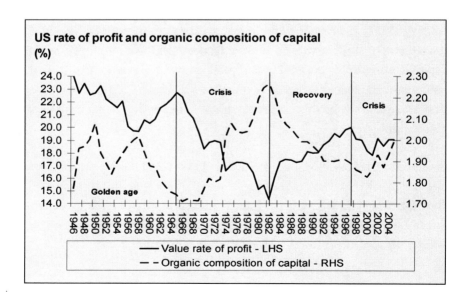

tive. With more and more labour in these sectors relative to productive sectors, the rate of profit would be lowered.

The key prediction that flowed from the profit cycle was that capitalism (at least US capitalism) was now in the early stages of a profitability downwave that was set to last until the rate of profit bottomed again, say around 2015-18.

Marx was right in saying that the tendency of the rate of profit to fall is the most important law of capitalist motion. From it flows all the other cycles of capitalist economic and social relations. And there are other cycles, including the cycle of boom and slump.

The capitalist stock market moves in cycles of bull upswings and bear downswings. This stock market cycle matched that of the profit cycle almost exactly. Thus capitalism (at least US capitalism) is now in a bear market for stocks and shares, where stock prices will continue to decline (not in a straight line) from a peak achieved in 2000 until a new trough around 2018.

Most interestingly, the long-known Kondratiev economic cycle of the movement of prices of production under capitalism also coincides with the movement of the profit cycle. In the post-war period, the Kondratiev cycle peaked in 1980, at the same time as the profit cycle troughed. The Kondratiev cycle (which is about double the length of the profit cycle of 32-36 years) is now in a downwave and we entered a new downwave in profitability in 1997.

Other economic cycles are not synchronised with the Kondratiev, profits or stock market cycles. The building and construction cycle completes over 18 years, half that of the profits cycle, but with different turning points. The troughs in the US building cycle were in 1973, 1991, with next due in 2009-10[3].

SUMMING IT UP

Similarly, the cycle of economic growth and employment appears to be about half that of the building cycle and one-quarter the length of profits cycle, again with different turning points, but due for the next trough or 'recession' in about 2010.

Indeed, what the evidence shows is that many of the economic cycles of capitalism are coinciding with troughs about 2010 in an economic environment of a Kondratiev price downwave and a profitability downwave. This augurs for a very ugly economic crisis in 2009-10, perhaps not seen since the 1930s[4].

I also looked at other profits cycles apart from that in the US. I found a similar cycle for the UK with fairly similar turning points. In contrast, Japan and Germany had different cycles, with Japanese capitalism apparently in a profitability upwave that began in 1998, while Germany is in the middle of a downwave that began nearly a decade ahead of the downwave in the US and the UK.

But the evidence, such as it is, suggests that most of the biggest capitalist economies will follow the US into economic crisis, as the pressures of a falling rate of profit exert themselves.

Finally, we made some tentative suggestions that flow and ebb of the profit cycle also had an impact on the intensity of the class struggle between the working-class and the capitalist class. When the profits cycle was in an upwave and capitalism looked healthy, its leaders were more confident; in contrast, workers were more passive and accepted the system as they tended to get more jobs and better living conditions.

Thus, in what we can call the Golden Age of capitalism after the second world war up to about 1964, most capitalist states had conservative governments that promoted the benefits of the 'free market' while the labour movement was relatively quiet. Socialism and militant trade unionism was broadly absent.

However, once the profits cycle entered a downwave and particularly as economies experienced successive economic recessions, labour disputes rose and governments came to office pledged to 'reforms' to improve things and control 'the ugly face capitalism'. Capitalists felt less secure and adopted more unorthodox theories that were even anti-capitalist. Socialist ideas and militant trade unionism flourished.

After over 20 years of reactionary politics, driven by a rising rate of profit from 1982-1997, improved economic growth and milder economic recessions that restored capitalist confidence and weakened socialist idoelogy, the US and most of the world capitalist economy has entered a new downwave in profitability.

Once the full impact of this downwave begins to bear down on economic growth, employment and living standards, then the intensity of the class struggle will rise again to levels not seen since the 1930s and 1970s.

That is where we are going: a falling profit rate to a new low around 2014-16; a series of economic recessions (at least two, in 2009-10 and 2019-20, and possibly more) at least as severe as those of 1980-2; and a new wave of political struggle against capitalism similar to that seen in the 1930s and the 1970s.

1. Andrew Kliman's brand new analysis on the US rate of profit also confirms this secular decline. See appendix A on measuring the rate of profit.
2. This is not Kliman's view but closer to that of Fred Moseley.
3. This was confirmed with the bottoming of the housing crash in the UK and the US around late 2009.
4. It came a little earlier with the Great Recession troughing in mid-2009.

Dr Pangloss rules

The *Financial Times* recently claimed the British economy has been doing rather well out of globalisation. But a closer look at the figures shows that what we have before us a growing polarisation, with the rich getting richer and the poor poorer. On a world scale, the position is even worse, which may possibly explain the growing instability all across the globe.

All is well — at least that is how the *Financial Times* reviews the state of the UK in a September editorial. Entitled "New Britain faces the world with confidence", the editorial starts with a confident assertion: "Though it has its problems, Britain is in good shape... the overall sense is one of progress and success".

And the primary reason, according to the FT, is globalisation. "It was globalisation, the vast expansion of world trade and migration during the 19th century, that brought Britain's greatest era of success... future governments must do as this government has done and let globalisation happen."

This Panglossian view of Britain and the world comes from the mouth of the leading forum of British capitalism, of course. Also, it is probably no coincidence that the editorial was written as New Labour holds its annual conference (possibly the last as 'New Labour').

Former FT economic leader writer and correspondent, Ed Balls, now an MP and Chief Secretary to the Treasury, Gordon Brown's right-hand man and likely future successor to Gordon as Chancellor of the Exchequer, may well have his writing hand in this piece. Britain's so-called economic success is the key selling point for Gordon in his quest to hold the Ring of power in Britain.

Dr Pangloss extends his influence across the big pond too. America's stock markets are nearly back to their all-time highs achieved in the heady hi-tech boom days of 2000. An investor in American shares back in March 2000, however, would still have made no money at all.

Okay, say 'the markets', things have been bad, but they are looking up. Corporate profits in the US, Europe and Japan have also hit peaks. Indeed, corporate profitability, that is profits relative to investment, is now nearly back to the level of 1997, the profit peak of the great stock market and economic boom of 1982-2000[1].

It's nearly back, but not quite. And here we can detect just a sign that all is not perfect in the most perfect of capitalist worlds. We could survey the world capitalist scene after 20 years of 'globalisation' in a more realistic way.

First, globalisation has brought us terrorism and the "War against Terror". That does not seem to be going too well. The US and its imperialist allies are locked into a never-ending occupation of Iraq with daily heaps of bodies (of course, it's mainly ordinary Iraqi people). The 'freedom forces' are penned up in their bunkers in the Green Zone of Baghdad, hardly venturing out. Thus, the militias of the various religious sectarian groups continue their murder and mayhem. Above all, Iraq slowly slips out of the control of US imperialism.

Across the border, Iran's mullahs preach defiance, while Hezbollah in Lebanon claims victory over the strongest army of the Middle East and the key henchman of imperialist rule in the region, Israel. And in Afghanistan, the religious fundamentalists of the Taliban successfully sting and cuff British armed forces in the harsh hinterland — when will British imperialism realise that they cannot tame Afghanistan, a cemetery for British soldiers for nearly two hundred years?

The FT tells us that all is well because this period is like the 'globalisation' free trade era of the 19th century that brought British capitalism its greatest success. Here the FT stretches history. British capitalism led the world economically from the time of the Industrial Revolution at the end of 18th century to say about 1870. From then on, in the period of 'globalisation', other capitalist powers, like the US, Germany, France, began to compete for spheres of influence and gain around the world. Free trade was no longer a boon to the UK.

Indeed, the current period is much closer to the struggle for markets that we saw at the end of the 19th century that Britain lost and eventually led to a world war in 1914 and again in 1945, before the US became the hegemonic power. Now in 2006, it is the US that is struggling to maintain its dominance: it is losing market share in exports; it is running up huge debts with the rest of world; it is finding it difficult to get other capitalist powers to support its interests in the Middle East and Latin America and it is losing any influence at all in Africa. Its influence in Asia through Japan is now threatened by a colossus, potentially bigger than itself, China. Far from globalisation heralding peace and prosperity in the world, it suggests increased rivalry and conflict.

British capitalism continues to rest its hopes on the US remaining top dog and remaining prosperous. Over the next 20 years, it is a gamble that will deliver, not "progress and success", but collateral damage not seen since the 1930s[2].

After all, let's be clear about some key facts on globalisation before we accept the FT's praise for it. Has it brought prosperity? Well, at the level of production, it has been a relative failure. Branco Milanovic is the leading economist at the World Bank. He has recently published a book called *World's Apart: measuring international and global inequality*[3]. Milanovic opens by saying that "the average world growth rate in output per head has declined in the last 20 years".

So, under globalisation, and even taking into account that the advanced capitalist countries have suffered only 'mild' economic recessions in 1990 and 2001; and even taking into account, China's staggeringly fast growth in the last ten years, the world average growth rate was still lower in 1979-2000 compared to 1960-78. Indeed, over the last 20 years or so, every year one country out of three has seen its GDP per capita decline — such is the inefficiency and instability of globalised capitalism.

And of course, these figures are averages. What Milanovic shows in his book is that inequalities between rich and poor countries and between rich and poor within each country and between rich and poor globally have increased under 'globalisation'. He finds that there "has been a steady and sharp increase in inter-country inequality", after being broadly constant prior to the launch of globalisation.

Even more startling is the inequality within the world's population wherever they live. According to Milanovic, "77% of the world's population live below the rich world's poverty line. There are 79 countries that are poorer than Brazil and they constitute 70% of the world's population." By his calculations, there is only 6.7% of the world's population that can be considered middle-class. He reckons that about 17% of the world's population can be considered rich. Even in the rich countries of the world, there are 92 million people who can be considered poor by world standards. In the poor countries, the poor constitute 93% or 4 billion people!

Economists measure the inequality of income by what is called the Gini coefficient. I won't explain how that works here, but suffice it to say that the higher the Gini coefficient between 0 and 100, the greater the inequality. According to Milanovic, the Gini coefficient has increased from the start of industrial capitalism back in the early 19th century when it was at 12 to reach 35 by the end of the 19th century (that is three times more unequal), to 65 by the early 1950s (five times more unequal) and to remain at this high level since then, despite China and India's fast growth in recent times. So globalisation under capitalism has been no great boon for more than 80% of the world's people.

While the world's stock markets bathe in the glorious September sunshine of huge company profits, bringing massive bonuses for the top executives and Wall Street and City of London financial traders[4], the rest of us feel a lot less sanguine about the world.

DR PANGLOSS RULES

The US is about to hold elections for its congress. Despite apparently everything being rosy, Bush continues to score lows in the opinion polls and the Republicans could be defeated in the elections despite gerrymandering and a lack of enthusiasm for the opposition Democrats. It's the same in the UK. Tony Blair polls at record lows and New Labour is behind the Tories in the polls.

But leaving aside both leaders' appalling foreign policy, is it so surprising when we realise that the so-called fruits of globalisation have not permeated down to most ordinary families in the US or Britain. In the US, the share of wages in national output is the lowest ever, while corporate profits hit its highest share since the Golden Age of the 1960s and this at a time when economic growth does not match the growth of the 1960s.

The 'overall sense of progress and success' that the FT refers to from globalisation seems absent from the data in the 'land of opportunity', America. According the US Census Bureau, in 2004, the top 20% of US households took over 50% of all income earned while the bottom 20% got only 3%. In 1980, at the start of globalisation, the top 20% took 43% and the bottom 20% just 4.2%. The top 1% is even better off. They took 11.2% of all income in 2004 compared to 6% in 1980. They have nearly doubled their share under globalisation. It was always very unequal, but it's even worse now.

If we look at wealth owned by households in the US and not just income earned in a year, the situation is even more shocking. According to the Federal Reserve Bank's latest consumer finances survey, the wealthiest 1% of Americans own 33.4% of all net wealth after deducting mortgages and other debt. That's up from 30.1% back in the late 1980s before globalisation took hold. The bottom 50% of Americans owns just a staggering low 2.5% of all household wealth!

And it is going to get worse not better[5]. Real wages are falling in the US. The median average hourly wage after inflation has fallen 2% in the last two years. For young people joining the labour market, they are finding that entry-level real wages are 4% lower than in 2001. Those with young families have seen their income fall 6% in the last five years.

The FT notes the problem of inequality in its editorial and admits that inequality in Britain has not altered under New Labour since 1997. It also notes growing inequality between the regions and the problems of providing enough infrastructure and resources to house growing numbers of immigrants, whose labour has enabled British capitalism to keep its head above water by taking low wages and working long hours and not using social services. But the FT sweeps all these problems aside in a blaze of sunny confidence.

Britain's capitalist survival has increasingly been built on becoming a rentier economy, relying on providing financial and 'professional' services to other capitalist nations who are producing surplus-value. Britain, as far as capitalism is concerned, has become a huge Switzerland, banking the world's profits, for a fee. The City of London is a giant aircraft carrier parked in the Thames, where world money flies in and out, with little touching the sides, except for those working on the carrier and living in London and the south-east. The rest of Britain is just a dark shadow to these people.

But if 60 million people must depend on the success of the world's stock and bond markets and above all on the continued success of the US economy, then they ought to view the next five years with trepidation. The housing bust is well under way across the pond and it promises to be the worst ever. Usually housing markets, when they blow out, tend to take 3-4 years before they reach a bottom. That puts the trough at around 2009-10, just at the time we could expect the next economic recession in the US, if history is any guide.

1. See the data expressed in the US profit graphic on page 36.
2. The credit crisis and the ensuing Great Recession of 2008-9 have delivered more damage to the capitalist system than any crisis since the Great Depression of the 1930s.

3. Branco Milanovic has recently updated his figures to show even greater global inequality — see the World Bank website.

4. No change there: Goldman Sachs have just announced a record payout on bonuses for 2009-10 at the trough of the Great Recession!

5. The latest figures from the 2008 US Census Bureau report show increased inequality.

From boom to slump

The financial press and the investment houses of global finance capital are in euphoria. The world's stock markets are booming. But a closer look reveals that all this euphoria is misleading and the real situation is far less healthy than would appear on the surface.

The US stock market index (called the Dow Jones industrial index), which measures the stock prices of the top 30 companies in the US, has just hit an all-time high. Other wider-based indexes, both in the US and Europe are also at five-year or more highs. Even the Japanese stock market, which plunged to incredibly low levels after the financial market bust of the late 1980s, has started to recover.

Even so, these new highs are somewhat misleading. The Dow Jones index may be at an all-time high of 12,000-plus. But it has taken six and half years to get back there after the dot.com collapse in stock market prices back in March 2000.

So if you had been stupid enough to invest in stock markets (as many middle-class people did and most of us were indirectly forced to do because our pension funds did) back in 2000, you would have made no money at all until now! You would have been better leaving your hard-earned savings (assuming you had any) in the bank.

Moreover, if the stock market indexes were adjusted for inflation since 2000, then the Dow Jones index has not reached an all-time high. To do that, it would have to rise another 15% before investors who bought stocks back in 2000 could claim to have made any money after deducting for inflation.

Nevertheless, the financial press and the investment houses of global finance capital are in euphoria. They are making huge profits — every day, the big investment houses announce yet more billions of profit made. This

FROM BOOM TO SLUMP

Christmas, their executives are expecting massive bonuses to their already bulging pay packets. Their earnings will be matching those of professional footballers. No wonder property prices in the 'best' parts of central London are rocketing!

These bonuses and the profits of finance capital also go a long way to explain why the stock markets are booming. Stock prices are rising fast because the level of profits for big business in Europe, Japan and the US seems to be at record highs.

According to the official data, the share of profits in annual national income is at a record high in the US, with the share going in wages (both for ordinary workers and their managers) at all-time lows. It's the same thing for Europe and Japan. The economic growth of the last few years since the mild global recession of 2001 has been mainly diverted into profits and workers have gained little or nothing.

It's the same thing with the profit margins. That's the measure of the rate of profit in a capitalist economy that the capitalist economists like to use. It measures the amount of profit made per unit of output. That is at an all-time high.

The rate of profit from a Marxist value point of view is very different from the bourgeois measure of profitability because it measures profit relative to the total cost to capitalists of investing in plant and the labour force.

Marx showed that capital accumulation would have a tendency to lower the rate of profit. That tendency for the rate of profit to fall could be counteracted for a while by higher exploitation of workers (as expressed in the higher share of profits in output which is what the capitalist measures currently show), or by lowering the costs of equipment and plant through new technology. But eventually, profitability would fall.

FROM BOOM TO SLUMP

The rate of profit in the US under the Marxist definition is still below where it was at its peak in 1997. It has recovered from a low in 2001, but it has still not surpassed 1997. If that is right, then the argument that capitalism is still in the early stages of profit downwave holds. According to my argument, capitalism is set for a tough time over the next decade similar to the 1970s and even more like the 1930s. If that is right, then the profitability of capitalism has probably peaked now and is set to fall from here[1].

Investors in the stock markets are currently enraptured by the news that big business profits have been rising in the US at over a 10% rate for 17 consecutive quarters. And in the current quarter (Q3'06), they will be up another 15%. Again these profit figures are misleading because much of the gains are concentrated in the finance sector. The most productive sectors of the economy, manufacturing and industry, have not recorded such mega results. The banks and finance houses have ripped off most of the profit.

That's not good news for the future of capitalism in the US, Europe or Japan, because it means that surplus-value extracted from the output of workers will not be re-invested in new technology and equipment to create more value, but instead will go into what Marx called 'fictitious capital', namely borrowing to speculate in the stock market or property, or will be invested abroad in exploiting workers in China, India etc[2].

Moreover many capitalist economists are now predicting that profits growth will slow to a trickle next year, as economic growth slows in the US and employment and investment costs mount. This is as good as it is going to get for capitalism.

Already, we know that the great driver of US capitalist prosperity — house prices — has collapsed. The US housing market peaked way back in mid-2005 and now, for the first time in 15 years, average house prices are falling. That is really bad news for the mass of Americans who have increasingly come to depend on maintaining their living standards by borrowing more on their houses as their value rose. They will not be able to do that any longer.

And they cannot expect to increase their incomes by working longer or taking extra jobs. Already Americans work more hours in one year than any other advanced capitalist country (with the exception of Japan). They work 20% more hours than French workers do in one year. It is a key reason why American capitalists have been making so much profit. American workers create more value (and because wages have hardly risen, more surplus value) than in any other capitalist economy.

But if Americans are going to have less money to spend because they cannot increase their borrowing any more and cannot work any harder, then demand for all the goods that they buy in the shops and demand for all services they pay for in restaurants, home maintenance, travelling etc., are going to slow down sharply. That means profits will no longer go on rising at such huge rates and may even start to fall by the end of next year.

It may well be that economic growth in the US will stagger on at a 2% rate for a few more years. This is less than the growth rate of 3% that would be necessary to sustain the relatively low unemployment that the US has at the moment. As we already see in the UK, where unemployment is already at a six-year high (even if it is still low by the standards of the 1970s), unemployment in the US will rise over the next few years.

The cycles of boom and slump in capitalism have not disappeared. They seem to operate on a 9-10 year cycle. There was a worldwide economic recession or slump in 1980-2. Then the world capitalist economy recovered and an economic boom ensued (with a slight 'pause' in 1986-7). Finally, capitalism fell back into recession in 1990-2, about 9-10 years after the previous slump. Again capitalism recovered and a new boom ensued (again with a bit of pause in 1994). It culminated in another recession (this time relatively mild) in 2001.

Once more, capitalism took another breath of life and began a new 'boom' (although this is one of the weakest in capitalist history). This has lasted five years so far. But if the cycle of boom and slump holds, then it should hit a new trough about 2009-10. The US housing slump will probably not reach its bottom until 2010, if previous real estate cycles in the US are anything to rely on. Also, profitability will be heading to a new low by then. Everything is shaping up for a very serious slump in world capitalism by the end of this decade at the latest.

The way to test whether this is right is to monitor the growth of profits in the US, the movement of house prices, and the level of employment. Expect all to fall over the next few years. That will wipe the smile off the faces of the stock market speculators. But the biggest misery will be reserved for those who must pay for the next world economic slump in jobs and living standards — us.

1. Subsequent data to 2008 show that the rate of profit in the US peaked in 2005 and declined thereafter.
2. The credit boom of 2002-07 was a grotesque example of fictitious capital or credit bubble that burst in mid-2007.

The economic witch doctor of capitalism

Milton Friedman died on 16 November, aged 94 years. He was one of the foremost bourgeois economists of the 20th century. His reputation among the right-wing capitalist leaders, especially those who drove the policies of reaction and counter-revolution against the gains of the post-war labour movement in the 1980s was second to none.

Indeed, Friedman was seen by Thatcher, Reagan, Pinochet and many others of this ilk as their main source of advice in rejecting what they saw as the compromising class collaboration policies of the misspent 1960s and 1970s dominated economically by the ideas of John Maynard Keynes. For them, Keynes, a Bloomsbury-set bohemian, who advocated government spending and full employment at the expense of profits and low taxes, was anathema.

It is no coincidence that the current US Secretary of State, Condaleeza Rice, among others, should be profuse in her condolences and in her intellectual debt to Friedman.

What was Friedman's biggest contribution to the cause of capitalism? His main theoretical and empirical arguments started from the assumption that the capitalist system of production and accumulation was without fault in its essence. As long as market forces were allowed to operate untrammelled, then the price mechanism of the market would ensure the proper allocation of resources and thus maximise growth without any crises.

This view was, of course, not original. It is the general ideology of modern capitalist economics, taught in all the university economic schools. But it is in direct opposition to the classical economists of the late 18th century and early 19th century like Adam Smith, David Ricardo, James Mill and Thomas Malthus, whose scientific inquiry led them to have grave doubts about the ability of capitalism to sustain long-term profitability and sustained expansion. For them, capitalism had serious defects, albeit either from agricultural monopolies, excessive competition or over-population.

Keynes too worried about the stability of capitalism. The experience of the depression years of 1921 and 1929-30 led him to conclude that capitalism could not guarantee steady economic growth without slumps and chronic unemployment at periodic intervals. So Keynes advocated making bankers keep their interest rates very low and for governments to borrow and spend money to sustain spending. That meant government had an important role to play in keeping capitalism stable.

Like the Austrian school economist, Friedrich Hayek, Friedman found these ideas as one step on the road to socialism, for him, a system of slavery. Friedman proclaimed the right of the individual to make as much money as he or she could without regulation. Such was his enthusiasm for this principle that in his last years he was a strong advocate of abolishing all laws against smoking, alcohol, and drugs, which he saw as an attack on individual freedom.

Friedman's most famous theoretical contribution was to argue that money was key to successful capitalism. It was the interference of the national bank in the US, the Federal Reserve, in the 1930s that caused the Great Depression, he argued. By restricting the amount of money in the economy, the Fed starved industry of the funds to grow. If it had stayed out of the equation, all would have been well. He and Anna Schwartz published in 1963, *The monetary history of the United States 1867-1950*, to justify this argument. The evidence and conclusions of that book have subsequently been contested by others.

In his propaganda against government interference, he argued strongly for the complete privatisation of nearly all state functions including ending state education, and arguing for a flat rate tax — so a millionaire would pay the same percentage as the poorest paid worker. He also opposed government control of the currency (he predicted that the euro would never be introduced in Europe and later, when it was, that it would collapse).

It is a rather sickening irony that a man who claimed he was opposed to big government was only too happy to advise the military dictator and Chilean coup leader General Pinochet in economic policies during the 1970s and at the same time the Stalinist Chinese regime — all in order to bring about raw-blooded capitalism.

Friedman is thus honoured in the church of capitalism. However, it is no accident that many of his policies have never been adopted nor will they be. The reality is that a completely free market without regulation would lead to anarchy and chaos for the capitalist system. Also, Friedman's policies would mean even more inequality of income and wealth than there is already, provoking reaction from working people. All-out Friedmanism would probably have brought capitalism to its knees.

His emphasis on controlling the money supply has been completely ignored in recent years as finance capital has exploded. Credit has never been more out of control in the capitalist economies of 2006. The capitalist apologists and leaders will mourn his passing, but not carry out his policies. The working class will remember the damage he has done to millions of people's lives.

Gordon's year

"Over the ten years that I have had the privilege of addressing you as Chancellor, I have been able, year by year, to record how the City of London has risen by your efforts, ingenuity and creativity to become a new world leader... an era that history will record as the beginning of a new golden age for the City...Britain needs more of the vigour, ingenuity and aspiration that you already demonstrate is the hallmark of your success". Gordon Brown speaking to bankers in his last months as Chancellor.

As I write, the UK's inflation rate has hit an 11-year high at 3% (excluding the cost of mortgages) or 4.4% overall. At the same time, unemployment is on the rise, if from very low levels. The misery index, a measure that combines the inflation and unemployment rates to provide a gauge on the general health of the economy is still low, but the direction up is clear.

Most forecasters are expecting a relatively benign year for the economy, with growth around 2.5%. But even the most optimistic economists reckon there are sizeable risks to their predictions.

The big one is stagflation, where economic growth slows but inflation goes on rising or does not slow. There is certainly a whiff of that in the British air this winter.   And we get slowing wage incomes along with higher inflation, the mass of British households can expect no rise in real incomes this year.

A key factor in relatively strong growth last year was the influx of immigrants from the new countries of the EU in eastern Europe. These hundreds of thousands have worked hard for long hours, usually in relatively low-paid jobs, without taking much in the way of benefits or social services, while contributing to tax revenues. It has been a significant boost to the UK economy, but particularly to the profits of big and small businesses desperate for cheap labour.

GORDON'S YEAR

Despite the help of these new workers, there remains little sign that the underlying productivity of British capitalism is improving enough to boost economic growth much above 2% a year. The reason is clear. British capitalism has reaped huge profits in recent years (the profit rate for UK non-financial corporations as measured in capitalist terms is now over 14%, while the cost of borrowing money to invest is just 6%).

But British capitalists have no intention of investing any of its accumulated capital back into British industries or services, except of course, in the hugely unproductive financial, property and business services sectors that increasingly dominate the UK economy. Investment goes overseas where returns are even higher.

The economic boom since 2001 has not been a product of investment into manufacturing or the infrastructure of the economy (roads, rail, housing etc). Nothing demonstrates that better than Britain's deficit on trade with the rest of the world. The trucks come across the Channel tunnel laden with imports and go back across to France relatively empty.

The deficit on exports and imports of goods has reached a record 6% of GDP. Including services, like insurance, design, professional consultancy etc, where Britain runs a surplus with the rest of the world, reduces that deficit to 4% of GDP. Then British capitalism gets profits and dividends from its huge investments abroad. That reduces the overall deficit to 3%.

The residual deficit has to be paid for. It is covered by large inflows of cash from the Middle East, Russia and other oil-producing dictatorships who park their money in London to take advantage of high interest rates (much higher than Switzerland, the alternative port of call). In this way, the British pound has not slid away despite the deficit the economy runs.

British capitalism is now almost completely parasitic. Long gone are the days when Britain was the manufacturing centre of the world (that was over 150 years ago), or even a major industrial power (finished by the 1930s). Since 1945, there has been a steady erosion of British manufacturing and engineering prowess and its replacement by the City of London, the banks, finance houses and ancillary services as the major earner of profits and provider of employment.

The City of London is now like a large aircraft carrier off the shore of the Thames, completely separated from the rest of the country. Its prosperity now depends on the ebb and flow of international capital and above all on the prosperity of the US economy and its equally overblown financial sector around Wall Street, New York.

Little do the financiers of Goldman Sachs worry about employment and incomes in Newcastle or Liverpool. Their grotesque incomes and bonuses (rather quaintly called 'compensation') are used to inflate luxury house prices (in Chelsea and Kensington, London they are up 28% in 2006, the highest rise since 1979!), not to spend on British-made goods.

This year, the bonuses for all 170,000 Goldman Sachs employees equalled the annual national product of Vietnam, a country of nearly 80m people. In the UK, £9bn were paid in bonuses to City of London traders with one GS trader alone getting £50m. No wonder that, under the mantle of New Labour, the inequalities of income and wealth in the UK (just as in the US under Bush) have increased substantially. On the day that Goldman Sachs announced its bumper bonuses for 2006, its cleaners went on strike and demonstrated about the appallingly low rates of pay (£5.35 an hour) their employer (part-owned by GS) gave them.

The left-leaning capitalist economist, Kenneth Galbraith, coined a phrase to describe capitalism when it was doing well: it delivered "private affluence, but public squalor". The incomes and wealth of the rich clearly demonstrate the first half of that equation.

The second half is revealed in all the things that would matter for the majority of Britons. Despite more government spending, our public services remain either in dire straits or ripped off for private profit.

GORDON'S YEAR

Take housing. In the 1950s and 1960s, under Labour and Conservative governments, public housing programmes were expanded so that at one point over one million homes were built in a year. But now 50 years later, the government cannot even guarantee that private sector builders can manage more than 50,000 homes — and most of these will be priced out of the range of those that badly need them. Of course, none of this affects the rich in their mansions in London, second homes in Cornwall and their buy-to-let investments.

Take transport. The national rail service was raped and butchered by the Conservative government of the 1990s to impose a ludicrous 'franchise' system that means capitalist companies can get taxpayer subsidies, hike fares to Europe-highest levels and still fail to provide a safe and punctual service to commuters and travellers. That forces more people into cars to clog up the roads and put their lives and limbs in danger. Of course, the rich in their gas-guzzling Chelsea tractors and first-class air travel don't care.

Take health. Despite more spending, the government continues to destroy this major achievement of the post-war Labour government — a universal health service free at the point of use — by making every unit operate on a so-called market basis, charging internally for services and hiving off sections to private health cowboys and gradually privatising through health foundation hospitals and private GPs and dentist services.

No wonder MRSA and other diseases spread through the hospitals, inadequately cleaned as they are by understaffed, poorly paid contracted employees. This does not worry the rich. They have private insurance and private hospitals, staffed by doctors, consultants and nurses trained by the NHS and often moonlighting from NHS hospitals.

Take education. Sure, new schools are being built (usually by handing over ownership to private builders, or handing over complete schools to individual capitalists). But teachers struggle to earn a living, classrooms remain crowded, college students have to pay big tuition fees and take out loans and standards slip further behind those abroad.

The middle-income families of Britain fear the worst and are desperate to send their kids to 'posh' schools to give them a chance to get up the social ladder. What could be more damning that a leading Labour cabinet minister, who used to be education secretary presiding over the closure of 'special schools' for those with learning difficulties, should decide to send her child to a private school despite several available state schools. Labour leaders have no belief or commitment to publicly-financed free education. Again, none of this worries the rich. They have their expensive private schools and universities.

The vast majority of Britons do not get huge bonuses, but work the longest hours in Europe with the shortest holidays to just about make ends meet. Massive borrowing at low interest rates has fuelled spending power. That sparked a housing boom of monstrous proportions, which eventually collapsed in 2004.

Now continued low interest rates and banks flush with cash ready to lend have revived the property market again. But the property and credit boom has left most British households with huge debt. Sure, these are mainly mortgages backed by inflated house prices, but debts they still are, now standing at 159% of average household disposable income — way higher than anywhere else in Europe or the US.

And during 2006, the Bank of England steadily hiked interest rates. As a result, the debt burden (what households have to pay on their debt in repayments and interest) has reached over 12% of disposable income, or back to the levels of the early 1990s and not far behind the level reached before the last economic recession in 1990.

Most significant, given the sharp increases in electricity and gas prices and taxes, British households now spend more of their income on nondiscretionary spending (necessaries like the mortgage etc) than since records began in 1988!

And it is big assumption that house prices will continue with their recent recovery when mortgage rates are heading upwards through 2007. Higher borrowing costs will curb the ability of the average working family to spend more. As a result, economic growth is going to slow.

This is the environment that Gordon Brown will succeed to the leadership of the Labour party and as prime minister. He will be the first Scottish prime minister since Ramsay MacDonald in 1929. MacDonald was the Labour leader who betrayed the labour movement in 1931 by breaking away and forming a national coalition with the Tories and the Liberals designed to impose severe cuts in social benefits and jobs on the working-class at the height of Great Depression.

This is not a comforting analogy with Gordon Brown. Will economic slowdown mean that he too will begin to make the working class pay to make capitalism work?

Capitalism unleashed

In his new book, *Capitalism Unleashed*[1], Andrew Glyn attempts to explain how capitalism moved from the crisis of the 1970s to recovery in the 1980s and 1990s. However, although full of interesting information, the book fails to provide an overall analysis and misses some essential aspects of Marxist theory.

Andrew Glyn is an economist at Oxford University. He has always been on the side of the angels. A doughty fighter for the cause of the labour movement, he has written and acted extensively for the interests of the working class and for the ideas of socialism[2].

He was at one time an economic advisor to the National Union of Mineworkers, the organisation that led the struggle against the imposition of the most ruthless policies of capitalism that were unleashed in the UK under the leadership of Margaret Thatcher in the 1980s.

In his most well known book, written back in 1973 with Bob Sutcliffe (*British capitalism, workers and the profits squeeze*)[3], Andrew explained how the Golden Age of modern capitalism came about from 1948 to 1973 and gave an analysis of why it came to an end and capitalism started to exhibit the symptoms of chronic crisis in the 1970s.

The analysis then of why capitalism fell into a period of crisis, of revolution and counter-revolution, was that the profitability of capitalist accumulation had begun to deteriorate to levels that created the conditions for crisis.

Glyn and Sutcliffe's profitability thesis was not Marx's, however, but one that relied primarily on the argument that full employment in the late 1960s meant that workers could organise to raise wage levels, while international competition did not allow capitalists to raise prices to compensate. Thus the share and mass of profits in the economy were squeezed and this forced down profitability.

CAPITALISM UNLEASHED

This explanation of the fall in capitalist profitability in the UK (and elsewhere) at that time was broadly wrong, in my view. In Glyn and Sutcliffe's explanation of the end of the Golden Age of capitalism from 1948-73, profits were squeezed by labour's share of value added growing and not by a rise in the organic composition of capital, which would be Marx's main argument for the decline in the rate of profit and eventually the mass of profit, and thus crisis.

The empirical evidence compiled by several people (including myself) is that the rate of profit in the OECD economies started to decline after 1964 well before labour's share rose. The rising organic composition of capital was the main cause. However, it is true that in the latter part of the sixties, profits were also squeezed by a rising share going to labour — something Marx envisaged in the later stages of the capitalist economic cycle.

Glyn and Sutcliffe at the time not only denied the role of a rising organic composition of capital empirically *but* also denied its role theoretically in explaining any decline in capitalist profitability. They fell back on a non-Marxist explanation based on Ricardo.

This was important, because if profits were only squeezed by labour power then capitalism could right itself by destroying wage gains. My argument is that even if wages are held down, capitalism cannot succeed indefinitely because of Marx's explanation of declining profitability. The evidence now confirms Marx's view not Glyn's.

But be that as it may — at least it was an analysis. What is lacking in this latest book by Andrew is just that. In *Capitalism Unleashed*, the reader is given, in Andrew's own words, "a short history of how this transformation" from the crisis of capitalism of the 1970s turned into a successful capitalism of the 1980s and 1990s, with fewer economic slumps, rising profitability, a significant weakening of the labour movement and the end of the Soviet Union and its replacement by capitalism.

A series of chapters describes how capitalist leaders adopted new policies that rejected accommodation with the labour movement and the working class, crushed the trade unions, reduced state spending on unproductive and unprofitable social welfare, and privatised and emasculated the state sector.

Also, in one of the most interesting sections of the book, Andrew shows how capitalism was launched on a new phase in its history as it became truly global with the emergence of the economic powerhouses of China and India and the widening of "free trade". This globalisation coincided with the introduction of new technology and the extension of the influence and role of finance capital globally.

All this is a very useful (if in parts opaque) account of the history of capitalism in the last 25 years. But the weakness of the book, in my view, is revealed in Chapter Six entitled *Growth and Stability*.

Here Andrew asks the question: if capitalism managed to remove most of the shackles of the labour movement and state regulation over its workings in the 1980s and 1990s, why did it fail to grow as fast as, or faster than, in the Golden Age of the 1960s? Capitalism had been unleashed, but it had not proved more dynamic. "Output per head has been growing more slowly since 1990 than it did in the turbulent period of 1973-9, never mind the Golden Age" (p151).

But Andrew's answer to his own question is not really forthcoming, except to suggest that maybe the economic dynamism has simply shifted from the more mature capitalist economies of the OECD to China and the emerging world. Also, because there is no analysis of why capitalism managed to turn things round and began a period of rising profitability and success (in capitalist terms) after the crisis period of the 1970s, there is no insight on where capitalism is going now.

The capitalist backlash against labour in the 1980s laid the basis for a renewed rise in profitability, but it was not just the reduction in labour's share that did the trick. It was the two deep economic recessions of 1974-5 and 1980-2 that cut back the cost of constant capital (plant, machinery etc) and thus reduced the organic composition of capital. That was the key factor in renewing the profit cycle for capitalism.

As for timing, capitalism entered an upswing in profitability from 1982 that culminated in a peak (in Marxian value terms) in 1997. This enabled economic growth to be faster than seen between 1964-82 but still not as fast as between 1948-64. It seems that capitalism (at least in OECD) is past its use-by date and cannot grow as fast as it did in previous upswings — again something that Glyn finds inexplicable.

Indeed, Andrew concludes, productivity growth in the last 25 years has been pretty "typical of most developed capitalist countries since 1870" and "performance over recent decades is within the 'normal' range" with no compelling evidence that there will be any decisive change from these long-run norms over the next decade or so" (p151).

Slightly slower (but more stable) economic growth under capitalism in the last 25 years hardly constitutes a crisis for capitalism in the rich countries, Andrew admits. As a result, he seems to conclude that there is no reason why the current scenario for capitalism will ever change, except for a few thoughts on China breaking down, a lack of resources and environmental problems or the collapse of America's consumer boom somehow.

Andrew seems somewhat at a loss on the direction of capitalism from here... "trying to work out more or less likely long-term scenarios is just peering into a highly uncertain future" (p155). Indeed it is, but that is part of the theoretical task, is it not? Perhaps, if he had returned to the approach of his book in the 1970s, which presents a theory of capitalist accumulation based on a law of profitability, he might have found some answers.

In my view, the last 25 years of capitalist success has been based on a recovery in profitability for the very reasons that Marx explained could happen. However, the next couple of decades will see a reversal of that process because Marx's most important law of the motion of capitalism will exert itself. Thus, falling profitability will turn capitalism back into crisis.

Instead, Andrew prefers to try and answer what he calls "the more immediate question": namely what can the labour movement and presumably leftist governments do to improve welfare now for the working-class in the environment of global capitalism? In his final chapter he outlines the inequalities, poverty and lack of welfare that continue to exist in large doses. He argues for less inequality, less poverty and more welfare, in particular pressing for a policy of a basic income for all, to free people from the misery of toil.

These are worthy objectives, but how can they be possible if an unleashed capitalism shows little real sign of crisis? As such, this last chapter of policy aims is no substitute or compensation for the lack of a convincing theory or analysis of why, how or when capitalism might yet falter.

I reckon that capitalism is again in a downswing similar to the period 1964-82. That heralds a period with more economic slumps than we saw between 1982-00 (just one in 1990-1), lasting up to 2014-16. Unless the working class seizes its opportunities over the next decade, then capitalism will find a way to revive itself at the expense of us all.

1. Andrew Glyn, Capitalism Unleashed, *2007.*
2. Andrew sadly died on 3 January 2008. He will be badly missed. See my obituary at http://www.Marxist.com/andrew-glyn-marxist-economist-socialist-fighter.030108.htm
3. See A Glyn and R Sutcliffe, British capitalism, workers and the profit squeeze, *1972.*

Equality, inequality and opportunity

Ben Bernanke is chairman of the US Federal Reserve Bank. As such, he heads up the most important central bank in the world. It is his job to review continually the state of US capitalism and then decide what action to take with monetary policy.

In doing that, under the aims laid down by the US Congress (the political arbiter for the US capitalist class), he must try and reconcile the objectives of good economic growth with keeping inflation down. In essence, he must make the two wings of capitalism happy: the manufacturing and business sectors want good profits and growth; the finance sector wants low inflation so that their income from interest rates is preserved.

At the Federal Reserve Bank, he has the economic weapons of: deciding the basic interest rate for borrowing and lending; the sole right to print money (dollars); and the power to insist how much the commercial banks must deposit with the central bank, thus controlling the quantity of money in the economy.

These are powerful tools in affecting the anarchic and unplanned expansion and contraction of capitalist growth. Since the early 1990s, the US economy has grown at about 3% a year with inflation lower than that. There has only been a mild recession in 2001. It's true economic growth has been relatively slow compared to the Golden Age of 1960s, but since 2001, profit growth has rocketed and the share of national income going to profits compared to wages has never been higher.

So it's no surprise to tell you that Ben Bernanke and his predecessor, Alan Greenspan, are treated like gods by the capitalist class in the US and in most of the rest of developed capitalist world. Because of that, Mr Bernanke's every word is drooled over by the capitalist press, the finance houses and the big capitalist corporations. And what Ben Bernanke has to say about the prospects for capitalism and even why and how the capitalist system works so successfully is closely followed.

Last month, in his wisdom, good old Ben decided to pontificate about the question of inequality of wealth and income in capitalist society. Global capitalism seems to be rolling along nicely at the moment — if you measure it by the size of profits being made by the big corporations and banks. Of course, it does not seem so great if you view it from the perspective of the unemployed, the poor, the hard-working mass of families in the 'rich' OECD countries; and even less so for the billions on less than $2 a day; living in horrific housing and sanitation and facing the risks of major environmental and climate hazards.

But good old Ben is aware that, although capitalism is pounding out good profits at the moment, there is growing criticism that the majority do not get the fruits of capitalist success. Indeed, the majority who depend solely on selling their labour time to survive are actually experiencing declining living standards. It has been well documented the average American household has seen no increase in living standards in the last 20 years[1]. And moreover, inequality of income (what you get in the pay packet every week or month) and wealth (what you own) is increasing in the US and in most advanced capitalist economies[2].

The grotesque news that the directors of the most powerful investment bank in the world, Goldman Sachs, were paid in bonuses alone tens of millions and the whole staff of 170,000 got over $9bn last year, while the cleaners in the bank's offices in London had to go on strike to get the minimum wage, is just one example of the extent of this inequality. We could go on… but let's hear Ben first.

In a speech to the Greater Omaha Chamber of Commerce on 6 February[3], Ben Bernanke explained that American capitalism stood for equality! But wait… this was not equality of income and wealth. No, this was equality of opportunity: *"a bedrock American principle is the idea* *that all individuals should have the <u>opportunity</u> to succeed on the basis of their own effort, skill and ingenuity"*, thus spake Ben.

However, he went to make it completely clear that enlightened capitalism did not actually stand for equality: *"although we Americans strive to provide equality of economic opportunity, we do not guarantee equality of economic outcomes, nor should we."*

Ben went onto admit that inequalities of 'outcomes' (as he calls it) had increased under capitalism. *"Rising inequality is not a recent development, but has been evident for at least three decades, if not longer."* He pointed out that the average American worker's income has risen 11.5% in real terms since 1979, but the poorest wage earner had only seen a 4% total real rise in 27 years. Yet, the top 10% of income earners got a 34% jump. Whereas the top 10% had incomes 3.7 times greater than the bottom 10% in 1979, now that ratio had reached 4.7 times.

When Ben looked at households, the situation was even worse: the top 20% of households took home 42% of all household income in 1979; now they take 50%. The bottom 20% of households took just 7% back in 1979; but now they get even less — just 5%! The top 1% of households in America has 14% of all income, up from 8% in 1979.

This is not good, Mr Bernanke told his audience in Omaha, Nebraska, the home of the Warren Buffett, the world's second-richest man and the world's most successful investor. What is the reason for growing inequality, he tentatively asked?

Apparently, it was not particularly due to increased demand for higher skilled workers who must be paid more. As Ben told the Omaha gang, super-rich income earners like football stars, chief executives of big corporations and Goldman Sachs employees do not have higher skills than their predecessors in 1979. Their skills are much the same; it just seems 'society' is prepared to pay finance executives and baseball players even more.

EQUALITY, INEQUALITY AND OPPORTUNITY

Ben admitted the globalisation may have reduced jobs for unskilled workers or at least lowered their wage bargaining power, but he did not think it was the main reason for growing inequality of income. He plumps for education as the key.

The continually changing nature of anarchic capitalism that is now global means that if you want a well-paid job you have to be well-educated and able to switch from industry to industry and be mobile. Those who get educated well and early will get more income. So Ben's answer is this: we do not need to reduce the wealth and incomes of the rich by progressive taxation or public ownership (god forbid!); and we cannot reduce inequality through public spending to improve the lot of the poor and unemployed. No, *"the challenge for policy is not to eliminate inequality per se but rather to spread economic opportunity as widely as possible... through policies that focus on education, job training and skills"*.

So that's it: more resources on education and skills training. Two immediate questions spring to mind: first, if more education is the answer to reducing inequality (or at least establishing equality of *opportunity*), why is inequality of opportunity growing?

Take the UK, under New Labour spending on education has increased as a share of annual income and government spending. This has happened for ten years amid much groaning and moaning by the capitalist class who complain that taxation to do it is too high and ruining them.

Yet after ten years, the UK rates of inequality of income and wealth have increased. And so is inequality of opportunity. It is now much more difficult if you are the son or daughter in a working-class family to move up the social ladder than it was 25 years ago.

The second question is that where is the money for education spending to come from? More spending on education must either come through the capitalist market sector (private schools and universities) that are out of the reach of most working families; or it must come through the state system (and that means more taxation). Are the working-class to be taxed more for their own minimum education or will the richest be taxed more? You know what the answer would be from the likes of Goldman Sachs, the Bush and Blair/Brown governments?

But most the fundamental point against Ben Bernanke's thesis that 'equality of opportunity' is the right objective not 'equality of outcomes' is that without greater equality of wealth and income there can be no equality of opportunity.

The reason that the rich are getting richer is that they are rich. The poor get poorer because they are poor. Inequality of income and wealth is endemic to the capitalist system of production and capitalism works best (at least for a while) by increasing inequality. The measures of inequality will never decline unless capitalism is curbed. Of course, if you curb a system, it does not work well; so you have to change it.

Ben Bernanke's speech to Omaha's rich was entitled *The level and distribution of economic well-being.* Marx considered the same topic over 150 years ago. His main message was that a fair and cooperative society (a socialist society) would ask every citizen to contribute according to their means and receive back according to their needs. It was not question of having equality of opportunity, but having the resources to live according your needs. If you had a large family, had disabled or sick people in your household, the need to educate, the need to retire, the need for hospitalisation etc, more resources would be provided by society.

Those resources would come from everybody's contribution to production (each with various levels and types of skill). But these resources could not be garnered and distributed and achieve "economic well-being" under a system of production specifically designed to ensure that the ownership of the means of production and distribution was in private hands (and by just a few people as well). In other words, the capitalist system cannot achieve equality of opportunity precisely because it needs inequality

of wealth and income to function. Only a socialist society works to reduce inequality through public ownership of wealth and democratically
planned distribution.

Recently, the UN commissioned a report on inequality in the whole world[4].
The report found that that *"for the world as a whole, the share of
wealth (property, investments and money) held by the top 10% was
85%!"* And one-quarter of those super-rich were in the US alone. The
poorest 50% of the world's 6.6bn population own just 1% of the world's
riches — so much for equality of opportunity.

1. US Bureau of Economic Analysis income data.
2. Federal Reserve Bank consumer finances survey 2007.
3. Federal Reserve Bank, 6 February 2007 speech.
*4. Anthony Shorrocks, Director of Research at the World Institute
for Development Economics Research of the United Nations University (UNU-WIDER).*

Will there be a slump?

As I write, the world's stock markets are hitting all-time highs in their prices. This is not only in Europe and the US, but even more in markets like those of India and China, where there seems no end to the spiralling upward of the burgeoning capitalists economies and their accompanying stock markets.

Most economists are forecasting global economic growth of over 4% in 2007, led by China and India and supported by Europe and Japan. Only the US economy is slowing as its housing market collapses. Even so, hardly anyone is expecting the US economy to drop into a slump.

Are all these optimists right? Is capitalism going to go on growing without any volatile downturn or slump in the next few years?

The answer to these questions, in my mind, depends on the capitalist profit cycle. Profits drive investment under capitalism. And investment drives growth, employment and this consumer spending. The motion of capitalist production starts and ends with profit.

And when you analyse the movements of the various cycles under capitalism: the stock market, prices in the shops, construction and housing, or output and employment, it is the profit cycle that links them.

 I have argued that the capitalist profit cycle spans about 36 years from trough to trough. The last trough in profitability was in 1982 and so the next one will be around 2015-18[1].

The stock market cycle almost matches the profit cycle in its timing, not surprisingly, as stock market investments depend so closely on the rise and fall of profits.

There are other cycles of boom and slump in the capitalist economy. There is a real estate/construction cycle. That cycle runs about 18 years from trough to trough, about half that of the profit cycle[2]. There have been three post-war troughs in the construction cycle: 1954, 1973 and 1991. The next one is due in 2010. In other words, the current downturn in the UK and US housing markets, after its peak in the UK in 2004 and in the US in 2005, should reach a bottom in 2010.

The output and employment cycle appears to be 9-10 years in length from trough to trough[3]. The last trough in the post-war period was the very mild recession of 2001. So the next trough should around 2010.

Within all these cycles, there a much shorter trade cycle of about 4-5 years from trough to trough. The last trough was in 2002 and so we can expect a 'pause' in economic growth this year, with another trough in 2010. That pause seems to be hitting the US this year, but may not necessarily cause a full-blown recession.

The profit cycle is key though. Because the troughs in the employment and building cycles in the mid-1950s coincided with a rising profit cycle, it did not produce any very deep recessions or downturns in economic growth and employment.

From 1964-82, the rate of profit fell. So what we got was successively worse economic slumps (1970, 1974 and 1980-2) alongside rising prices — in other words stagflation. In 1974, the profit, employment and housing cycles all troughed together and world capitalism suffered its first post-war simultaneous economic slump. The 1980-2 recession was deep and long lasting because it was when profitability reached lows.

The next upwave of profitability (1982-97) coincided with the downwave in the Kondratiev prices cycle[4], which we are still in. Thus rising profitability was accompanied by falling inflation, from 15% in 1982 to just 2-3% by the late 1990s. Rising and high profitability (by 1997-00) also meant that the output and employment troughs of 1991 and 2001 were not nearly as deep or severe as 1974 and 1980-82. The construction cycle troughed again in 1991, making the 1991 recession much more severe than the 2001 recession when the housing market in the US and elsewhere was booming.

We are now in another profit downwave that should not bottom until around 2015. So output and employment slumps should be as severe and long lasting as they were in 1974-5 and 1980-2.

This profit downwave now coincides with the downwave in the prices cycle that started in 1982 and won't reach its bottom until 2018. So it is likely that in future economic slumps, prices could fall absolutely as they did in the 1930s, the last time the profit downwave coincided with the downwave in prices, and as they did in Japan from 1989 for a decade.

The next troughs in the construction cycle, the growth cycle and the short-term trade cycle are due in 2010[5]. There has not been such a coincidence since 1991. And this time (unlike 1991), it will be accompanied also by the downwave in profitability within the downwave in prices. That suggests around then, we can expect a very severe economic slump of a degree not seen since 1980-2 or more likely since 1929-32, the last time all these cycles troughed or were in downwaves.

Of course, as Marxists know, the war of 1939-45 was no coincidence, but was a product of the continued failure of capitalism to restore its health by an arms race, the physical destruction of capital and the whipping-up of nationalist fervour among the masses by the ruling classes of each capitalist state.

In my view, the fact that the largest capitalist economic powers of the 1930s (the US and the UK) were in a period of prices and profitability downwaves explains why capitalism did not seem to be able to recover.

There is one other aspect of the capitalist economic cycle. There are four phases in the cycle of innovation that set the structure of the techniques of production in any era.

WILL THERE BE A SLUMP?

Let me explain. From 1948-65, was the phase of take-off for the mass production of autos, electrical goods and other household consume items that had started to grow in the 1930s. These innovations, based on transistors etc, now became the dominant sectors for profit and growth, while the older heavy industries of steel, shipbuilding, mining began to decline.

From 1965-82 the mass production of electrical goods and autos entered a mature phase. They dominated as economic sectors, but no longer grew very fast and, in this period of profits downwave, increasingly did not produce the huge profits of the earlier phase. Alongside these dominant technological sectors were new, small, but now growing industries around computers (big macroframes) and hi-tech innovations that had been in just a discovery, inventor stage before.

From 1982-97, profitability recovered, but the mass production sectors were saturated: on the whole consumers in the advanced capitalist economies did not need or could afford more than two cars, five TVs or microwaves etc. Manufacturers of these items faced fierce competition on price as consumers increasingly decided only on price for these commodities. Alongside, the new hi-tech sector began to take off and in the profits upwave, the returns on these new products (PCs, the internet, Microsoft, e commerce) were spectacular.

From 1997 onwards, the old mass production sectors have been in serious decline — at least in the top capitalist economies. And the new hi-tech sectors are now also entering a period of maturity (and dominance), where profits will be large, but profit growth will be low (especially as this coincides with the profit downwave).

Sure, beneath surface, the innovations of the period 1982-97 (as yet unclear, but probably nano technology, genetic technology etc) will begin to grow into commercial sectors. But this will be in a downwave period, unlike any other previous period since the second world war. And in the 1930s, the downwave delayed the real growth of the mass production sectors until afterwards. The new technologies could be similarly stunted.

WILL THERE BE A SLUMP?

The conclusion from analysing the profit cycle is that the world capitalist economy may not enter a major slump just yet. But capitalism (at least the G7 economies) is now heading for a combination of troughs in all its economic cycles (the motion of capitalism) that will coincide about 2010. The profits cycle is in a downwave alongside the prices and construction cycles. Capitalism is in its Kondratiev 'winter' period[6] — making it very vulnerable to crisis.

So the stock markets may have some to run. And the world's capitalist economies may continue to motor a while longer (in the case of China, perhaps until the 2008 Beijing Olympics is over). But the boom, extended as it is, by huge dollops of credit and speculation (what Marx called 'fictitious capital') is just propagating the conditions for a global slump not seen since the early 1930s.

1. See chapter 6.
2. See chapter 10.
3. See chapter 11.
4. See chapter 9.
5. The Great Recession came in 2008-9.
6. For an explanation of the 'seasonal' periods of the Kondratiev prices cycle and their connection with the Marxist prices cycle, see chapter 10.

Reclaiming Marx's Capital

Reclaiming Marx's Capital: A Refutation of the Myth of Inconsistency by Andrew Kliman, published by Lexington Books

This is an important book. In a nutshell, what Andrew Kliman shows is that Marx's laws of motion of capitalism (how capitalism works and does not work) are logically consistent and theoretically valid.

Kliman's book is a compilation and summary of all the efforts of a few Marxist economists over the last 30 years to defend Marxist economic theory from critics (both bourgeois and those claiming to be Marxist)[1].

Over the last 100 years, various bourgeois economists, starting with the Austrian Eugen Böhm-Bawerk in 1896, the Russian Ladislaus von Bortkiewicz in 1896, the Italian Piero Sraffa in 1960 and the American economist Paul Samuelson in 1971 have all claimed that Marx's labour theory of value and its application to understanding how profitability under capitalism would move was logically inconsistent and/or just plain wrong.

So overwhelming were these arguments that most economists, including most Marxist economists, accepted them. The eminent Marxist economist Paul Sweezy swallowed the criticisms hook line and sinker in 1949 when he republished both Böhm-Bawerk and Bortkiewicz's papers.

Later in the 1970s, most Marxist academics accepted the arguments of Sraffa and the Japanese Marxist economist, Okishio, that Marx's errors meant that his law of the tendency of the rate of profit to fall under capitalism was wrong theoretically. They included Michael Kidron and Andrew Glyn in the UK, among many others.

For them, Marx could not explain the nature of capitalist exploitation consistently and could not provide a logical explanation of capitalist crisis either. Thus, Marx's economic theories were shelved except by a few (including David Yaffe[2], Guglielmo Carchedi, Alan Freeman and Andrew

Kliman), who were quickly dubbed 'fundamentalists' unable to accept reality.

What were the main criticisms of the bourgeois and Marxist critics of Marx? The first deals with Marx's transformation of values of each commodity (as measured by the labour time going into producing them) into prices of production (as measured by cost of production and the average profit).

Marx knew that his labour theory of value did not mean that each commodity sold in the capitalist market would be priced according to the labour time needed to produce them.

Competition under capitalism meant that profitability would tend to be equalised or averaged out across the economy. If a company or industry had a higher rate of profit, capital investment would move towards that sector and away from another in order to reap that extra profit.

This would lead to an averaging out of the profit generated from the labour employed in all sectors. The labour value embodied in each commodity would be transformed into a price of production that was based on the average profit across all sectors. That would differ from the labour value in the commodity, which was based on the labour time involved. Some of the surplus value generated from workers in one sector would have been transferred to another sector.

But, Marx argued, this did not mean that the labour theory of value no longer provided an explanation of capitalist production because, in *aggregate* across the whole economy, the total value of all commodities would still equal the total prices of production; total surplus-value would equal total average profit and the rate of profit in value terms would equal the rate of profit in price terms for the whole economy. Thus, indirectly but decisively, the labour time appropriated by the capitalist into the value of production of commodities explained the prices of all commodities.

It was this transformation that Bortkiewicz said did not work[3]. He argued that Marx had made a crucial error in his analysis. If the value of a commodity is transformed into a price of production by an average profit, then Marx should also transform the values of the original investment in capital equipment (constant capital) and labour force (variable capital) into prices of production too. But if Marx had done that, then his formula would not lead to total values equalling total prices of production and/or total surplus-value equalling total profit. Thus Marx's theory of value falls to the ground.

Kliman shows conclusively in his book that Bortkiewicz's 'correction' of Marx's 'error' (so readily accepted by many for over 100 years) is wrong. There is no need to transform the values of the inputs into the production process based on prices of the outputs. That is logically and temporally wrong.

If you make a pair of trousers and price it according to the cost of the textiles and something for the wear and tear of the machinery and for the labour time involved, you don't then *reprice* the labour time or the machines you used according to the price of trousers you have just made. That's because you have already spent the money on the machines, textiles and labour. To do so is not only logically incorrect; it makes no sense of what happens in the real world. Thus Bortkiewicz's correction is wrong and Marx's solution to the transformation problem is perfectly valid.

The other main criticism of Marx was on his law of the tendency of the rate of profit to fall. For Marx, this was the most important law of the motion of capitalism, because it showed that capitalism had an inherent tendency towards crisis and collapse. Capitalist production is production for profit and if profit should fall, capitalists may well stop production.

Marx argued that the capitalist economy reproduces by increasingly using technology and equipment in place of the labour force in order to drive down costs and raise the productivity of labour. But, as the cost of machinery rises relative to the cost of employing labour (what Marx called a rising organic composition of capital), the rate of profit will tend to fall because if it takes less labour time to make a commodity, its value (or price) would fall and thus tend to squeeze profitability.

This law has been criticised and mauled by a succession of bourgeois economists. And in the 1970s it was rejected by those who claimed to be Marxists. They argued that Marx's conclusion was inconsistent with his assumption: because the rate of profit could not fall if the organic composition of capital rose. This was not an empirical question; it was logically impossible.

The most elegant mathematical refutation of Marx along these lines came from Nobuo Okishio[4], basing his ideas on Piero Sraffa, in turn a follower of the classical early 19th century economist David Ricardo.

Marx had said that no capitalist would willingly introduce a new method of production unless it increased his profitability. In other words, investment in new equipment must raise profitability for the capitalist, not lower it. That seemed to contradict Marx's law that increased investment in technology relative to the labour force would tend to drive down profitability.

Marx resolved this contradiction by explaining that, while the first capitalist would increase profitability by introducing a new technique before others, once all the rest had done so, profitability would fall back and to an even lower level than before.

Okishio denied this. His mathematical formula showed that, assuming there was no increase in real wages for the workers, any increase in the use of new technology would raise profitability and would never cause it to fall. After all, if the workers produced more in the same number of hours, productivity would rise and thus profitability: QED!

Okishio's theorem was soon accepted as a devastating demolition of Marx's position. If you wanted a cause for the rate of profit to fall, you would have to look elsewhere, probably to a rise in the share of wages relative to profit (as argued by Ricardo back in 1819 and Sraffa in 1960 — and later empirically by Andrew Glyn in the 1970s[5].). It meant that any explanation of crisis under capitalism could not rely on Marx's own theory.

In his book, based on previous works and the work of others, Kliman provides a convincing refutation of Okishio's theorem. Okishio's theorem, ostensibly a correction of Marx, made a similar mistake to Bortkiewicz. If a new technology increases the productivity of the labour force, it lowers the value of labour time in the production of commodity. According to Marx, that will lower the value or price of production and tend to lower profitability, other things being equal.

But, according to Okishio, a rising organic composition of capital will not squeeze profitability because a higher productivity of labour will immediately (simultaneously) lower the costs of production involved in the new equipment and the wages of the labour force used in production and thus their prices.

But again this is illogical, as Kliman explains. You cannot reduce the cost of production using the new prices achieved with the new technology because you have already spent it at the old prices. The new prices only apply to the next round of production. The process of production is not simultaneous, but temporal. You can do anything with mathematics, but if your assumptions are unrealistic, you will come up with unrealistic outcomes.

Moreover, Kliman shows that Okishio is not really correcting Marx, but completely distorting Marx's theory. Marx assumed from the start that the prices of inputs to production would differ from the prices of the output; he was not a simultaneist.

Thus, the work of Kliman and others has been to reclaim Marx's economic theories through what they call a temporal single-system interpretation (TSSI). It is temporal because Marx's theory is dynamic. The prices of the inputs going into production do not change simultaneously in line with the prices of the outputs after production.

And it is single-system in that Marx's labour theory of value is not divorced from the prices of capitalist production, but is integrally connected to them. You cannot have profits without surplus-value and you cannot have surplus-value without the appropriation of labour time by capitalists from workers. Thus Marx's economic theory of exploitation is logically consistent with the process of capitalist production. The creation of profit depends on the creation of surplus-value.

There is one very important point in the book that Kliman emphasises. Kliman is not saying that Marx is empirically correct. It may not be that the rate of profit under capitalism will fall as the organic composition of capital rises, or the organic composition of capital may not rise under capitalism. Marx's law of motion of capitalism may not fit the facts to explain economic crisis. That is the job of others to show or not.

I can remember the debates in the mid-1970s that some of us had with Andrew Glyn and others over whether Marx's 'orthodox' theory of the rising organic composition of capital and the tendency of the rate of profit to fall was valid both theoretically and empirically. We knew instinctively that Marx had not got it wrong and his iterative solution to the introduction of new technology and the rate of profit made sense. But we struggled with the arguments of the neo-Ricardians of the Sraffa variety or the Marxists who followed Sraffa. Their revelations about Marx's 'mistakes' in *Capital* and their apparently impeccable algebra left us puzzled, even floundering.

What Kliman has done is summarise the arguments of the defenders of Marx's economic theory. He shows that a proper reading of Marx's *Capital* reveals a coherent theory of capitalist production from the labour theory of value and a logically consistent explanation of the movement of profit.

He has stripped away the obfuscations of the neo-Ricardians. Marx did not make theoretical errors (at least in the areas that the critics have claimed and others have accepted for over one hundred years since Volume 3 of *Capital* came out). And for that, Kliman must be thanked.

Kliman makes every effort to make his book simple and easy to follow. But even so, many of the arguments are complex and those who do not have some knowledge of Marxist economics may find it difficult. But it is worth persevering, because those who digest the arguments in the book will come away with formidable weapons to defend Marxist economic ideas.

1. See Andrew Kliman, Alan Freeman and Julien Wells eds, The new value controversy and the foundations of economics, *2004.*
2. See Yaffe's early defence in The Marxian theory of crisis, capital and the state, *1972.*
3. Ladislaus von Bortkiewicz, Value and price in the Marxian system, *1952.*
4. N Okishio, Technical change and the rate of profit, *Kobe University Economic Review, 1961.*
5. A Glyn and B Sutcliffe, British Capitalism, the workers and the profits squeeze, *1972.*

The mass of profit and crisis

The data for the US economy show that the rate of profit has resumed its downward phase after a significant recovery from the low of 2001. In 2006, the rate of profit fell and that was repeated in 2007.

The falling rate of profit does not generate an economic recession or slump, it merely indicates that it is coming, if the fall is sustained. Indeed, as the rate of profit falls, capitalists make even greater efforts to boost the mass of profit by expanding constant and variable capital. So the mass of profit will rise as the rate of profit falls.

"The number of labourers employed by capital, hence the absolute mass of the labour set in motion by it, and therefore the absolute mass of surplus labour absorbed by it, the mass of the surplus value produced by it, and therefore the absolute mass of the profit produced by it, can consequently increase, and increase progres-

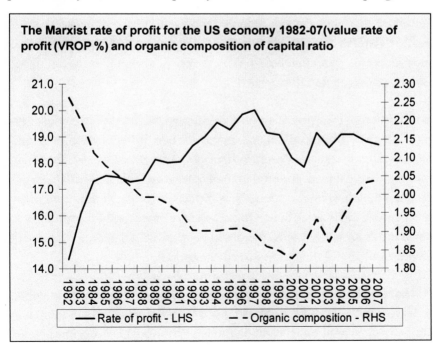

The Marxist rate of profit for the US economy 1982-07(value rate of profit (VROP %) and organic composition of capital ratio

sively, in spite of the progressive drop in the rate of profit. And this not only can be so. Aside from temporary fluctuations it must be so, on the basis of capitalist production." Capital (1959, p. 218)

The trigger point for economic crisis will be when the rate of profit falls enough to bring about a slowdown and contraction in the mass of profit. At that point, capitalists will stop investing: there will be a strike of capital. That was certainly Marx's view: *"Accumulation depends not only on the rate of profit but on the amount of profit" Capital (1969, p. 536). "A portion of the capital would lie completely or partially idle (because it would have to crowd out some of the active capital before it could expand its own value), and the other portion would produce values at a lower rate of profit owing to the pressure of unemployed or but partly employed capital ... The fall in the rate of profit would then be accompanied by an absolute decline in its mass ... And the reduced mass of profit would have to be calculated on an increased total capital." Capital (1959, p. 252)*

But more than this, we can pinpoint another trigger within the mass of profit. Capitalists must eat and live. Capitalism may be a system of production for profit that is driven by the cry of accumulate, accumulate! But capitalists cannot live on air.

So a portion of the mass of surplus value must be diverted into consumption and away from available resources for new investment in plant and labour. Thus the mass of profit produced in one period can be divided in the next period into an accumulation of constant capital and variable capital plus capitalist consumption. Now if the mass of profit produced in the previous period is unsufficient to sustain investment and for capitalists to consume at previous levels, there will be a crisis. So another trigger for slump would be a fall in capitalist consumption[2].

As the rate of profit falls over a period, the pressure is on both an eventual reduction in the mass of profit and probably before that, on a reduction in capitalist consumption. If capitalist consumption begins to decline or even not increase at previous levels, capitalists will stop accumulation. So economic recession will begin even before the mass of profit falls[3].

Can this argument be validated by empirical evidence? It certainly can. Let's look at the US economy since 2005 to see if the level of the mass of profit and capitalist consumption can reveal a capitalist slump. First, look at our regular graphic showing the US rate of profit. The fall in the rate was resumed in 2006. What happened to the mass of profit?[4]

Well, the mass of profit kept on rising right through to 2008, even though the rate of profit was falling. But in 2009, the mass of profit fell — the Great Recession had arrived. Capitalist consumption was an even better indicator of impending slump. It rose through to 2007 but then fell slightly in 2008, before the mass of profit. It was a clear forward indicator of the Great Recession.

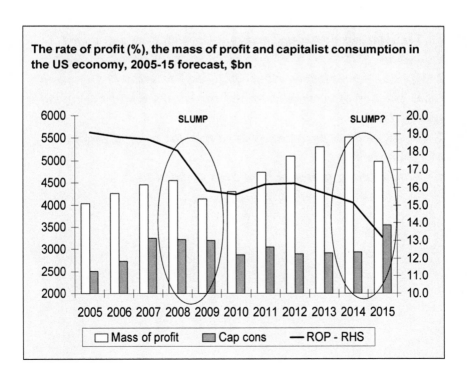

The rate of profit (%), the mass of profit and capitalist consumption in the US economy, 2005-15 forecast, $bn

If we make reasonable assumptions about future accumulation of capital and the rate of surplus value from 2009 onwards, we can forecast whether we are in for another capitalist slump.

On those assumptions, the rate of profit should make a marginal recovery up to 2012 and then start to fall again. However, capitalist consumption will continue to be squeezed and although the mass of profit would go on rising up to 2014, eventually the capitalists will have had enough accumulating at the expense of their living standards. They will reinstitute a strike of capital to boost capitalist consumption. A new slump will ensue around 2015.

The rate of profit will now reach a low not seen since the bottom of the last downphase in the profit cycle, in 1982, and it may even be lower. The organic composition of capital will have reached a new high not seen for 70 years. The slump will have to be substantial to destroy capital values sufficiently to restore profitability.

1. The data have been updated to 2009 with forecasts added through to 2015.
2. Much of this argument has been taken from Henryk Grossman's book, The law of accumulation and the breakdown of the capitalist system, 1992.
3. See Appendix B for an analysis of how the mass of profit can vary with the rate.
4. The following passages have been updated to 2009.

The Great Recession

— during

The Great Depression was (and in many ways) remains a great puzzle as there were millions of the world's citizens who wanted to consume more housing, food and clothing; and producers by the hundreds of thousands who wanted to manufacture more housing, food and clothing and yet the two sides could not get together. Why? What was preventing these economically improving, mutually beneficial exchanges from taking place? What was it that pre-vented people from working and producing more? ...At this mo-ment, (the answer) remains largely unknown". Randall E Parker from The Economics of the Great Depression, *2009*

Stock markets in turmoil

Over the last few days, world stock markets have taken significant plunges. It all appeared to start in China. The Beijing government hinted that speculation on the Shanghai stock exchange was getting out of hand and the government may have to introduce a special tax on capital gains being made. That produced a 10% fall in prices, the biggest daily drop in ten years.

It was ironic that the Chinese government should make this call. Only six months before they had declared open day for stock market speculators, easing restrictions and announcing big sales of shares in state companies. The stock market jumped 100% in just half a year! Now the pain is following the gain. It also shows how the turn towards capitalism driven by the so-called "Communist" leaders has exposed China's economy to the gyrations of capitalist volatility.

But the stock market plunge did not just affect China. It soon spread to the stock markets of Japan, Europe and the US. They fell by 3-4% in a day, not a huge fall but significant after the steady rise that these markets have seen since last summer.

That a hiccup in China should ripple throughout the world's stock markets shows how globalised capitalism, particularly its finance sector, has become. Truly, chaos theory applies in the anarchy of world capitalism: when the Beijing butterfly flaps its wings, the snow falls on New York.

The problem was compounded by two other events. US economic data were released that suggested that the US economy may be slowing down much faster than markets expected. It appeared that real GDP growth in the US in the last quarter of 2006 was only just above 2% rather than 3.5% previously estimated.

Also, the former chairman of the US central bank, Alan Greenspan, made a video speech to investors in Hong Kong (for $150,000 by the way!) in which he said that there was a possibility of economic recession in the US in 2007.

All this was enough to spook investors into selling their stocks. Yesterday, the US stock market seemed to stabilise. But today the falls have continued in China, Japan, Europe and the US.

How far can this go? It depends on how you analyse the causes of the fall-back. The capitalist optimists argue that there is nothing wrong with the fundamentals of capitalist growth: employment is good, profits are good, interest rates are lowish, inflation is under control. So this stock market fall is just a healthy "correction" that will end soon, before the market starts going up again — just as it did last summer after a "correction".

This is the view of the majority and the current Federal Reserve Chairman who succeeded, Greenspan, Ben Bernanke. Speaking to Congress, yesterday, Bernanke was at pains to tell the senators that all was well. The US market stabilised (briefly) on his words.

However, there are others who argue that the US financial markets have become way overpriced because of 'excessive' credit in the economy. Huge money piles are being ploughed into buying up companies through so-called 'private equity' deals and into lending money for property and share deals. Money is not going into productive investment (indeed investment into new plant and machinery is hardly growing in the US), so it is being squandered.

Such is the excess that any sign that the great manufacturing powerhouses of Asia, particularly China, could be slowing down and thus driving up inflation and slowing world growth could easily set off a collapse in stock prices and drive the world into recession.

My view is different. The key to understanding the health of capitalism is profitability. US and global profits have rocketed up since the recession of

2001. However, much of these profits are not available to industry (they have been siphoned off from the productive sectors of the economy into the financial sector). Moreover, although profitability has risen in the last five years, supporting higher stock prices, it is still below the levels achieved in 1997.

Most important, profitability is set to fall from here. US productivity growth is slowing and costs of production are rising compared to growth in sales. Sales are dropping off as the US housing market slumps. Also, the cost of borrowing has risen as the Federal Reserve has hiked up interest rates.

The profits squeeze will steadily grow over the next few years. That will weaken enthusiasm for the stock market. Eventually profitability will fall to levels that will provoke an economic slump and a sustained fall in the stock market.

This current stock market fall probably won't lead to any crash and an immediate economic recession. But it is an indicator of the future deterioration of the health of global capitalism that will unfold over the next few years.

More stock market nerves

The nerves of stock market speculators cannot be in too good a shape these days. Wall Street has just suffered its second biggest point drop in four years. This immediately spread to Asian stocks markets that suffered serious falls.

World stock markets continue to take a turn for the worse. The latest concern of speculators is not just a possible slowdown in the US economy hitting economic growth in the rest of the world. It is also the collateral damage from the falling US real estate market.

In the great bubble that was US housing in the five years up to summer 2005, many Americans started to speculate in house purchases, while others were desperate to get on the housing ladder. So they looked for mortgage loans that they could ill afford. The banks and finance houses of Wall Street were happy to lend these dubious borrowers the money, given the boom in the homes market.

These 'sub-prime' loans, as they were called, were hugely risky for the borrowers and would be a disaster for the banks if the housing market collapsed. And it did. House prices have dropped from rising 15% a year in 2005 to an absolute fall now.

As a result, many sub-prime borrowers have gone bust and cannot pay their mortgage payments. The latest figures showing nearly 14% of such borrowers in default sparked off the fall in stock markets yesterday.

Of course, most mortgage borrowers and homeowners are not sub-prime. These high interest-rate loans are just 10% of the total mortgage market. But the worry is that many banks have packaged up their loans in the sub-prime market and 'sold' them on to other banks. This diversification of risk means that sizeable sections of the mortgage industry are 'exposed' to the sub-prime market.

STOCK MARKET NERVES

Now the second-largest sub-prime lender, New Century, has said that it cannot pay back its creditors and lots of small sub-prime lenders have gone to the wall. The risk of a general financial sector default has risen.

Some bourgeois investors are worried that a further collapse will weaken the US economy further and cause a 'domino' effect across the world.

Stock markets are now down by about 6% since the latest scares began, still less than the sell-off in May 2005. But even if markets should eventually recover again as they did last year, this ripple is yet another confirmation that it is only a matter of a relatively short time (six months to three years) before a major downturn in the financial sector (and with it, the rest of economy) takes place.

The rocky road to ruin

Over the past 15 years production has risen at about 3% a year in the OECD countries, while money supply, mortgage and company debt, personal borrowing and the massive so-called derivatives market based on this credit have increased at over 25% a year! Result? A huge bubble which is now bursting, starting with Northern Rock in the UK.

They started queuing first thing in the morning. They wanted to get their hard-earned savings out as soon as possible. Northern Rock, Britain's fifth-largest mortgage bank was going bust. It had announced that it could not raise enough funds in the interbank market to finance its mortgage lending or meet its obligations any more. Disaster!

Tens of thousands of savers who had put their money in Northern Rock faced huge losses. As they said in the queues: "We are elderly and this is our life saving," said Sheila Smith, who came with her husband, Arthur, to withdraw all their money from the bank's Moorgate branch in central London. "We can't afford to lose it."

A 61-year-old retired health service consultant from Sidcup was following suit, having spent more than an hour getting into the city after a morning of failed phone calls to his local branch. "I put all my savings in one basket and the best thing to do is to get out of this basket," he said. Michael Ribotham, 74, could not see any point in leaving his money in a bank with such big problems. "I'm not young and don't have a chance to make it back again."

There were similar stories at a branch in the bank's home of Newcastle upon Tyne, whose football team carries the Northern Rock logo. "I've been thinking about it all night," said 72-year-old pensioner Mary Bowman, who had £38,000 in a Northern Rock Silver Saver account with her retired miner husband. "It's our burial money and everything," she said.

ROCKY ROAD TO RUIN

It was no good the government, the Bank of England or so-called experts announcing on the radio and TV that there was no need to panic, that deposits were safe. First, the banking industry's so-called deposit insurance only covered the first £2000 of savings and then only 90% of the next £33,000. After that, any savings were not covered and anyway it could take months before getting money back if Northern Rock collapsed.

David Clark, a 61-year-old builder, said he did not believe official assurances about anything financial: "It's just like football managers. Their jobs are guaranteed, then they are sacked the next day."

June Barnes, a special needs guide, and her husband Edward, a retired road worker, left the branch with £500 of their £20,000 savings, the most they could withdraw, and plan to come back every day to do the same. "It's all right people saying don't panic, but at the end of the day you've worked hard for what you have in the bank," said Mrs Barnes.

Many in the queues just did not believe the government. "Tony Blair lied to us about Iraq and many other things. Gordon Brown went along with him: why should we believe these people now?"

The collapse of Northern Rock sums up the mushrooming financial crisis that is spreading across the capitalist world. The last 15 years since the last major economic recession of the early 1990s has seen an expansion of capitalism built on an unprecedented growth in financial credit globally. While annual real production has risen at about 3% a year in the OECD countries, money supply, mortgage and company debt, personal borrowing and the massive so-called derivatives market based on this credit has increased at over 25% a year!

Never has capitalism been so dependent on its financial sector. Never has the financial sector been such a major contributor to profit. This is what Marx called 'fictitious capital'. The boom of the 1990s and of the last four years or so has not been mainly based on an expansion of real production (at least not in the advanced capitalist countries). No, it has been based on huge spending by American and British households, financed by a vast increase in debt. Households no longer save anything, they just borrow.

How can they do that? Well, it's because there has been a boom in the paper prices of stocks and shares (which bust in 2000) and above all in housing. Across most of the advanced capitalist world, cheap credit and wild mortgage lending by banks has inspired a massive increase in the price of real estate.

Much of the world's value-creating production has been siphoned off by the banking system (mainly based in New York and London) into a Ponzi-like[1] pyramid of credit that fuels an unproductive sector of land and bricks. China and Asia's massive export surpluses have been 'recycled' through the banking system into buying mortgage debt, bonds and shares of American households and companies.

This has been possible because American and British banks have developed 'clever' new ways of spreading the risk of lending. If they lend billions in cheap mortgages, they then take the mortgages and 'batch' them up into debt packages that they sell onto other banks, hedge funds and other financial institutions around the world.

They called these new debt instruments 'asset-backed securities' because they were backed by assets (namely mortgages and houses). Investors buy them because the interest on them is much higher than anything else and it is safe — isn't it?, because everywhere house prices are rocketing and people can afford to make their payments. So risk is spread around and everybody is happy.

Well, not any more. If credit is expanded at geometric rates and the production of real things that add value cannot keep pace, then inflation begins to enter the capitalist system. For years, inflation did not appear because the cheap slave labour of billions of workers in China, India and Latin America kept prices of traded goods low. But that began to stop about a year ago as labour markets tightened in Asia.

Also, as more and more money went into the financial sector or into 'serv-ices', labour shortages and higher costs appeared in the OECD econo-mies. The central banks of these countries began to hike interest rates to control inflation. Mortgage rates began to rise and the cost of financing homes.

What kicked off the crisis was the collapse of the US homes market. From mid-2005, prices stopped rising at astronomical rates, then slowed sharply and finally by the end of 2006 started to fall. This was particularly bad news for those borrowers who had lied about what they earned or were offered mortgages with no attempt by the banks to check on whether the borrowers had incomes to justify repayments.

These were called 'sub-prime' loans (not the best prime ones). Only 10% of the US mortgage market was in sub-prime loans, but the problem was that the banks had 'batched' all these loans in packages with prime loans and sold them on around the world. So nearly every bank in the world had bought part of these 'junk' loans or asset-backed securities. Then the asset part disappeared in a puff of smoke. So all the banks were all liable, as sub-prime borrowers started to default on their payments. The world credit crisis began.

The irony is that Northern Rock never lent to American houseowners, never mind the high-risk ones who are now defaulting in droves and bad debts on its British mortgages are close to record lows. Yet it is the first bank to need bailing out since new rules allowing rescues were introduced in 1988.

The reason is that Northern Rock was only in the mortgage business because it could borrow money from other banks at very cheap rates to finance mortgage lending. Back in the early 1990s, Northern had been a steady building society based in Newcastle, only lending based on depos-its it got from people who put them with it.

But then came the property boom and the great 'new ways' of raising credit. Northern turned itself into a bank with shareholders and launched an aggressive strategy of lending cheap to householders. In January this year, the management were being feted by their shareholders for boosting profits and taking the biggest share of new mortgages in Britain — they got awards for being so clever!

Then came the credit crunch. Because house prices were collapsing in the US and mortgages were being defaulted, banks were no longer sure that the all the mortgage debt was worth what they had paid for it. So they stopped buying any more. Lots of small funds in this mortgage-backed security business went bust, as did a big US mortgage bank, American Mortgage Securities. Then America's biggest mortgage lender, Countrywide, announced huge losses and job cuts.

The banking world panicked. They stopped lending, even to each other. The crunch spread around the world. European banks that had bought these junk bonds from American banks also went under (IKB and Saxon in the US). Northern depended on borrowing from other banks as its savers in Newcastle and around Britain were not enough to finance its breakneck pace of lending. Now it could not raise money. After a few weeks of struggle as the interbank loan markets stayed dry and interest rates rocketed, Northern Rock gave up the ghost and asked the Bank of England to bail them out.

The banks may be in the line of fire now, but it will be ordinary working people who will feel the pain: the savers, the home owners as home prices plummet in the UK and, of course, the workers in the banks and mortgage lenders who will soon lose their jobs.

Mortgage rates are now rising. The cost of owning a home in Britain will become even more nightmarish. Already, mortgage interest payments are taking up a bigger share of our income — the average is 17.4% — than at any time since the early 1990s housing crash. And the average rate has risen from 4.67% in July 2005 to 6.1%. Any additional rise will further stretch borrowers.

The long-forecast end to Britain's 18-year housing boom is drawing closer. In September, there was a 2.6% drop. A survey by Rightmove, the property website, showed the average asking price in the UK was £235,176; down from £241,474 in August. And the average property sat on the market for 86 days compared to only 70 in May. The number of properties for sale per estate agent has also risen; from 52 in December to nearly 66 today.

The reaction of the institutions of capitalism and the New Labour government has been nothing short of a joke, if it wasn't so painful for ordinary people. Only two days before the Northern Rock crisis broke, the governor of the Bank of England, Mervyn King, had told a parliamentary committee that there was no way that the Bank would 'bail out' banks and investors who got into trouble because they has invested speculatively and unwisely in sub-prime loans and other risky ventures.

And yet King had to do a somersault when it was clear that Northern Rock was going under and announce it would after all fund Northern. The new Chancellor of Exchequer, Alastair Darling, who took over from Gordon Brown when he became prime minister, had obviously panicked. He demanded that King provide funds immediately to Northern. He realised that thousands of Labour voters would be demanding blood if their savings were forfeited and their mortgages called in.

Even more serious, it was clear that if Northern went down, so would a number of other banks with similar balance sheets and there would be the biggest banking crisis since the 1930s. The Bank's actions did not stop the run on the Northern branches. The shares of other banks also tumbled and the cost of borrowing between banks continued to reach extreme levels. Britain's banking system was seizing up.

So late on Monday evening, 17 September, Darling announced (stuttering and stammering his speech, looking like a rabbit caught in the headlights) that all the deposits of Northern Rock savers would be honoured by the government. In effect, the government had nationalised the bank. Also, he was opening up the condition that if other banks go under, their depositors would also be repaid in full. So the whole banking system in Britain was now backed by the taxpayer.

Quite right that hard earned money saved by British people should not be lost because of the casino gambling of the global banking system going wrong. But if deposits are to be saved at the taxpayer's expense, should not ownership of the banks also pass to the people? What could be a more conclusive condemnation of capitalism than this boom and bust cycle in global financial markets? People's money is not safe with capitalists — only a democratically accountable state system can make it so.

And this financial crisis and credit crunch is just the beginning. From here, tightening credit markets and rising interest rates will mean falling profit-ability for capitalist companies and slowing production, possibly even economic slump, as American, British and European householders have to tighten their belts.

First watch out for serious falls in the profits of the big banks around the world. That will be followed by job cuts throughout the financial sector. And job cuts will mean less income to finance property purchases and mortgages. House prices could plummet.

Never in the history of capitalism has the financial sector been so important to the health of capitalism. In its maturity, capitalism is increasingly no longer a system that raises the productive forces. It is more and more a financial parasite unproductively resting on top of the productive sectors of the global economy (mainly in China, India etc).

That is especially so in Britain, the financial parasite extraordinaire — a giant Switzerland, that sucks in the earnings of other countries (oil-producers in the Middle East and the manufacturers of Asia) and recycles it. British capitalism now makes little itself. Instead, it is just the banker to the world. As such, the British capitalist economy is the most vulnerable to a global financial crisis and any ensuing economic slump. And British workers and their families will suffer more than most.

1. Named after the most notorious of these scams carried out by Charles Ponzi in 1920.

Credit crunch!

Everywhere the cry is: credit crunch! You can smell the sweat on the brows of bankers as their necks are squeezed by the tightening credit noose. In all the offices of the great investment banks of Wall Street, the City of London and gnomes of Zurich, you can hear the hissing sound of the global financial bubble bursting and deflating.

Whereas just a few months ago there seemed no end to the upward drive of stock market prices and availability of loans to buy companies, build skyscrapers or invest in ever-mushrooming condominiums from San Diego to Shoreditch and Shanghai; now all has changed. An abyss has opened up before the financial sector of capitalism.

Every day another huge global bank announces that it has had to 'write off' the value of assets that it has bought (mortgage loans for houses in the US or bonds that are 'backed' by the value of mortgages in America). It's $10bn for Citibank, $5bn for HSBC, $8bn for Merrill Lynch and so on. So far, the banks have fessed up to $60bn of losses.

And heads have rolled. The head of Citibank, the biggest bank in the world (until a Chinese bank surpassed it last month when it launched on the stock exchange), has been sacked and forced into taking a redundancy package worth $150m. He was followed by the head of the biggest investment bank in the world, Merrill Lynch.

And around the world, smaller banks and financial institutions have not just lost money, but have gone bust. In the UK, it was Northern Rock, a lender of mortgages in the north of England. Big mortgage lenders have gone bust in the US. The biggest American lender, Countrywide, is on the brink with huge losses recorded. Desperately, the big banks are trying to drum up a special fund worth $75bn to help fund lots of small 'Special Purpose Vehicles' that they originally set up to make extra profit.

CREDIT CRUNCH!

Even supposedly 'safe and prudent' financial institutions like company or local government pension funds have been burnt. Few people in the remote Norwegian town of Narvik, 200km north of the Arctic Circle where the sun has disappeared until January, were likely to have given a lot of thought to the credit squeeze sweeping the global money markets — that is, until it now threatens their wages over Christmas.

Narvik, along with three other similarly isolated towns of Hemnes, Rana and Hattfjelldal, has become the latest community to discover just how directly even the most remote places can be affected by the financial turmoil after it made multi-million dollar bets on complicated US-linked financial products.

The towns invested about $96m (€65m) in complex products linked to unspecified municipal bonds in the US, designed by Citigroup, and sold to them by Terra Securities, the investment banking arm of one of Norway's leading banking groups. Now representatives of the towns have admitted that recent market movements linked to the credit crisis had destroyed most of the value of their investments.

The great credit crunch is not located just in the US, but is everywhere. And it's only just begun. The OECD estimates that the final losses from this credit contraction will be $300bn. Other bank estimates put the hit at $400-500bn, or about 1% of global annual output.

It's going to be that big because the start of the problem was in the US housing market. Way back in the early 2000s, a huge boom began in the US residential property market, not dissimilar to the boom in the commercial (factories and offices) property market that started in the mid-1980s in the US. As money flowed into the property market, mortgage rates plummeted and banks began to offer easier and easier loan arrangements.

Whereas before, the usual US mortgage for 75% of the value of the house was at a fixed rate for 30 years, while house prices rose at a moderate 3-5% a year, now you could get a 100% (or even more) mortgage at a special discount rate of near zero for the first few years, with even the cost of paying that 'back ended' to the cost of the loan, which could be just ten years.

Moreover, if you could not prove that you had a good steady job with income to pay the loan, it did not matter. Because house prices were now rising at 15% a year, you could easily cover the cost by selling on or borrowing more later. Banks would lend what they called 'sub-prime' mortgages (so-called because they were made to riskier borrowers) without compunction.

The housing boom took off as the Federal Reserve Bank cut interest rates down to 1% and the head of the bank then, Alan Greenspan, declared publicly that it was a great idea to borrow more and spend to keep the US economy motoring. However, in June 2005, things began to turn for the worse. First, rising inflation forced the Fed to reverse its policy and begin to hike interest rates. It did so for the next 18 months from 1% to 5.25%. Mortgage rates rose sharply and borrowers began to feel the pinch.

Most important, house prices had got so far ahead of incomes, which for the average American family had hardly moved, that lots of new homes coming onto the market were no longer affordable. Builders found that they could not shift their new condos without massive discounts and incentives. Eventually, even that was not enough and those sub-prime borrowers who had bought without adequate incomes or had done 'buy to lets', with the hope of 'flipping' their purchases quickly into sales, could no longer afford it.

Defaults on sub-prime mortgages rose from 3% to 15% in a year. Lenders suddenly found that their highly lucrative mortgage incomes were dropping fast. And here is where the problem got so much worse.

In the great new world of the global finance capital, the mortgage lenders had not kept these mortgages on their books. They went to other banks and particularly to smaller financial organisations like hedge funds (funded by blocks of capital set up by some financiers using the money of very rich people and promising them huge returns) and said: look why don't you buy a block of mortgages from us?

Some mortgages will be prime (good credit) mortgages and some will be sub-prime. But a batch of this mortgage debt (a mortgage-backed asset) will pay a lot more than interest at the bank or even interest from a government bond. And don't worry, it's really safe because house prices are going up and up and anyway your batch of mortgages includes lots of good safe ones.

And then the banks went to insurance brokers and said: why don't you offer insurance on these mortgages defaulting? It's not going to happen so you can make money selling premiums to the buyers of our mortgage-backed securities. And they did.

Soon everybody and his dog was buying and selling mortgage securities around the world. Sub-prime mortgage securities reached $3trn globally and prime mortgages reached another $25trn.

This was similar to what the savings and loans banks in the US did in the 1980s. They were very small savings banks that collected the savings of all the people in the small towns of mid-America. Then they lent their money to local businesses to build offices, factories and develop.

A boom in commercial property broke out as interest rates fell and the owners of these small banks thought they were onto a winner. They began to lend to commercial businesses in a big way and got involved in lots of big commercial projects offering very good fixed rates of return. But then, interest rates began to rise as inflation exploded in the late 1980s. These banks found they had to pay higher rates to depositors, but could not raise rates to their business borrowers. The banks went bust, or their owners did a runner with the local people's deposits.

Both the savings and loans disaster in 1980s and the sub-prime crisis now are examples of how a corrupt and greedy capitalism tries to maintain economic momentum by turning to unproductive sectors because the productive sectors have weakened.

In the US, the rate of profit earned by all sectors of capitalist investment peaked in 1997[1]. As explained by Marx, capitalists are continually trying to increase the profit they make out of their workers. If they don't, then their competitors will undercut them in price or invest more to lower costs.

This competition drives capitalists to find new ways of raising profits. Once they have exhausted the exploitation of the workforce, they can only raise profit by using new labour-saving forms of technology. That requires extra capital invested in machinery and plant over labour. This rising proportion (that Marx called the organic composition of capital) begins to drive the rate of profit down just as the mass or overall total of profit rises. Eventually, the falling rate of profit will exert enough influence to stop the mass of profit rising.

That process began in earnest in 1997. Eventually the hi-tech boom of the 1990s burst in a stock market collapse of 2000 and the mass of profit stopped rising in 2001 and there was mild recession. But the recession was only mild because capitalism tried to keep the system going by the expansion of credit into unproductive areas like finance and property. The boom in property provided a cushion against the collapse of productive forces. It even reversed the fall in profitability for a while, from 2002 to 2006. Employment and economic growth also picked up.

But to achieve this, there had to be a huge expansion of money credit, indeed the largest in capitalist history. Marx called this fictitious capital. Credit is money supply (printing banknotes and increasing bank reserves), debt (issuance of bonds and loans) and stock market values (increased prices for buying and selling shares in companies). When this expands way beyond the accumulation of real capital, it is fictitious. The prices of shares, bond and houses do not match the value appropriated by capital-

CREDIT CRUNCH!

ists from the sale of things and services produced by workers in factories, offices and transport facilities, namely profits.

So, just as the rate of profit started to fall, fictitious capital exploded (graphic)[2]. In the first seven years of the decade of 2000, fictitious capital grew at over 25% a year compared to the growth of real production in the capitalist world (up a maximum of 5-7% a year). Money supply printed by the central banks rose about 7% a year, while banks increased loans by over 10% a year. And then there was the issuance of bonds by big companies and governments. That form of credit rose by over 15% a year to reach $73trn by 2006, or around 140% of world annual production.

But the most staggering part of the explosion of fictitious capital was in the value of what are called derivative contracts. Of the $70trn in debt, about $11trn was 'sold on' over and over again in various contracts derived from that debt. These derivatives, in essence bets on the future value of a bond, a mortgage or a share, rose in value to a staggering $550trn, or 11 times annual world output.

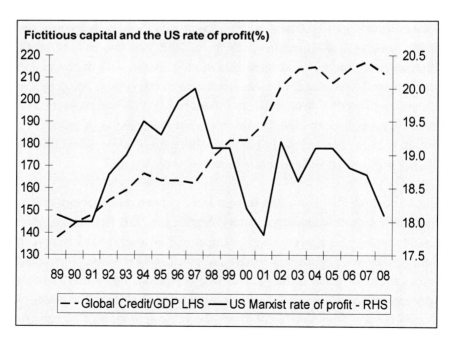

Fictitious capital and the US rate of profit(%)

-- Global Credit/GDP LHS — US Marxist rate of profit - RHS

This made for easy money, allowing borrowers to buy property, shares and other assets by the bucketful. But most of this expansion of credit was into unproductive sectors of the capitalist economy — sure, it delivered jobs and income, but as Marx explained, under capitalism, it was unproductive because it did not create value that could be used to reinvest in new production and drive the economy forward. Indeed, as more and more money went into the stock or property markets, less and less was available for investment in industry, new technology or better skills for the workforce.

It has been a feature of modern capitalism in its declining phase for capital to be invested more in unproductive rather than productive sectors. For example, the financial sector now contributes 30% of the profits of capitalist businesses in the US. Strip that away and the productive sectors of the economy are not doing well. Indeed, the underlying rate of profit has fallen over a period of decades, even though there are long periods when it rises[3]. The credit crisis is the other side of the coin. Once the US property market began to collapse from summer 2005 onwards, so the massive credit boom was revealed for what it was — a fantasy, not based on real values.

Now the credit bubble has burst just like the hi-tech dot com bubble burst in 2000; and just like the savings and loans bubble in commercial mortgages did in the mid 1980s in the US; and just like the credit bubble in Japan did at the end of the 1980s.

Banks are now losing money hand over fist. So are the clever hedge funds and insurance brokers. Credit is contracting fast, as fictitious capital goes up in smoke and the real level of values is revealed. This real value will be found at a much lower level of production, employment and income — and of course, at a much lower level of profit.

The collapse in credit will be just as severe over the next few years as the expansion of fictitious capital was in the last five. And this time, the profit cycle is also in a long-term downward cycle that still has some way to go to reach the bottom. And we remain in a long-term downward cycle for share prices, which express the confidence that capitalists have in their own system. Finally, the global property market is dropping too, not just in the US, but also in the UK, Europe and later in parts of Asia.

Everywhere the arrows are pointing down for capitalism. This synchronised downturn in profitability, credit, stock and property prices heralds a major economic slump by 2009-10, or even earlier. The credit crunch will lead to the worst global failure of capitalist production since 1980-2 and perhaps even as bad as 1929-33.

1. See chapter 6.
2. The graphic has been updated to 2008.
3. See chapter 7.

Panic!

Panic! The world's stock markets had their sharpest fall since 9/11 on Monday 21 January. It is supposed to be the most miserable day in the year in the Northern hemisphere, where the daylight is short, the weather is bad, people have colds and flu and they have run up debts from Christmas. But this year, it really was a Black Monday for capitalism.

World stock markets are now down over 20% from their highs set just last November. That technically is called a 'bear market'. Stock markets have had their worst start in a year for 30 years and in the case of the US and the UK, the worst start ever since records began!

Why the panic? Up to Christmas, stock markets were generally static, not falling much. Capitalist investors were 'in denial' as the psychiatrists say. They knew that there was a problem in credit and debt markets, because of the collapse in the US housing market and the losses then suffered by the big banks and other financial institutions that had bought so much of the so-called sub-prime (risky) mortgages. But stock market investors thought that this would not affect their investments because it would not touch the nicely growing capitalist 'real' economy of making goods and delivering services.

Of course, this was wishful thinking. After Christmas, one big bank after another announced yet more losses as they 'wrote down' the value of their debt securities they had bought on the expectation that house prices would keep on rising. To date, the banks and financial institutions have written off about $120bn. They may well have to admit to losses four times greater than that before they are finished, or 1% of world GDP.

Then the evidence about the state of the US economy began to filter through to the minds of capitalist investors. Profits results from the big companies were down hugely, not just in the financial sector (20% of the US stock market), but also in other companies like Microsoft, the auto companies and other important services-based firms. US corporate profits looked to have fallen by about 5-10% in the last quarter of 2007. It will get worse in 2008.

Also, the US economy is now slowing down fast towards what is called economic recession, when national output actually drops. The housing sector was in free fall, with prices dropping 5-10%, sales down 50% and mortgage defaults in the risky 'sub-prime' sector rising to 20%. But it was not just there. The Christmas sales for the big US retailers were appalling, with no growth at all over 2006. And other services are falling back.

The credit and debt markets (mortgages, credit cards, auto finance) have seen large rises in the cost of borrowing, even though the US Federal Reserve Bank had started a series of interest-rate cuts. The Fed, the Bank of England and the European Central Bank have launched a coordinated injection of $500bn of credit into the world's financial system. But it is not working to turn the housing market around or stop the recession. So stock markets have panicked.

And they are right to do so. As the US economy heads into recession, it will drag the rest of the world down with it. Already, the UK housing market is heading the same way as in the US. House prices have fallen for three consecutive months in Britain and will fall further, even though the Bank of England plans to cut interest rates. The UK consumer spent little over the Christmas period because most British households are already highly indebted with big mortgages and credit card debts.

UK manufacturing is in the doldrums because the pound has been way too strong, keeping export prices too high. That's happened because the UK trade deficit (even bigger than that of the US as a share of GDP), has been financed by attracting 'hot money' from Russians, Arabs and other oil-rich ruling classes (who buy homes, football clubs and British stocks). Thus the UK economy had staggered on, living off rising property prices and foreign borrowing. That is all coming to an end.

Now stock markets have noticed that Europe and Japan will slow down too. Just three months ago, most capitalist economists said that Europe and Japan would grow at around 2.5-3.0% in 2008, with the UK and the US a little slower. China and India would rocket along at around 10% a year. Now they have changed their tune. Most expect a recession in the US and slower growth in Europe and Japan. They still hope for good growth in China and India.

But it's going to get worse than that. With the UK and the US in recession, expect Europe and Japan to grow no more than 1% this year. And China and India will slow too to about half their current growth rates. That's bad news across the board.

It means higher unemployment (probably double current rates in the US and the UK) and smaller pay rises (possibly none at all), although the bonuses to the fat cats in the City of London and Wall Street won't drop much. It will be particularly bad for those economies that are increasingly dependent on finance capital rather than productive sectors of manufacturing and transport.

The UK is the most dependent of all the big seven economies on finance, property and so-called professional services (legal, insurance, consultants). So this world downturn will hit it hardest of all.

Capitalism beared

Under capitalism if there is no profit, there is no production even if people need things or services. Therefore, over the last 25 years there has been a massive expansion of the unproductive sectors of the capitalist economy, i.e. a massive increase in fictitious capital. This is now expressing itself in what may be the worst crisis for more than 30 years.

As I write, world stock markets are still reeling from yet another shock to the system brought on by the so-called credit crunch that has enveloped capitalist financial markets since last summer.

The latest shock was the biggest yet. Late on Sunday night, 16 March, the US Federal Reserve Bank announced that Bear Stearns, America's fifth-largest investment bank, was bust. So it had agreed that JP Morgan-Chase, an even bigger bank, would take over Bear Stearns. JP Morgan was to pay just $2 a share and it would not be paying cash, but just offering JP Morgan shares to Bear Stearns shareholders. At the same time, the huge loans and bonds of $30bn that Bear Stearns had on its books would be guaranteed by a loan from the Federal Reserve to JP Morgan.

In effect, JP Morgan was getting Bear Stearns and its business for virtually nothing. It was paying $256m (and not in cash) for a bank that had buildings alone worth $2bn and whose shares were worth over $100 each just a few months ago! And the risky loans that Bear Stearns had, and which had forced it to the wall, were going to be guaranteed by the Fed. What a deal for JP Morgan!

The US state authorities were doing this because they knew that Bear Stearns could not meet its obligations to other banks and creditors. It had run out of cash and nobody in Wall Street, New York's financial centre, would lend to it. If it went bust, however, then all the other banks in Wall Street and in Europe too would incur huge losses on their loans and contracts to Bear Stearns and perhaps force some of them into bankruptcy too.

CAPITALISM BEARED

The Fed had to act in bailing out the great capitalist financial system. So it has taken on a considerable obligation to the rest of the banking system on behalf of the taxpayer — that's us.

The Fed's action echoes what happened with Northern Rock in Britain. There a medium-sized mortgage lender that had pretensions to become a bigger bank went bust when it could not borrow enough money to pay interest or principal to the banks and investors who bought its mortgages.

In this case, the Bank of England refused an offer from Lloyds Bank to buy Northern Rock for a pittance with guarantees on its loans, like the Fed did with JP Morgan to buy Bear Stearns. Instead, it opted to try and save the bank by providing taxpayer funds directly.

The Bank of England's plan did not work and it racked up huge obligations — nearly $100bn compared to $30bn the Fed just provided. Eventually, the government was forced to nationalise NR with the aim of sacking most of the workforce and selling off much of the mortgages to get our money back.

Whatever the solution opted for by the state monetary authorities in the US or the UK, it shows that the credit crunch has reached such proportions that large banks are now going to the wall. No wonder former Fed Chairman Greenspan called the global financial crisis the worst since the 1930s. The financial sector of capitalism is tottering.

How did it get into this sorry state? The key to understanding the crisis is the changing relationship between the productive and unproductive sectors of capitalism. Capitalism is a system of production of things that people need for profit. Production is not for need, but for profit. If there is no profit, there is no production even if people need things or services.

By that definition, the productive sectors of capitalism are those that generate profit. Marx explained that only labour can generate value and profit arises when the value of goods or services sold on the market exceeds the cost of employing labour and investing in plant and raw materials to make goods or services.

Some sectors of capitalism may seem to make a profit, but in reality are really just extracting or redistributing profits actually generated in other sectors of the economy. Thus, real estate companies can make a profit on buying and selling properties and on the fees they charge. But nothing has been produced in that process. Profits are also made when private builders build a house and sell it. But here something that people need is produced. From the point of view of capitalism, the productive sector is house building but the unproductive sector is real estate, because that is where the profit that real estate agents make is originally generated.

For capitalism, the productive sectors that generate profit are broadly manufacturing, mining, transport and communications. But these sectors must buy the services of lawyers, estate agents, advertisers and above all they must borrow from the banks and financial institutions to finance investment and pay their employees. These sectors are necessary to lubricate the wheels of capitalism, but they are unproductive because they do not generate profits for the whole economy, but merely get a bite out of the revenues produced by the productive sectors.

Just as 'necessary' and unproductive for capitalism are the government sectors of health, education, police and the armed forces. They are necessary to preserve the health and skills of the workforce and keep 'law and order'. But they do not generate surplus value or make a profit in themselves.

What has happened over the last 25 years particularly has been a massive expansion of the unproductive sectors of the capitalist economy (at least in the mature advanced capitalist economies of North America, Western Europe and Japan). As capitalism has matured it has become increasingly less oriented to production. The shrinking productive sectors have had to finance an ever-growing unproductive sector or mature capitalist economies have had to extract profits from the fast-rising productive sectors in China, India and Latin America.

As a result, economic growth in the mature economies has slowed to a trickle compared to the golden decades of the 1950s and 1960s. Sure, economic growth has not been as convulsive and volatile as in the 1970s, but it has averaged no more than 3% a year in the advanced economies compare to 5-6% in the post-1948 period.

That's because more and more investment has been diverted into unproductive sectors that have given only the appearance of more profit. And worse, as profitability declined in productive sectors, the monetary authorities tried to boost growth by lowering interest rates and printing more money. Money capital grew, giving the appearance that there was plenty of capital or profit to reinvest.

But as Marx would say, this was fictitious capital. It was not real because it was not based on profits made in the productive sectors of capitalism, but merely the result of the printing of paper money, or the making of contracts for bonds, mortgages and other financial instruments. In the last 15 years, completely new and ever more exotic financial instruments were created to finance the buying of stocks and shares, buildings and homes and even some investment in real production.

This fictitious capital reached astronomical levels. The world's annual output was worth about $53 trillion in 2007. However, bank loans reached $40 trillion, the stock markets of the world reached $50trn, the bond and mortgage markets reached $70trn and most astounding of all the derivative markets (contracts to buy or sell bonds, stocks or loans by a certain date) reached $500 trillion, or ten times world GDP!

Clearly, world capitalism had become unreal. This could not last. The trigger was housing. This, after all, was one the biggest parts of fictitious capital. Cheap mortgages and a huge influx of money enabled even average earners to get onto the housing market from about 15 years ago.

Everywhere the housing market took off: rising prices bred even bigger mortgages and even higher prices. The appearance of prosperity led home-owners to borrow money and spend like there was no tomorrow.

And the banks not only provided ever more mortgages to people who could not afford them; they also sold on those mortgages as bonds to other banks and investors greedy for the higher interest and prices that they earned.

Then about mid-2005 American house prices began to stop rising so fast and even started to fall. Prices had got so high that more and more people could not afford to buy, even with cheap and easy mortgages. The productive sectors of the economy were just not generating enough wage increases and profit rises to pay for high house prices. Just as the stock market bubble had burst in 2000, leading to economic recession in 2001, now it was the turn of the housing market bubble.

House prices in the US have now slumped over 10%, with falls as big as 30% in key states like California and Florida. People began to default on their mortgages. Banks that held them were forced to write off these debts. But many of these mortgages had been packaged off as bonds to others. Investors now found that their bonds were worthless. They had borrowed on the value of these bonds and now could not pay back their creditors. Soon the credit crunch was swinging right through the financial sectors of America, Europe and Asia. Eventually we have come to Bear Stearns.

When banks have to pay losses with their shareholders' money, they are forced to find more investors or they must cut back on lending. That's because they cannot lend more than say ten times the value of their investor's capital or the deposits they hold. Most of the time, investors and depositors don't want their money all at once, so banks 'leverage' up, assuming that they only need to pay out on about 10% of their liabilities at any time.

CAPITALISM BEARED

If their capital disappears as they pay off losses and if depositors all demand their money back at once, they face bankruptcy. They must be careful and cut back on their lending or go bust like Bear Stearns. They must deleverage.

Banks and other financial institutions are now deleveraging like mad. They won't lend to home owners or manufacturers, or they will lend less and at higher interest rates. Fictitious capital is disappearing and the poor state of real capital is being revealed beneath a welter of worthless paper.

This spells economic slump. Capitalist profitability goes up and down in cycles according to Marx's law of the tendency of the rate of profit to decline. This is a tendency: profitability does not always decline. Indeed, in the US, the UK and Europe, it rose from 1982 to 1997. But now we are in the middle of the down phase in profitability that is likely to last until 2013-15.

In the down phase, falling profitability can sometimes lead to an actual fall in the mass of profits generated by capitalism producing a bout of economic recession where production slows, unemployment rises and investment falls until profitability is restored.

This process is now happening. US corporate profits are now falling and soon European corporate profits will too. Then investment will slow or stop and unemployment, which has been falling in the US and Europe since 2002, will start to rise — and fast.

The last economic recession was in 2001 and it was very mild because, although profits fell, the huge boost of fictitious capital into the housing market kept up consumer spending. Now we are entering an economic recession when housing markets everywhere are heading downwards and credit has dried up. This is going to be the worst economic downturn for capitalism since 1991 or 1981, maybe as bad as 1974-5.

Black swans and economic recession

British capitalism is in big trouble. The annual inflation rate has hit 3.3%, its highest level for 16 years. The governor of the Bank of England, Mervyn King, has been forced to send a letter to the Chancellor of Exchequer, Alastair Darling, to explain why the Bank has been unable to keep inflation from rising at more than 2%, which is the target set by the government for the Bank.

In the letter, King explains that inflation has got completely out of control. Global fuel and food prices have rocketed. World agricultural prices have risen 60% in the last year; oil prices are up 80% and wholesale gas prices are up 160%! That has meant significant increases in living costs for average working family in the UK. For example, the average gas bill is up 7%, electricity bill up 10%, the water bill up 6%; rail season tickets up 5% and, above all, the cost of an average tank of petrol or diesel to fill the car or lorry is up 20-35% in a year. Overall, the weekly shopping basket is up 8%. Inflation is recorded at only over 3% because the cost of other items like clothing or electrical goods has fallen.

And it is going to get worse. Mervyn King forecasts that the inflation rate will climb to over 4% a year and stay up there through most of 2009, at best. And the acceleration in inflation is happening at the same time as the UK economy is heading into slump as a result of the global credit crunch and the collapse of the housing market.

Most economic forecasters are now admitting that British capitalism is grinding to a halt. The bosses union, the CBI, reckons that economic growth this year will be just 1.3% and next year not much better. That would be the lowest rate of growth since 1992, the last great economic recession.

Even this forecast is probably optimistic. That's because a key factor driving British capitalism over the last decade or so has not been investment in manufacturing and other productive sectors of the economy, but in real estate (housing) and unproductive speculation in stock and shares, bonds and money in the City of London.

Now the credit crunch is causing huge losses in the financial sector and the UK housing market is collapsing like a pack of cards. House prices on most measures are falling by around 5-7% a year now and most forecasts suggest that the total decline could reach 20-30% by end of 2009.

So young people and others who joined the 'housing ladder' at its peak in summer 2007 will find that their property is worth only 70% of what they paid for it by then. And many will have taken out large mortgages to pay for their flat, many up to 100%. Their homes will be worth less than the debt they owe. That's what is called 'negative equity'.

And with mortgage rates rising all the time, hundreds of thousands of British families are going to be unable to meet their payments over the next couple of years and will be forced to sell or have to walk away from their homes.

So the great consumer spending binge is over. Everybody will be tightening their belts as wage rises fail to keep up with inflation and unemployment rises. That's a recipe for outright slump, not just an economic slowdown.

Unemployment is already starting to rise. The number of claimants for unemployment benefit in May rose for the fourth consecutive month and the official unemployment rate rose for the first time in years to 5.3%.

With unemployment heading above 6% and inflation towards 5%, the misery index (the addition of the two rates) will be in double figures soon. And the last time that happened, British capitalism was reduced to its knees.

What can the Bank of England and the government do about this to avoid a slump? The short answer is nothing. Mervyn King is in a deep quandary. If he raises interest rates in order to drive down inflation, he will just make it worse for British businesses and households to fund their investment and spending. That will deepen the oncoming recession. On the other hand, if he lowers interest rates, he could inspire more borrowing and more inflation. So he will do nothing.

The truth is that the spectre of 'stagflation' is now hanging over the UK economy. That is where the economy stagnates and does not grow, but the economic slowdown does not get inflation down either. Such a situation has not existed since the 1970s and early 1980s and the strategists of capital are now really worried that it could reappear, proving yet again that capitalism cannot avoid the continual cycle of boom and slump, which is inherent in the mode of production for profit, not need.

The supposed solution of the politicians (including New Labour ministers), the bankers and the bosses to this dilemma should be no surprise to Marxists. It is not that the bankers and financiers that got the economy into this mess should be penalised. Oh no. The answer is that workers and their families should take the hit.

The cry of the politicians and economists is that workers must accept lower or no wage rises to stem inflation. Public sector workers are being forced to accept less than a 2% pay rise when inflation is now well above that and accelerating and employers in the private sector are trying to do the same. And yet we know that the reason for inflation is nothing to do with wage rises and that is admitted by the economists and the Bank of England. So the capitalist solution is blatant — working-class families must be forced to reduce their already low standards of living.

The economic crisis is not the result of workers like the oil tanker drivers asking for too much (they had not had a pay rise since 1992). It is a product of the failure of capitalism globally. The housing slump is not confined to Britain, but started earlier in the US and has spread to Spain,

BLACK SWANS AND RECESSION

Ireland, Australia and elsewhere. The financial crisis is not confined to Britain, but started in America and has spread to the UK, Europe and Asia. Nothing is clearer: capitalism is destroying people's hard-won living standards built up over the last decade or so and the leaders of capitalism want the working-class to pay for their losses.

There is a theory doing the rounds of capitalist economists at the moment. It is called the Black Swan theory, developed by an American financial analyst, Nicholas Taleb. Before people discovered Australia, it was thought that all swans were white. But the discovery in the 18th century that there were black swans in Australia dispelled that notion.

Taleb argues that many events are like that. It is assumed that something just cannot happen: it is ruled out. But Taleb says, even though the chance is small, the unlikely can happen and when it does it will have a big impact. Taleb cited the 9/11 Twin Towers attack as a modern example. The global credit crunch and the ensuing economic crisis has been suggested as another example of the Black Swan theory.

From a Marxist dialectical point of view, the Black Swan theory has some attraction. For example, revolution is a rare event in history. So rare that many (mainly apologists of the existing order) would rule it out as impossible. But it can and does happen, as we know. And its impact, when it does, is profound. In that sense, revolution is a Black Swan event.

But where Marxists would disagree with Taleb is that he argues that chance is what rules history. Randomness without cause is not how to view the world. This is far too one-sided and undialectical. Sure, chance plays a role in history, but only in the context of necessity.

The credit crunch and the current economic slump could have been triggered by some unpredictable event like the collapse of some financial institution last August or the loss of bets on bond markets by a 'rogue trader' in a French bank last December. For that matter, the recent food price explosion may have started with a tsunami or an unexpected drought in Australia. And the oil price explosion may have been the product of the 'arbitrary' decision of President Bush to attack Iraq.

But those things happened because the laws of motion of capitalism were being played out towards a crisis. Capitalism only grows if profitability is rising. And corporate profitability peaked in 1997, fell back to 2002, recovered somewhat up to 2005, but began falling again after that. With profitability declining, the huge expansion of credit (or what Marx called fictitious capital) could not be sustained because it was not bringing enough profit from the real economy. Eventually, the housing and financial sectors (the most unproductive parts of capitalist investment) stopped booming and reversed.

Similarly, the food price explosion was man-made, not an act of God. Global warming, droughts and floods are man-made. The food and energy deficits are due to weak capitalist production combined with strong demand from China and other fast-growing economies and the failure of capitalism to diversify into clean alternative energy production.

So the current economic crisis was no chance event that nobody could have predicted. Marxists and even some capitalist theorists forecast it. The economic slump that British capitalism is now entering (along with many other capitalist economies around the world) is no Black Swan. It is an inevitable consequence of the capitalist system of production.

Credit crunch one year on

One year after the beginning of the credit crunch, the earthquake in the global financial system has left banks, insurers, pension and municipal funds, hedge funds and private equity companies tottering and falling. Collateral damage has been immense and the after-shocks are still to come.

On 6 August 2007, America's second-largest mortgage lender American Home Mortgage Investment Corp filed for bankruptcy. Three days later, France's biggest bank, BNP-Paribas announced that it was freezing redemptions on three of its investment funds in sub-prime mortgages. Immediately, the European Central Bank announced it was injecting E75bn into the financial system. Only a few days later, the US Federal Reserve Bank reacted with a 50 basis points cut in its funds rate and injected extra liquidity into the system. The credit crunch had begun!

How did it come about? Well, the trigger (but not the gun) was the collapse of the US housing market and the debacle of the so-called sub-prime mortgage market. As in many countries of the Anglo-Saxon world (the US, the UK, Australasia, Ireland, Scandinavia, the Baltic states) and even parts of Europe (Spain, Hungary etc), there had been a massive boom in house prices, particularly after the mild economic recession in the OECD of 2001. House prices had never risen so much and so fast.

Cheap credit from the banks and mortgage lenders enabled home owners to borrow hugely on the back of their house values. At one point, according to the great guru of American finance himself, Alan Greenspan, American home owners were taking $1trn each year out of the 'value' of the their homes to spend. This fuelled consumer spending and economic growth, as well as the stock market.

But it was all based on a lie. No real values were being created. Indeed, US and British householders were saving nothing. Household savings rates had dropped from 13% of disposable income in the 1990s to negative in 2005. The credit-fuelled economy was a huge bubble waiting to burst. And so it did.

Eventually house prices got so high in the US that first-time buyers could no longer get on the ladder. They had been encouraged and cajoled to do so with sub-prime mortgages, in effect loans that required no deposits, no proof of income and no initial payments for the first six months etc. These loans were cynically sold to people (often on very low incomes in poor housing areas, mostly black and Hispanic) who very soon realized that they could not maintain the payments. Eventually, the housing bubble was pricked, beginning in 2006 and gathering pace to the collapse of summer 2007.

It was then that the banks and other financial institutions realized they were in trouble. They had made these loans and had then packaged them up as bonds or securities to be sold and sold again around the world to all sorts. The risk of default on the mortgages was thus spread around or 'diversified'. In reality, it just meant that when the housing bubble burst, it affected not just mortgage lenders but all sorts of investors, big and small.

Take one. Irvine, California, was a planned community nestling between Los Angeles and San Diego. A year ago at this time, Irvine was home to 18 sub-prime lenders, including many of the leaders in the field, New Century Financial. Irvine had become the center of the sub-prime industry almost by accident. As the business of writing mortgages to riskier borrowers grew rapidly in the middle of the decade, many top employees at the established sub-prime firms struck out on their own, setting up shop nearby.

But the industry imploded even faster than it grew. New Century had become the second-largest sub-prime lender in the US. It filed for bankruptcy last April and essentially halted operations a month later. "Honestly, some people are still sitting here with their jaws dropping, saying 'How did it happen?' It was just so fast," said Jacquie Ellis, CEO of the

Irvine Chamber of Commerce. "Typically when you have a downturn, it's a slow decline. That's not what happened here."

By the end of the year, almost 9,000 'subprime' jobs were gone from Orange County. Many of these people have been unable to find new jobs. And economic officials say that was only part of the economic pain. Suppliers and service firms from hotels and restaurants to printers and software developers that had come to depend on the lenders for a bulk of their business have had to cut staff as well.

Ellis said one hotel in town has lost $1m in annual bookings as a result of the subprime collapse. And small businesses, such as local trophy shops that produced the monthly sales awards, have been hurt. "Everybody was riding high, it was like fat city," said Ellis. "All of a sudden you look around and think, 'Joe across the street lost his job,' or 'Oh, my gosh, Sally next door lost her job.'"

The impact of this credit crunch was global. Narvik is a remote seaport where, along with three other Norwegian municipalities, it has lost about $64m in complex securities investments that went sour.

The residents want to know how their close-knit community of 18,000 could have mortgaged its future — built on the revenue from a hydroelectric plant on a nearby fjord — by dabbling in what many view as the black arts of investment bankers in distant places.

In 2004, Narvik and the three other towns took out a large loan, using future energy revenue as collateral. They invested the money, through Terra Securities, which offered a better return than traditional investments — namely US sub-prime mortgages. In June 2007, as the sub-prime problems were brewing, Narvik shifted some money into an even more complex investment, again through Terra Securities.

Within weeks, as the sub-prime market deteriorated, this investment declined in value and Narvik got a letter from Terra Securities, demanding an additional payment of $2.8m. The chief investigator of Norway's financial regulator, Eystein Kleven, said Terra Securities' Norwegian-language prospectus did not mention such payments, or other risk factors.

Terra Group, which is in turn owned by 78 savings banks and remains in business, has rejected calls for it to compensate the towns. Norway's finance minister, Kristin Halvorsen, has ruled out a state bailout and Citigroup, which shut down one of the money-losing investments that Narvik bought, said it had no legal obligation.

The investments represented a quarter of Narvik's annual budget of $163m and covering the losses would necessitate taking out a long-term loan, which the town could only pay off by cutting back on services.

And it was not just the small town lenders and councils that took the hit. The great credit bubble burst eventually took down some of the giants of the global finance. In March, the US Federal Reserve was forced to rescue the fifth-largest investment house in Wall Street, Bear Stearns, when the securities firm faced bankruptcy and its failure could have led to a widespread financial collapse. As Ben Bernanke, the head of the Fed put it: "The adverse effects would not have been confined to the financial system but would have been felt broadly in the real economy through its effects on asset values and credit availability".

The Fed agreed to give emergency funding to Bear Stearns after a run on the company wiped out its cash reserves in two days. During the weekend following the rescue, Fed officials helped arrange a takeover by JP Morgan at a fraction of Bear Stearns's market value.

All this was a far cry from the comments of Bernanke when the credit crunch first broke last summer. Then he said the bursting bubble would cost no more than $50bn and there would be just a few failures of some small regional banks invested in real estate.

CREDIT CRUNCH ONE YEAR ON

As we review the collateral damage now, the current score of bank losses globally (and still counting) is $500bn, ten times Bernanke's forecast. Moreover, up to 30 regional banks and mortgage lenders have gone bust in the US; and we know about Northern Rock in the UK (bailed out by £30bn of taxpayers money); as well as the 'rogue trader' scandal of $6bn in France's Societe Generale — and we could go on.

Indeed, any reasonable estimate of the total financial damage globally puts the figure at over $1trn (the IMF) or even $2trn. That's compared to world GDP of about $60trn, or 3% of world GDP. That is how much global growth is likely to lose over the next year. Given that global economic growth, including fast-growing India and China, is about 5%, that would take world growth below the 2.5% that the IMF reckons is needed to sustain employment and incomes on average in the world. And in the more advanced capitalist countries of the US, Europe and Japan, economic growth is likely to be below 1% or even negative in the next year.

Figures for the economy in the last few weeks suggest that now all of the G7 economies (the group of the major advanced economies including US, UK, Japan, Germany, France, Italy and Canada) are already in a recession or close to tipping into one. Other advanced economies or emerging markets (the rest of the Eurozone; New Zealand, Iceland, Estonia, Latvia and some South-East European economies) are also on the tip of a recessionary hard landing.

And once this group of 20-plus economies enters into a recession, there will be a sharp growth slowdown in the BRICs (Brazil, Russia, India and China) and other emerging market economies. For example, a country like China — that even with a growth rate of 10%-plus has officially thousands of riots and protests a year — needs to move 15m poor rural farmers to the modern urban industrial sector with higher wages every year just to maintain the legitimacy of its regime. So for China a growth rate of 6% would be equivalent to a recession. It now looks like that, by the end of this year or early 2009, it will have that.

CREDIT CRUNCH ONE YEAR ON

The housing collapse and the sub-prime mortgage debacle was the trigger for the credit crunch. But it was not the gun. The gun was the anarchic and crisis-ridden nature of the capitalist system of production. The bullet was declining profitability.

Capitalism, contrary to the views of the dumbest of capitalist apologists (usually the heads of government like George Bush or Gordon Brown; or the heads of the central banks and finance houses), does not grow in a straight line upwards. The very nature of production for private profit with companies, individuals and investors competing and gambling against each other leads to excessive and blind investment and expansion. The result is a massive waste of resources and damage to people's lives.

Credit bubbles and subsequent crunches are not new. Indeed, they happen whenever the productive sectors of capitalism start to experience slowdown, namely profitability (the rate of profit) begins to fall. Then capitalists and financiers try to compensate by investing more into areas that are less productive, but provide better returns for a while (real estate, stock markets, fine art, gold etc).

What is different about this credit crunch is that it involved new ways of expanding credit beyond the productive capacity of capitalism. Traditional bank lending gave way to loans that were converted into weird and wonderful new forms of bonds and securities that were sold onto all and sundry as 'safe and profitable' investments. And bets and hedges called derivatives were also sold and bought on top of them. The global credit market (including loans, bonds and derivatives) expanded from three times world GDP to 12 times in just ten years.

So this credit bubble (the expansion of fictitious capital, as Marx called it) is different because it was huge and it was global. The collateral damage on its bursting will be the same: huge and global.

As the credit boom exploded, profitability of the productive sectors began to decline, particularly after 2005[1] . The credit bubble expanded even more in response. But just like a yo yo, credit growth reached its limit and has now jumped back with a vengeance.

The credit contraction is now experienced every day by people trying to get a mortgage for a house; borrow money to invest in new equipment or expand a business; or just to make ends meet. The banks won't lend or if they do it is at exorbitant rates. With the banks squeezing credit, households must save, not spend; and businesses must contract, not expand.

The credit crunch one year later means global economic recession one year (or more) onwards. That means housing repossessions, business bankruptcies, rising unemployment, falling real incomes and more loss of productive capacity. This is the bleak reality of the capitalist system of production.

Sure, now all the talk in the councils of government and high finance is that they have learnt the lessons of the crunch and they will 'regulate' and 'monitor' to ensure that it does not happen again. It won't — in the same way. But as sure as the night is black, if capitalism continues as the system of human organisation, there will be more crunches and economic crises, even if the apologists' lies and excuses take a different form.

This latest global economic recession will be one of the most severe; perhaps matching that of 1980-2. Eventually, global capitalism will recover, say from 2010 onwards. But this recession won't be the last before 2020. There will be another, perhaps even worse, before the next decade is out.

1. See Chapter 24.

Financial meltdown

Financial markets in Wall Street, New York, the City of London and all over are in turmoil. In just 24 hours, two out of the four largest investment banks in the US have disappeared. All this confirms what Marxists have always maintained: capitalism does not operate in a smooth and steadily increasing way to progress. It operates violently, lopsidedly, in cycles of boom and slump. Now more banks are set to fail and there will be more misery in the financial markets. Working people are also set to suffer as massive job losses are announced.

As I write, financial markets in Wall Street, New York, the City of London and all over are in turmoil. Lehman Brothers, around for 158 years, has declared bankruptcy and 25,000 employees around the globe have lost their jobs. Merrill Lynch, the world's largest investment bank, has been taken over by the largest high street bank in America, Bank America.

Bank America was virtually ordered by the US financial authorities to take over Merrill Lynch, paying $50bn. Otherwise, that bank too would have gone bust, putting thousands more out of work. Even worse for capitalism, it would have meant that both Lehman and Merrill Lynch would have defaulted on their contracts and obligations and thus brought down many other banks (15 were rumoured to be in trouble). Along with Bear Stearns (wiped out last March), three out of the top five investment banks in the US have now vanished in a puff of financial smoke. And finally, the world's largest insurance company, AIG, announced that it needed to raise $40bn within hours if it was not to default on its obligations and appealed to the Federal Reserve for a loan before it was too late!

All this took place only one week after the world's largest semi-government mortgage lenders Fannie Mae and Freddie Mac had to be nationalised to protect American homeowners and the mortgage industry from going bust. These two lenders had over 40% of all mortgages in the US and 85% of recent new mortgages. It would have meant the total collapse

of the housing market if they could not do business. So the Bush administration was forced to nationalise them!

How did this terrible mess for capitalism come about?

The capitalist economists have no real idea. Some say it is the fault of
greedy chief executives of the banks who have gone into reckless investments and lent too much money to people who could not pay it back.
Some say it is the fault of the Federal Reserve and other central banks for
keeping interest rates too low and thus encouraging too many people to
borrow too much or too many banks to lend too much. Others say it was
the failure of the central banks to 'regulate' the banks and investment
houses to make sure they had enough funds to do their business instead of
borrowing to lend etc.

But perhaps the story of the British travel agent XL, which also collapsed
this week, leaving hundreds without jobs and tens of thousands unable to
get home from their holidays, has the most interesting clues to why this
global financial tsunami is sweeping away so many big financial institutions.

XL chief executive explained tearfully to the press that his company had
gone under without warning for two reasons: the sharp rise in the price of
oil had dramatically increased the company's costs for air fuel; but when
he tried to raise more finance to cover this, he was unable to get any
banks to provide funding at rates or terms that made it viable to continue.
And there we have it. Such is the stranglehold and fear in the global credit
crunch that banks are no longer willing to lend money at reasonable rates
or on reasonable conditions to businesses. And those that are hard pressed
are forced into bankruptcy — expect much more of this over the next
year.

Why are the banks unable to lend? It's because they have lost so much
money on the writing down of the assets they bought over the last five or
six years. Now they must retrench and stop lending. Now they must find

new capital and investors before they can start relending. In the mean-time, they are too scared or unwilling to lend, even to other banks (that's why Bear Stearns, Lehman, Northern Rock and others went bust — no-body would lend to them).

What are these assets that have lost so much value? In the main, they are called mortgage-backed securities. In the old days of the housing market, banks or building societies would attract cash deposits from savers like you and me (we should be so lucky!) and then use these deposits to lend to people who wanted to buy a home. From deposit to mortgage — sim-ple.

However, some bankers started to be more 'innovative' in order to make more profits. They started to borrow funds from other banks and then lend that on as mortgages. This 'wholesale funding' became particularly popular with US and UK banks, like Northern Rock, which had been a rather sleepy building society until the mid-1990s when it converted into a 'bank' with shareholders and an aggressive management out to make money for its investors (not savers).

But that was not the end of it. Many banks came up with another wheeze. They would take their mortgages and batch them up into a basket of different quality mortgages which they would sell off as a bond or security to other banks or financial investors. By creating these securities and selling them off, they 'diversified' their risk to others. Also they set up separate companies that took all these liabilities completely off their books.

That meant they could go out and borrow more and do more mortgage business. Soon many banks that used to have enough cash and stocks to match at least 10% of the loans, now had reduced that to just 5%, or in the case of the big American banks and mortgage lenders to just 2%. Lever-age (borrowing) was now 50 times the money the banks actually had to meet any losses.

FINANCIAL MELTDOWN

But no problem — the US housing market was racing upwards. So as fast as banks lent money, they made it back in the rising house prices. Home owners could afford to pay them back and take out even bigger loans. Banks could lend to people who hardly had any income because they could count on the value of the home rising to cover their loan.

But then it all went horribly wrong. From about 2006, house price rises began to slow and then began to fall. Once house prices headed downwards, so did the ability of mortgage borrowers to pay back their loans and their willingness to take out bigger and better mortgages. The mortgage market slumped. Soon the mortgage lenders were losing money and behind them, the owners of all these mortgage-backed securities found that their 'assets' were not worth what they paid for them. And just everybody and his dog in the financial world had these securities. The risk had been diversified so that everybody got hit when things went wrong.

Why did the housing market go down? Why did it not carry on in a straight line upwards and it had done for nearly 18 years? I venture an answer. First, there are cycles of motion that operate under modern capitalism. The most important law of motion under capitalism is profitability. As Marx showed, the rate of profit is key to investment and growth in a capitalist system: no profit, no investment and no income and jobs. But profitability moves in cycles: for a period, profitability will rise, but then it will start to fall.

But the profit cycle is not the only cycle of motion under capitalism. There is also a cycle in real estate prices and construction. The real estate cycle seems to last about 18 years from trough to trough.

There appears to be a cycle of about 18 years based on the movement of real estate prices. The American economist Simon Kuznets discovered the existence of this cycle back in the 1930s. We can measure the cycle in the US by looking at house prices. The first peak after 1945 was in 1951. The prices fell back to a trough in 1958. Prices then rose to a new peak in 1969 before slumping back to another trough in 1971. The next peak was in 1979-80 and the next trough was in 1991. The spacing between peak to peak to trough to trough varies considerably. It can be as little as 11 years or as much as 26 years. But if you go far enough back (into the 19th century), the average seems to be about 18 years.

The last peak in US real estate prices was in 1988. Assuming an average cycle of 18 years, then house prices should have peaked in 2006. The last trough was in 1991. Assuming an 18-year cycle, then the next trough in US house prices should be around 2009-10.

The real estate cycle does not operate in line with the Marxist profit cycle. The latter is a product of the laws of motion of capitalist accumulation. It operates in the productive sector of the economy, namely contributing to the production of value.

In contrast, the real estate cycle operates in the unproductive sector of the capitalist economy. New value created and surplus-value appropriated in the productive sectors of the capitalist economy are siphoned off by the unproductive sectors as the owners of capital spend their profits and workers spend their wages. Housing is a big user of consumer income. So the cycle in house prices reflects the spending behaviour of capitalists and workers, not the profitability of capital.

For these reasons, the real estate cycle has different timings in its turns than the profit cycle. The profit cycle reached a trough in 1982 before rising for 15-16 years to peak in 1997. In contrast, the US real estate cycle troughed some nine years later in 1991 and only reached its peak in 2006-7. The next trough is due no earlier than 2009-10.

This huge rise in house prices, exhibited around many parts of the world as well as the US, represented a massive diversion of resources by capitalism into unproductive sectors that produced no new profit through investment in technology and productive labour. As a result, it actually reduced the ability of capitalism to invest in new technology to boost economic growth. It was entirely a process of creating fictitious capital.

FINANCIAL MELTDOWN

That is shown buy one stark fact. You can measure the movement of house prices from 1991 to 2006. In 1991, the US house price index stood at 100; by 2006, it had reached 200, a doubling in price. But the costs of building a house including land purchase had not risen at all. So house prices were way out of line with the real production value of a home. The housing market had become a huge financial speculation. When home prices got so far out of line with the incomes of those who were buying them, the market finally toppled over.

Capitalism does not operate in a smooth and steadily increasing way to progress. It operates violently, lopsidedly, in cycles of boom and slump. The path of chaos and anarchy applies to the cycle of profit and also to the cycle of housing construction.

So what now? Well, more banks are set to fail. There will be more misery in the financial markets. More to the point for working people not worried about whether rich investors lose money, jobs throughout the financial services industry are going to go. And we are not talking about the fat cats at the top who caused this mess — they will leave with their payoffs and pensions intact. We are talking about the tens of thousands on moderate pay packets who put all their savings into the shares of the banks they worked in, and which are now worthless.

And more, the collapse of the financial sector will lead to a serious economic downturn. It is already underway with the US, the UK, Europe and Japan going into economic slump, where output will stop increasing, companies will fail and unemployment and inflation will rise sharply.

The politicians are lost in all this. Whether it is a right-wing Republican administration or New Labour, they know not what to do. Indeed, in many ways New Labour has been so tied to the model of American capitalism with its 'free choice' and 'open deregulated markets' that it is even more in denial than the Republicans. In America, they have nationalised the mortgage lenders. In Britain, they just look shocked and babble about the 'worst crisis in 60 years'.

Eventually, capitalism will recover, unless governments come to power mandated to end the rule of capital. But it will recover only by restoring profitability. To do that, many jobs must go and many companies must be swallowed up by richer ones. That process has started in the financial sector. It will continue across the whole economy.

Socialism for the rich, capitalism for the poor

After a week of turmoil on financial markets, on Saturday 20 September, President Bush said he was proposing to spend $700bn of taxpayers' money to buy the rotten mortgage assets held by the banks on Wall Street. He said he was doing this to help the average American family with their homes and jobs.

At the same time Gordon Brown, at the annual Labour party conference in Blackpool, England, was telling delegates the same thing to explain why he intervened personally to ensure the Lloyds Bank bought Britain's biggest mortgage lender, HBOS last week.

Both were lying. They were not taking these actions to help working people. They did it to save finance capital from disaster.

The Bush-Paulson plan to buy to rotten mortgages, along with the nationalisation of the two biggest mortgage lenders only ten days ago, will mean that the US government will soon own the vast majority of Americans' mortgages. It will mean a large part of American household debt in the hands of the state. Overall, it is the biggest nationalisation in world history, equivalent to $6trn, or 45% of annual US output.

But, of course, the devil is in the detail of the terms. This is not expropriating the banks. On the contrary it is saving them — with nearly full compensation, so they can resume their operations and restore their profitability.

In turn, US government debt will rise 40% of GDP to nearly 100%! And what will the taxpayer get for this huge bailout? Just a load of defaulted and non-paying mortgages, along with higher taxes, cuts in public spending on health, education and social security.

SOCIALISM FOR THE RICH

And behind those bad debts lie a trail of misery for millions of Americans who will lose their homes and eventually their jobs. Nothing much will be done for them. It won't stop the unfolding slump in world capitalism that we are entering with rising unemployment, falling real incomes and declining public services.

Instead most of the money will go to help the fat cats of Wall Street get out of their mess. You see, when it comes down to the impending collapse of capitalism, suddenly socialism is a good idea. It's just this is socialism for the rich, while the rest of us have to continue to live under capitalism.

A kick in the face for capital

Such was the indignation of ordinary Americans that yesterday the much trumpeted $700 billion bailout was voted down in Congress, sending shockwaves around the world's financial institutions. Whatever they do now, a new package or no package will mean serious economic downturn and reveal the real nature of capitalism to all.

What a kick in the face for America's capitalist elite! The US House of Representatives voted to reject the Emergency Economic Stabilisation Act put forward by Treasury Secretary Hank Paulson, Fed Chairman Ben Bernanke, President Bush, Vice-President Cheney, the majority Democrat leader of the House, the Republican minority leader of the House, both candidates in the upcoming presidential election, Barack Obama and John McCain and all the American media.

Hank Paulson wanted to take $700bn of taxpayers' money, equivalent to 6% of America's annual output, and not spend it on new hospitals, Medicare, more schools and better education; No, not on that. Paulson wanted to spend it buying up the bad and rotten debts of the big banks and financial institutions so they could start making profits again.

But the American electorate was not having it. Congress members were deluged with emails, letters and phone calls from constituents demanding that this legislation be thrown out. It did not matter that the 'great and the good' were saying this payout, equivalent to the entire cost of the Iraq war, would have 'safeguards for taxpayers'. They knew it was just a bailout for the rich at the expense of the majority of working people.

The fat cats of Wall Street were led by the Treasury Secretary Hank Paulson, the former head of Goldman Sachs, the most powerful investment bank in the world. Paulson used to get $40-50m a year in salary and bonuses. He wanted to save his former bank and all the others.

KICK IN THE FACE FOR CAPITAL

Paulson represents just 1% of the population, those 450 billionaires in America and 3m millionaires who between them own 25% of all America's wealth. The credit crunch was losing them money big time. He aimed to get taxpayers' money to bail them out.

Fear and terror were proposed to the people if this law was not passed. The world would come to an end, he said. Well, not enough Congressmen and women, even though many took money from finance capital, would agree.

A majority of Republicans, driven partly by an extreme ideology against so-called "government interference in markets", and partly by pressure from the electorate that can vote them out of office in just five weeks time, rebelled against their leaders. Also, many Democrats backed the views of their constituents against their sycophantic leaders. The vote to bail out the rich was lost.

What happens now? Well, the rich elite will make strenuous efforts now to reverse this decision. There are two possibilities for capitalism. The first is that the vote stays lost. Then more banks will fail (three big ones failed on the same day that Congress voted) and the stock market will fall further (it was down by the biggest amount since 9/11). America would be staring depression in the face, equivalent to the 1930s.

Paulson is right: failure to bail out his friends will mean a strike of finance capital; another squeeze of credit and then companies will stop producing, profits will fall (they are already falling at over 10% a year now) and jobs will be lost, as the housing market dives further.

The second is that the vote eventually goes through. That will mean massive government spending to bail out the banks and huge printing of money to help the fat cats. That will mean inflation alongside stagnation of the economy in America, Britain and Europe.

So the alternatives are depression worldwide or stagflation worldwide. We are beginning to see the reality of capitalism in crisis.

Credit crunch — who pays?

Britain's second-largest bank, the Royal Bank of Scotland, which owns NatWest and has recently bought Holland's largest bank ABN-Amro, has announced that it lost £4bn in the last three months as a result of the world's great credit crunch.

RBS says that it must write off £5bn in loans and debt securities that it had on its books as worthless. And it now must ask existing shareholders to stump up more money — as much as £10bn — to buy new shares in the bank so it does not go bust.

And this is happening just a few weeks after the head of the bank, Sir Fred Goodwin, had declared a whopping great profit for the bank and made it clear to all and sundry that the credit crunch would not affect RBS and it had no need for extra funds.

This news shows that the credit crunch is going to hit Britain in a big way. Up to now, Britain's main high street banks had not seemed to have suffered much — they were all announcing big profits and there was little talk of large 'writedowns' of worthless assets.

The collapse and subsequent bailout by the taxpayer of Northern Rock was an exceptional event due to the 'bad policies' of one set of managers.

At the same time, the government of Darling and Brown, the leaders of industry and the City of London were arguing that the British economy was still growing well and while the financial sector was on a 'sticky wicket' due the housing and mortgage crisis in the US, Britain was "well-placed" to avoid the worst.

Well, that story now looks shot full of holes. RBS is not a small mortgage lender from the north-east like Northern Rock that got too big for its boots.

CREDIT CRUNCH — WHO PAYS?

It is a major international bank with interests in Europe, Ireland and the US. But when you delve into its accounts, you find that all was not well.

The bank is one of the weakest in Europe. Relative to all its loans and debt securities that were made or purchased, it had the least amount of shareholder investment. Indeed, it had safe funds worth only 4% of all the loans and assets on its books — the barest minimum allowed under international banking regulations. And, more than anyone else, it had bought those 'toxic' mortgage securities from American banks that were backed by the value of American homes. So much of its assets and its profits were based on the now falling value of American houses.

At the same time, it had just bought another huge bank, ABN-Amro, after a bitter merger fight fora huge amount of money at the top of the market just before the share prices of all the banks plummeted in the credit crunch. And RBS, like all the other British banks, was now facing up to a housing market slump in the UK in 2008 that the US had seen in 2007.

And boy — is that housing slump coming. After peaking last summer, UK house prices had been slowly sliding downwards. Now the pace of decline is accelerating. Most expert analyses have come round to the view that house prices will fall a minimum of 10% from their peak last summer — it is more likely to be 15%-plus before the market bottoms some time in 2009-10. So a house worth £250,000 last summer will be lucky to be worth £200,000 before the end.

And here is the problem. Over 50% of mortgages issued by the likes of RBS and Northern Rock in the last few years have been for over 80% of the value of the property. And that does not include all those mortgages made to people just trying to make money from renting out flats (buy-to-let, as it is called).

So if house prices drop 15%, many homeowners are going be under water in what is called 'negative equity', where their house is worth less than the mortgage loan they have on it. If these homeowners walk away or default on their payments, the banks are going to take substantial losses.

And it is not just British homes. Many companies that bought their offices on loans from the banks will also be under water and there will losses on commercial mortgages too.

It is often argued that a housing slump won't have such a big impact as it has in the US because British banks did not go in for reckless lending to people who could not afford to pay it back as they did in America — the so-called sub-prime market.

Well, the figures don't agree. IMF and OECD researchers reckoned that the UK's level of mortgage debt to household income and level of house prices to income are so high that UK housing is more overvalued than any other in the advanced capitalist world — British houses are facing price subsidence.

A recent survey by a credit agency found that sub-prime borrowers who had taken out mortgages on dubious income statements were ten times more likely to default and there were plenty of places all over the UK of towns where people desperate to get onto the housing ladder now faced default. Places where sub-prime mortgages were more than 10% of homes included Manchester, Cardiff and Wolverhampton. While in London, more than 25% of all homes with mortgages were buy-to-let loans, facing 'negative equity'.

A huge tsunami of unpaid debt is about to hit British capitalism. What the RBS announcement shows is Britain's bankers are finally recognising that the tide is coming in fast and they are battening down the hatches.

CREDIT CRUNCH — WHO PAYS?

It is unlikely that any big bank will go bust — first, they will raise more money from their shareholders to finance their past bad decisions; and second, the Bank of England (and that means us the taxpayers) will bail them out if necessary.

The Bank of England, having put its head in the sand for months and months, is now waking up to the disaster. It has finally started to cut interest rates (although it remains worried by a rise in inflation that it cannot seem to control).

But more — it has decided, on our behalf as taxpayers, to start buying or swapping the bad loans and debt held by the likes of RBS for UK government bonds. So the banks get nice safe bonds for their rotten mortgages to put on their books and they no longer have a problem. The problem becomes one for the government.

Brown and Darling, after much kicking and screaming, finally took over Northern Rock and had to recognise £50bn of loans to the bank that are now the liability of the state. This new Bank of England measure will put even more liabilities on the government books. But it had to be done or there would be a major banking crisis in 2008.

Thus capitalism works its mysterious ways: the capitalists don't want any 'interference' from the state and democratic accountability when they are making huge profits; but when things go pear-shaped, they demand funds from the state but with no recourse and no control.

Who will suffer from the coming UK housing slump? Well, first it will be the workers in the financial sector, the City of London. It is estimated that about 40,000 will lose their jobs for a start.

On the whole, these won't be the fat cats on the boards of directors of the big financial institutions like Sir Fred Goodwin (they are always 'knights of the realm'). No, if they get the push it will be with a 'golden hand-shake' of millions and their pensions intact[1]. The head of Northern Rock took nearly a million and a pension for presiding over a strategy that brought it to its knees.

Yet thousands of Northern Rock employees are losing their jobs with no handshakes, pensions or prospects of future work. The job cuts in the City of London will be aimed at those in the back rooms. They may be earning £30-50,000 a year — not bad by most people's standards, but not millionaires.

The government reckons UK economic growth will be about 2-2.5% this year well down from 3.25% last year. But that is now regarded as very optimistic. The IMF, basing itself on the global credit crunch and housing collapse in the UK, reckons growth will be closer to 1.5% for the next two years. It is likely to be worse than that.

But all these forecasts lead to one thing — everybody, not just City work-ers, are going to suffer. The UK is more dependent on the financial sector in its economy that any other major capitalist country (unless you count Switzerland as major). Job losses and rising unemployment will be the order of the day.

The government has announced another fall in the jobless figures. Of course, this is mainly a statistical trick. Those who claim jobseekers al-lowance are under 800,000. Even in booming Britain, they cannot get a job because they are so undereducated or unskilled that there are not enough low-skilled jobs available for them (there are only 700,000 'no skills' vacancies at the last count).

This is not a true reflection of the real level of unemployment in Britain. Indeed, the total number of people in work has hardly changed in the last

CREDIT CRUNCH — WHO PAYS?

30 years despite an increase in population and in people of working age. There are millions who are in 'fulltime' education where they are hopefully getting qualifications that will get them work. Also, there have been millions of women that have come into semi-skilled work over the last few decades while millions of older unskilled men have just gone.

Where have they gone? Well, the Tory myth is that they have all signed on for 'incapacity benefit' claiming that they are ill or disabled and cannot work. This benefit is not means tested and worth more. This myth that there are 2.6m loafers and shysters not willing to work has been accepted by New Labour and they are cracking down.

Interestingly, the 8% of the UK's working population on this benefit is not much higher than the 6% in the US where the rules are supposed to be tougher.

And when the government did a survey of people on incapacity benefit, they found that half a million were suffering from depression or had clinical mental illness.

Only a small minority had alcoholism or drug abuse. Moreover, only about 0.5% were faking. Sure, many of these millions were capable of doing some work, but most lacked skills, half were over 50 years, or they had sick family members to look after, or needed transport to get to jobs.

The reality is that if you added to the 750,000 claiming job seekers allowance another 1.5m claiming disability allowance who could work but cannot get a job, then Britain's unemployment rate is not 5% but probably double that already. And the hard times are still to come.

1. The head of the Royal Bank of Scotland, Sir Fred Goodwin was at the helm of a bank that lost £24bn, the biggest loss in UK corpo-

rate history. He subsequently resigned as chief executive and left with £20m compensation and a pension worth £700,000 a year. Despite demands from the government to return that compensation, he refused. RBS has subsequently sacked thousands of employees, but not on similar terms.

All Keynesians now?

January 2009

There have been dozens of books on the global credit crunch. There was one by Charles Morris, banker and lawyer, which came out last March (*The trillion dollar meltdown*). Then there were more recent books by top American economists, Robert Shiller and Mark Zandi that were published this summer (*The sub-prime solution; how today's global financial crisis happened; and Financial shock*).

And then there is the book by one of the most notorious of financial speculators, George Soros, infamous for making billions of dollars on predicting (or forcing) the collapse of the British pound in 1992 (*The new paradigm for financial markets; the credit crisis of 2008 and what it means*). Soros has now become a 'socialist', attacking the Iraq war, 'free market economics' and inequalities of wealth and income. This new volume again attacks the excesses of modern capitalism!

Even earlier than all these, two City of London economists, David Roche and Bob McKee published a slim volume, back in September 2007, that exposed the Ponzi-style expansion of fictitious capital built up over the last ten years and predicted its collapse (*New monetarism*).

But now, British economist, Graham Turner has published a book (*The credit crunch*). Turner is an independent consultant who worked in the City of London for many years. What singles out this book is that it claims to approach the problem from a socialist perspective, or at least it has been adopted by the left. Turner has spoken at many left forums in recent months.

What is Graham Turner's message? He outlines his aim in the preface: "the roots of this crisis must be understood to ensure there is no repeat of the flawed economic policies that have created the biggest credit bust

since the 1930s. If we understand the causes, the damage can be miti-
gated".

And what does Turner think are the causes? Is it due to the anarchy of
capitalism, the laws of motion of capitalism that include the tendency of
the rate of profit to fall; or the huge expansion of fictitious capital designed
to avoid a slump?

Well no. Apparently the reason for the credit crunch is the growth of free
trade that led capitalist companies to move their production to cheaper
labour areas. This forced central banks in the west to keep interest rates
low in order to keep up demand and spending. Debt rose to excessive
levels as a result.

Turner says he is not against free trade. For him "it is a good thing, but not
when it is used by companies simply as a ruse to cut costs". But is that
not just one of the inevitable consequences of free trade (trade without
tariffs and quotas on the movement of goods) under capitalism? How
can you have free trade under capitalism that is not damaging to working
people's jobs?

What should we do to avoid future crises? "Governments will have to
realign their policy away from the exclusive promotion of big business that
lies at the heart of recent credit bubbles". So governments must not 'ex-
clusively' promote big business — in other words, we need more of a
balance.

Turner argues that we need a new economic agenda that "balances the
interests of companies and workers more evenly and promotes a free
trade that does not fuel the boom and bust seen today". So there we have
it: we need a capitalism that is fairer and more even so that free trade
does not cause slumps.

Turner expresses a naivety about the nature of capitalism that is disap-
pointing. It is in the nature of capitalism to generate inequality and injus-

tice in seeking profit and it is in the nature of capitalism to deliver periodic economic slumps as it grows. There can be no 'good and fair capitalism', and, for that matter, Turner does not explain how we could get it in this book.

Having said all this, this book does provide many insights into how this credit crisis developed and how it has unfolded. In particular, the chapter on the impact of the credit bubble and burst on emerging economies is revealing. He also very clear and correct in his condemnation of the spurious arguments of Ben Bernanke, the head of the US Federal central bank that the crisis was a problem of 'excessive saving' by mercantilist Asian economies and not more the result of excessive spending in the West on housing financed by a credit bubble. And there are many interesting points about why and how Japan got into permanent depression in the 1990s.

But here lies another theoretical flaw in Turner's reasoning and thus in his prescriptions to solving the crisis. Graham Turner is clearly a Keynesian through and through[1]. At the end of nearly every chapter, he refers to John Maynard Keynes as providing the theoretical explanation for the mess and also providing the policy measures for the way out.

Turner argues that the credit crunch led to debt deflation. By that he means that people, banks and corporations could not pay their debts and the value of debt therefore plummeted. This led to a vicious circle in which investors would no longer invest and preferred to hold their capital in cash. Thus money capital was trapped and credit became scarce and unavailable for investment.

Keynes called this the liquidity trap. Keynes argued that this was a cause of the Great Depression of the 1930s. What needed to be done was for central banks to cut interest rates to the bone. For Keynes, though, monetary policy could not be effective on its own in solving a crisis. So governments had to start spending and make tax cuts, and not worry about how to pay for it. This is called expansionary fiscal policy. Just print money until the economy comes out of its slump.

Turner makes the same argument to solve the current crisis. For him, the real risk is that central banks won't cut interest rates quick enough and governments won't spend and borrow quickly enough. The reason that Japan stayed in depression was because the authorities sat on their hands for too long.

Turner's arguments are somewhat ironic. For it appears that capitalist governments are all Keynesians now (again). The US Federal Reserve under Ben Bernanke has released over $2trn of funds to bail out the banks, refinance the money markets and even subsidise insurance and auto companies. And it has cut interest rates to 1% at a time when inflation is still at 5%. The Bank of England has (belatedly) launched a cycle of interest-rate cuts and the New Labour government is about to announce a massive package of spending and tax cuts to be paid for by borrowing.

After the Great Depression and the post-war slumps, all capitalist governments adopted Keynesian views, culminating in President Nixon's statement in 1970 that we are all Keynesians now. But the crisis of the 1970s pushed capitalists to try and break the labour movement and restore profitability that had reached new lows by the end of the 1970s. This led capitalists to revert to monetarist economics.

Government spending was out. As the then UK prime minister James Callaghan told the Labour party conference in 1978, "you can't spend your way out of recession". And he then imposed a round of spending cuts that led to 'the winter of discontent' in 1978-9 and the eventual defeat of Labour by Thatcher's Tories.

And yet spending the way out of recession is just what New Labour is proposing to do now and what even the US government is doing. Gordon Brown has dumped his long-held belief that capitalism can grow 'endogenously' without slumps. Keynesianism is back with a vengeance. So Turner's answers to solving the crisis are about to be played out.

Will they work? Did Keynesianism work in the 1930s? It was not really adopted in the UK then, but in the US, the New Deal programme under President Roosevelt went some way to taking it up with low interest rates and public works programmes. What was the result? There was a re-covery in the US economy from the bottom of the slump in 1932 up to 1937. Then the economy entered a renewed slump that was only ended with the arms race spending that preceded the Second World War. It took a war economy to end the Great Depression, not low interest rates and government spending.

For Marxists, capitalism goes into economic slump because profitability drops so much that the mass of profit starts to fall. This leads to capital-ists stopping investment in real production. If credit is provided, investors use their money to invest in other assets that are not productive like prop-erty or speculating in shares. Thus this capital becomes fictitious. It will not stop the eventual slump, but merely delay it.

Once enough capital value (of money, labour and plant) is destroyed and profitability is restored, those capitalists that are left will start to invest again and the 'liquidity trap' will end. Just as huge dollops of credit will not stop a slump under capitalism, neither will huge dollops of credit revive capitalism, if profitability is not right.

The best analogy is this. Marxists say that the capitalist engine works on the petrol of profit. The petrol tank is always leaking and eventually the engine will stop. Keynesians say the problem is not a leaky petrol tank. No, the engine needs oil to lubricate its financial components and some-times the oil gets trapped in the sump and does not lubricate. The sump needs to be filled to overflowing, then all will be well.

But Marxists say that even if your oil sump is full and all the cylinders are fully lubricated, without the petrol of profit, nothing will start working.

ALL KEYNESIANS NOW?

Sure, capitalism works better if its pistons are lubricated, but putting too much oil in can also drown the system. The capitalist engine cannot work without fuel, of which there can never be too much.

Slumps cannot be avoided under capitalism, because they are necessary to restore profitability when it gets too low — it means filling up the tank. The liquidity trap may be broken by Keynesian policies of low interest rates and public spending, but it won't get capitalism going again. That only happens when profitability is restored.

Turner's Keynesian solutions will prove inadequate, as will his naïve hope that all we need to do is "to even out the playing field, reduce corporate power or increase the strength of labour".

1. Graham Turner has said since that he is no more Keynesian than he is a monetarist or a Marxist and that he draws on all these theories. Certainly, in his latest book on the crisis, No way to run an economy, *released as we go to press, he takes a more eclectic view, leaning more on Marxist ideas for what he calls the structural causes of the crisis, but still relying on Keynes for the policy solutions.*

Unprecedented!

"A British bank is run with precision! A British home demands nothing less! Tradition, discipline and rules must be the tools; without them – disorder, chaos! Moral disintegration! In short, we have a ghastly mess". Mr Banks in Mary Poppins

"Mr Darling used to boast to Wendy that her mother not only loved him, but respected him. He was one of those deep ones who know about stocks and shares. Of course, no one really knows, but he seemed quite to know and he often said stocks were up and stocks were down in a way that would have made any woman respect him". JM Barrie from Peter and Wendy.

Unprecedented! That was the mantra of the broadcasters, pundits and newspapers throughout September, as the credit crisis took a dark turn. Credit markets (mortgages, loans for cars and goods, company bonds and overdrafts) just dried up. Banks stopped lending even to each other. Liquidity disappeared like water into the Sahara desert. Interest rates rocketed despite the best efforts of the central banks to provide unlimited credit at almost any price.

The capitalist financial machine seized up. Banks started to go bust and even countries went bankrupt (Iceland). Nothing has ever been seen like it — for the first time in the hyperbole of the news media, it really was unprecedented.

The difference between what banks were charging each other for loans and what they could borrow from the Bank of England, the Federal Reserve Bank of the US or the European Central bank reached unheard of levels.

This spread fear and loathing through the capitalist financial system. Stock markets rocketed up and then fell like a rollercoaster with every piece of news. The volatility index of the US stock market hit unprecedented levels.

Governments of every political hue were thrown into a frenzy of activity. First, the right-wing American Republican government announced that it was nationalising the biggest mortgage lenders (already semi-government agencies); then it proposed a massive bailout package of $700bn to buy up all the rotten 'toxic' mortgages and bonds that the banks held and were now worthless after the collapse of the US housing market.

But it didn't work. The crunch grew ever tighter. Finally, the British government bit the bullet that it had been avoiding. Gordon Brown and Alastair Darling, after months of dithering and denial, decided to part nationalise the British banks with taxpayers money. The Europeans quickly followed suit and even the Americans decided to adopt a similar approach. They all had to admit that capitalism could not be saved without state intervention.

As the last few weeks have passed, credit markets have started to ease a little and stock markets have stopped plummeting and even recovered somewhat. It appears that the end of capitalism has been averted — at least for now. And all thanks to state interference — the enemy of 'free markets'.

Take a moment. How did all this come about? How did this seemingly 'fundamentally healthy' all-powerful financial system become a 'ghastly mess'? How did a seemingly strong and ever more 'prosperous' and 'endogenously growing' (to use Gordon Brown's phrase), capitalist economy just drop like a toboggan over a precipice?

To my mind, it was a combination of what Marx called the most important law of motion of the capitalist system and the new forms of anarchic excess in capitalist expansion. Take the first component. Marx explained that the most important driver of capitalist growth is profitability. Without profits, there will be no investment, no jobs and no incomes. Capitalists will not allow production without because they own and control the means of production. But capitalist expansion does not proceed in a straightforward and orderly progression. Instead, it jumps forward and slumps back in an anarchic, unequal and wasteful manner, creating and then destroying jobs, incomes and lives.

Indeed, profitability moves in cycles. Marx's law of the tendency of the rate of profit to fall explains that, as capitalism expands, there is a downward pressure exerted on the profit 'earned' from the capital (money, plant, equipment and labour) invested by capitalists. For some time profitability can rise, but eventually the rate of profit begins to fall, laying down the conditions for a crisis — namely a strike of capital, what Marxists call a 'slump' and what capitalist economists call a 'recession'.

In the major capitalist economies, the last up phase in the profit cycle peaked in 1997. It had lasted about 16 years from the 1982 trough. From then on, profitability began to decline. After the dot.com hi-tech stock market bubble burst in 2000, it dropped sharply, causing a recession in 2001. It then recovered from mid-2002 to reach a peak (but a peak below that of 1997) in 2005. After that, profitability began to slide again. And in the latter part of 2007, the total mass of profits, not just the rate of profit, fell. A capitalist crisis was brewing.

The movement of profits is the main law of motion under capitalism, but it is not the only one. There are other cycles driving capitalist production up and down. One is the building and construction cycle: again lasting about 16-18 years in its up and down phases. The housing cycle started at its bottom in 1991 and rose at an ever increasing pace in the main capitalist economies, almost without a break to reach a peak in house prices and sales in 2007. But then the bubble burst, as the sheer height of house prices finally outstripped the ability of purchasers to buy, even with higher incomes or ever bigger and cheaper mortgages.

Capitalism moves in a succession of booms and slumps — that is normal. But each boom and each slump has different characteristics from another; and what triggers the bust can be very different. In 1974-75, it was rocketing oil prices. In 1980-2, it was a housing bust. In 1991-2, it was the collapse of the Soviet bloc and another housing downturn. In 2001, it was the collapse of the hi-tech mania.

But this time, in 2008, it was a humungous credit crunch. The 1991-2 recession was in a period where profitability was in its upward phase. In 2001, profitability was in its downward phase, but the housing boom was still strong. So in both cases, the recession was mild or short-lived. In 1974-5 and 1980-2, profitability and housing were both going down, so the recessions were vicious and long-lasting. The global recession of 2008-10 looks like those.

This cycle of boom and slump had its own peculiar characteristic. The boom was driven by housing, sure, but in particular by the expansion of new forms of credit. When profitability starts falling, as it did after 1997, capitalists look for ways to maintain profit growth. There are many: colonial expansion, an arms race or an outright war; or nearly always an expansion of credit: or what Marx called fictitious capital.

He said fictitious because it was not a real expansion of values created by labour power, but the apparent expansion of value through rising stock prices, rising levels of debt and rising house prices. Investment of profits made went more and more into unproductive areas that produced apparent quick bucks.

So capitalists invested not in new equipment and plant, or new techniques so much, but more into real estate or into the stock market or into buying what appeared to be very profitable bonds. In this way, profits rose, at least for a while.

In 1980, just 5% of US capitalist profits came from the financial sector (namely from bank loans, buying bonds and stocks). By 2007, it provided 41% of all US profits! Money was being made more and more from investing in money! You know that does not make sense and you would be right. To make money from money cannot last because eventually profit must be generated from the production of real values.

This was a giant Ponzi scheme, named after the man who invented the idea of paying investors big returns by attracting new investors in a pyramid of money with no actual business involved. Eventually, the pyramid topples over under its own weight.

And so it was this time. The Ponzi pyramid this time was built by investing in the great housing boom through buying a share of the mortgages lent by the banks at increasingly attractive terms to increasingly risky borrowers who could only afford to service them as long as house prices kept rising at exponential rates. Investors like a small Norwegian council or the British Cat Protection League would be persuaded to buy a bond that paid very high rates. This bond was backed by a myriad of various mortgages in far-off America batched together and sold on. The bond was rated 'triple A' by ratings agencies to give it a high standing so that investors could feel confident that their taxpayers' or cat lovers' money was safe.

On this basis, the banks 'sliced and diced' up the mortgages to make yet more bonds and sell them onto other investors — thus the risk was spread far and wide. The further it spread, the more the banks could issue more. On top of this, they began to sell insurance on these bonds to make more money. As they were triple A rated, it was no problem.

But it was. The housing market toppled. Prices began to fall and mortgages began to look sick, especially the so-called sub-prime ones sold to people with little income to pay them. They began to default and lose their homes. And the banks were left with 'toxic' assets. The credit pyramid crumbled. And this particular credit collapse is unprecedented.

However, government action (taxpayers money and huge government borrowing) has come along to save the fat cats in Wall Street and the City of London from pulling us all down into the abyss. Of course, that does not mean that a recession has been avoided. At the very best, a Great Depression as experienced in the 1930s has been averted (although then it may be too early to say). But the boom and slump of capitalism has returned.

Only fools and knaves argued that the cycles of capitalism had gone forever. There were and still are plenty of fools and knaves. Take Mr George Mudie, a Labour MP on the esteemed UK parliamentary Treasury committee (supposedly composed of people who know about the economy and finance). Just last April, the honourable Mr Mudie pronounced: "I do not see how anyone can table a motion that suggests we are nearing a recession and that we are in all sorts of economic gloom... I cannot see how anyone can come to the House and say there will be a recession." Mr Mudie's words were repeated and echoed by PM Gordon Brown, Chancellor Darling, America's Treasury secretary, Hank Paulson and many others of the 'great and good' (or is that fools and knaves?) — until recently.

Suddenly, Alastair Chancellor Darling reversed course and said the UK faced the worst crisis in 60 years, just before he announced (reluctantly) the nationalisation (temporarily) of the banks.

All the great and good now scream for regulation and control of the excesses that brought capitalism to its knees. But they sang a different song just months ago, demanding yet more 'deregulation' and 'free markets'. Indeed, the UK's Financial Services Authority, supposedly the guardian of the public interest against reckless and fraudulent behaviour by the banks and financial institutions, has had to apologise in public for its failure to notice anything wrong!

But don't worry Gordon Brown is now appointing people to clean up the City of London. Who? Well step forward Lord Adair Turner, former head of the bosses union, the CBI and vice chairman of the bust American investment bank, Merrill Lynch. And with him will be Sir James Crosby, the former head of HBOS, the failed UK mortgage lender. And then there is Sir John Grieve, the former deputy head of the Bank of England and responsible for financial supervision. Talk about poachers becoming gamekeepers!

Now there is much talk of ending the lavish salaries and bonuses of the financial fat cats. But don't hold your breath. In 2008, bonuses in the City of London will hit a record £16bn, more than triple that of 2001. At the same time, employers announced that they would try and defer pay rises for their workers to 'control costs'. In the US, Wall Street bonuses will reach $70bn this year even though stock prices of the banks have plummeted and the government is to plough $700bn into the banks to save them from their follies.

And remember just 1% of American households own 25% of all America's wealth in homes, stocks and businesses, while half of Americans have lost as much as $2trn in the last 15 months from the value of their pension funds invested in the stock market. Both Americans and Britons about to retire will take a huge cut in their retirement incomes. So much for control of the fat cats.

And when we move from the UK to the world, we can see who is going to pay for this slump. According to a UN report, upwards of 20m people globally are set to lose their jobs next year as a result of the coming recession, taking global unemployment to 210m in 2009, the first time it has topped 200m – unprecedented!

Nothing can stop the oncoming recession. The IMF now expects global growth next year to be just 3%, which means rising unemployment in the majority of so-called 'emerging economies' like China, India, Brazil, Argentine, Turkey and eastern Europe. In the advanced capitalist economies, British, American and European national output is already falling along with Japan. There is going to be 'negative growth' this year and next.

UNPRECEDENTED!

In the face of disaster, many capitalist apologists are ditching their cherished beliefs in free markets, deregulation and balanced budgets and turning back to the ideas of John Maynard Keynes, the British aristocrat and economist of the inter-war years. He argued that there was nothing wrong with the capitalist system of production. It was the financial sector that was the problem. It suffered periodic credit crunches and slipped into what he called a liquidity trap where banks would not lend to businesses or workers.

That sounds familiar. Keynes' solution, along with lower interest rates and government-backed liquidity was state spending and government projects to provide income and jobs. It seems that Chancellor Darling plans something similar; and all round the world governments are raising borrowing and running up deficits to 'unprecedented' levels.

But it won't work. At the heart of the crisis is the lack of profitability. Profits have been falling quarter by quarter and are set to fall further until enough fictitious and real capital is destroyed in value to create a bottom in profitability.

A slump is needed to cleanse the capitalism system of 'excess capital', expressed in 'overproduction'. There will be no bottom until mid-2009 at the earliest, probably later. Then there will be a gradual and weak recovery. But profits will not return to levels of 1997 or even 2006. We are still in the downphase of the profitability law of motion of capitalism. Eventually, another slump will occur, probably about 2014-15, which will be deep again.

The Great Recession

It is the working class of the world who will really suffer from the present crisis. Globally, the UN estimates that unemployment will reach 220m this year. Out of a global workforce of about 3 billion, that's "only" 7%. But this figure leaves out millions of hidden unemployed who just cannot even begin to look for work. And as a percentage of those working in sweat shop and factories around the globe, it is more like 20%.

As I write, the New York stock exchange index fell to its lowest level in six years as the big financial institutions and investors in company stocks slipped into the depth of despond about the state of the world capitalist economy.

And these investors have every reason to feel depressed. The world economy, by most estimates from the major international institutions, will contract this year for the first time since the 1940s. And by the world, they mean everywhere, not just in the advanced capitalist economies.

China is now slowing to an official real GDP growth rate of just 5% a year from 11% last year (and in reality is probably hardly growing if the measure of electricity consumption by businesses, factories and homes is anything to go by).

It's the same story across the rest of Asia. Japan has just announced that its economy shrank by the biggest amount in 27 years in the last quarter of 2008. Singapore and other south-east Asian economies are also diving, as their exports to Europe and the US screech to a halt.

The worst-hit are the former 'Communist' countries of Eastern Europe. Having thrown in their lot with capitalism after the collapse of the Soviet Union, the ruling elites of these countries must now explain to their people why their economies will contract by as much 10% in one year!

THE GREAT RECESSION

Even more disastrously, many of these countries (Hungary, Poland, Czech, Romania, Bulgaria and the tiny Baltic states) had promoted a huge property boom similar to that in the US, the UK and parts of Western Europe. People, thinking they were now to benefit from the fruits of capitalist progress, took out big loans, not in their own national currencies, but in cheaper foreign currencies like Swiss francs, euros and even Japanese yen.

That has now backfired badly. As their national currencies have plummeted in value, by over 30% in just the last few months, the cost of paying their monthly mortgages in euros etc has rocketed. So many people are losing their jobs and their homes at the same time.

Of course, the locus of this economic slump, the deepest since the 1930s, was in the biggest capitalist economy, the United States. This huge economy, producing around $14trn a year in output value, is now falling back at a rate of 5% a year. Unemployment is racing upwards, millions of home-owners face the threat of eviction, wages are being cut and the value of pension funds built up by millions of working people for their retirement have been cut by 40%.

In desperately trying to bail out the banks and financial institutions that triggered this crisis, the Obama administration is ploughing trillions of dollars of state funds and paying for it by increasing the public sector debt to 100% of annual output. The cost to the taxpayer is twice the size of the cost of the Vietnam war and approaching half the cost of World War 2! Down the road, working people will not only have to pay for this capitalist mess through job losses, wage cuts and home foreclosures, but also through sharply increased taxes to pay for helping the bankers.

It's the same story, only worse, in the UK. The property slump (with home prices heading for a cumulative 30% fall) has made a joke of the old Thatcher slogan of a 'property-owning democracy'. The stock market slump in the City of London has been just as big as in the US — again making a cruel laugh of the stock market boasts of the privatisation era of the 1990s. Remember, we were told by the sellers of state assets, that we could make profits by buying all those shares, and even more by getting shares for free if we agreed to allow building societies to become banks; banks to become real estate agents; and retailers to become mortgage lenders.

Now the value of the biggest building society in Britain, the Halifax, is zero, swallowed up in the semi-nationalisation of the banking system. British Telecom, once the state-owned telephone company, privatised in the 1980s and revamped in the 1990s, is now virtually bust in this crisis.

The UK economy is contracting by up to 4% a year and will have the worst economic performance in 2009 of all the top seven capitalist economies — so much for New Labour's (in particular, Gordon Brown's) boast that the 'boom and bust' British economy was over under their stewardship. New Labour has been even more naïve about the credit crunch and even more 'in denial' than the Conservative opposition.

Overnight, from being the standard bearer of the 'free market', offering minimal regulation of the City of London; favouring a reduction of taxes to big business; and a major supporter of privatisation, Gordon Brown has become a fervent supporter of Keynesian policies of public sector spending and borrowing; of the regulation of the banking sector; and wanting to 'control' the huge bonuses paid to the top executives in the City; and even applying virtual nationalisation of failing banks.

What hypocrisy! Gordon Brown used to argue that British capitalism, with the right policies adopted from America, could be made to expand 'endogenously' without slumps or 'cycles'. That was the theme of his main economic advisor, Ed Balls, now in the government. Now Mr Balls tells us we are in the worst economic slump for 100 years!

And what of the bankers who kicked this all off with their greed? The heads of the British banks recently went to parliament to explain how this had all happened. They started off by saying they were very, very sorry….but. But there was no way anybody could see this was going to happen. It was like a tsunami sweeping away all their clever plans and investments overnight. They told the politicians it was a chance in a million that nobody could have predicted, just as nobody thought there were black swans in the world until Captain Cook got to Australia in 1780.

The same excuse was echoed by Gordon Brown at the G7 finance ministers meeting before he had an audience with the pope (I hope they both prayed hard!): the crisis was like a hurricane that came from nowhere.

According the head of 'Financial Stability' at the Bank of England, the bankers did not see the credit crunch coming because their 'risk models' only went back ten years and did not take into account that capitalism has had slumps before that!

Indeed, the banks' risk models said that the chance of what has now happened was one in 13.5 billion years! As scientists currently reckon the universe is about that age, that means what has happened to the British and world economy in the last 18 months, according to the bankers, was impossible. So much for risk models and stable capitalism.

Of course, all these explanations are really pathetic excuses. There were a few voices even among capitalist strategists, apart from Marxists, who forecast the calamity that was coming from the massive expansion of 'fictititious' capital in form of cheap credit, rocketing property prices, ever-expanding stock market prices that were not matched by any equivalent expansion of real production values. But those voices were swamped by the screams of ecstasy from bankers with their big bonuses and from rich investors with their rising wealth in property and shares.

Now, whether it is the bankers, the investors, the regulators or the pro-capitalist politicians, they are all screaming murder, while at the same time, saying it had nothing to do with them and could not have been predicted or avoided.

And all the dirt and sleaze is now crawling out of the woodwork. The workings of capitalism are always full of theft, swindles and cheating. But they are often remain hidden when all seems well and everybody is making money. But now it is the opposite, some of the swindlers are being found out, like scum coming to surface of stagnant water.

Bernard Madoff is an eminent New York financier. He had investment funds that you had to be invited, as a rich person, to invest in! He had been head of the New York stock exchange's regulation committee. He supported with funds many politicians and arts centres. He is the very epitomy of capitalism — a crook. Every year he was able to provide his clients with regular 10%-plus gains on their investments, whatever the fluctuations of the stock market. How was this brilliant work possible? Well, we now know it was a swindle.

Madoff was using each new amount of money invested to pay back the existing investors when they wanted their money. Of course, many did not ask for it back and happily received their annual accounts showing their gains (these were completely phoney). Using new money to pay old is called a Ponzi scheme, after the man who first adopted this form of swindle.

Once the credit crunch began, more investors needed their money back and suddenly Madoff did not have enough new investment money to cover paybacks. Eventually, he owned up, claiming that he did it all on his own for over 30 years to the tune of losses worth up to $50bn — the biggest swindle in the history of the world!

Many so-called 'financial experts' had invested client money with Madoff because as experts they knew he was good. The British 'superwoman' financier, Nicola Horlick, had told her investors that Madoff represented exactly the sort of expertise that people like her provide and justified why he and she should be paid mega millions in fees and bonuses. Her advice has led to losses of $70m for her clients. This is yet another reason for never believing anything a capitalist expert tells you!

One fraud usually leads to another. The Madoff collapse has meant that other dodgy financiers who had invested with him were also exposed. 'Sir' Allen Stanford is a Texan billionaire who has a set of banks across the Americas and is the biggest employer in parts of the Caribbean, where he has become a major sponsor of cricket, the sport of the British Empire.

Cricket organisers in the UK and the West Indies have fawned over him for his money; while poor Antiguans depend on him for jobs and their savings. Now Stanford has been cited by the US Securities and Exchange Commission for a similar Ponzi-type fraud worth up to $8bn. Investors and savers around the Caribbean look like losing all their money too.

As capitalism descends deeper into slump, it is not just all the 'fictititious' capital that is being destroyed. Capitalism can only reach a bottom if it also destroys the value of real capital too. In order to restore profitability for capitalist industry, workers must be sacked and wages cut to lower the cost of what Marx called 'variable capital' and the factories must be closed and businesses put into bankruptcy in order to reduce the cost of what Marx called 'constant capital'.

Once production costs are cut back significantly, then profitability will stop falling. After all, there will still be businesses left, there will be still workers in jobs and there will still people with homes — just a lot less of them. Then the world capitalist economy will start a slow and painful process of recovery.

When will that be? How long is a piece of string? Most capitalist slumps last about 18 months or so. This one began somewhere in the first half of 2008. So it will likely not reach a bottom before the end of this year. But this crisis is way worse than any capitalist slump that we have seen since the 1930s — and it could be worse than that. So it could well last into 2010.

That would especially be the case if each national capitalist economy starts to turn on the others to protect itself. 'Globalisation' was the theme of the 1990s, where national capitalist states combined to reduce trade barriers and allow the 'free' movement of finance. Now the trend is towards the protection of national interests. Barack Obama talks of a 'Buy America' campaign and Gordon Brown bellows for 'British jobs for British workers' in a feeble attempt to curry votes. What Brown is really offering is 'British dole for British workers'.

The Great Recession

— after

"To kill an error is as good as a service as, and sometimes even better than, the establishing of a new truth or fact."
Charles Darwin

"There is nothing new except what is forgotten"
Rose Bertin

Human nature and capitalist crisis

Alan Greenspan has just turned 83 years old. He was Chairman of the US Federal Reserve Bank for over 19 years before he stepped down in January 2006, just as the great boom turned into the awful credit crunch and brought global capitalism to its knees.

Greenspan presided over the biggest credit boom in capitalist history and the largest rise in property prices that the US had ever seen. He was praised to the heights during those years and as the helmsman of capitalist success globally and in America. Bob Woodward, one of the journalists who exposed the Nixon Watergate scandal back in the 1970s, wrote a book about Greenspan in the year 2000, in which he described him as 'the maestro'[1].

Back then, Greenspan claimed the hi-tech and internet revolution of the 1990s set the scene for an uninterrupted period of economic growth for capitalism based on increased productivity from new technology. But then came the so-called *dot.com* bust, when thousands of tech companies went bust and stock markets collapsed (they have not returned to the levels of 2000 even now).

Then Greenspan described the booming property market of the early 2000s as an exciting way to expand the economy and the new forms of credit like derivatives that it engendered as wonderful innovative instruments to reduce risk and boost growth. Then came the property bust of 2007 onwards and the biggest credit crunch in human history. It's not a great track record.

Over the Easter weekend, Greenspan was interviewed on the US cable TV business channel, CNBC, about why the great boom turned into the biggest economic slump for capitalism since the Great Depression of the 1930s. He said it was not because he and other bankers who ran the citadels of finance capital were stupid.

HUMAN NATURE AND CAPITALIST CRISIS

That conclusion was in sharp contrast to the answers that the top bankers in Britain gave to the House of Commons Select Committee. When they were asked what went wrong, they said it was a financial *tsunami* that came from nowhere, that nobody could have predicted, a one in a billion chance — not their fault.

Greenspan differed. It was not because the bankers were stupid; "they knew what was going on; it's just that they thought they could get out before everything came to an end". As Chuck Prince, the head of the now bankrupt US investment bank Bear Stearns said at the time: "we know the party will come to an end, but while it lasts, we have to keep on dancing".

Greenspan argued that what brought everything down was sheer greed. The bankers knew they were being reckless; they knew that what goes up must eventually come down. But they just went on because they had to make more and more money for their shareholders and for their bonus payments. Greed was the driver. But Greenspan said greed is "human nature", so this boom and bust will happen again some time in the future.

There we have it. For Greenspan and the ideologists of capitalism, it is 'human nature' that caused the crash and the slump, not the particular form of social and economic organisation that he operated under and supported. But human beings can be 'greedy and selfish' and they can be 'cooperative and selfless'. It depends on the circumstances.

Capitalism is a system of production of goods and services for profit; it is built on competition, on the drive to make more money (not things or services people need). It is a system designed to promote greed and selfishness. The 'human nature' that Greenspan blames for the economic crisis is nothing more than the capitalist system at work.

The booms and slumps of the global economy began with capitalism. In a recent study by Carmen Reinhart and Kenneth Rogoff of the US National Bureau of Economic Research (NBER) on banking crises[2], they found that from the very early beginnings of capitalism in the 14th century up to the present day, there have been booms and slumps brought on by the operation of a system of production based on profit, competition and private appropriation of value.

Reinhart and Rogoff concluded that, as capitalism spread its tentacles across the world from the 18th century onwards, so the frequency and scope of economic crises grew. Sure, there had been crises of production before capitalism, based on famine as harvests failed or due to conquests from foreign invasions. But economic crises due to the failure of money, credit and banks are uniquely capitalist.

According to the NBER, there have been 64 'official' slumps in capitalist production since 1854 — 'human nature' is powerful, it seems. What a waste of output, economic resources and above all, what damage to people's lives in the loss of jobs, homes, well-being and even early deaths that slump and economic depression brings.

Most important, Reinhart and Rogoff concluded that as capitalism was increasingly free from government regulation and control and became more 'globalised', so crises grew in number and impact. Indeed, this latest period of globalisation since the 1980s was not one of success in reducing booms and slumps, as the likes of Mr Greenspan and other capitalist economists have argued, but quite the reverse. The last 25 years have seen more financial crises than ever: in emerging economies (1980s and 1990s), Asia (1997-99), Japan (1990s), US loan companies (1990s); Nordic banks (1990s) and so on.

Alongside the waste of resources from capitalist slumps comes inequality and injustice. Branco Milanovic of the World Bank has analysed the level of inequality of income and wealth in the world of capitalism. In 2002, he found that if he divided the world's population into three groups: those with incomes greater than the average income of Italians could be regarded as rich; those with incomes less than the poverty levels of the advanced capitalist economies could be considered poor; and those in between could be categorised as middle-class. Milanovic found that 78% of the world's 6bn population were poor and 11% were rich, with another 11% being middle-class.

In 2007, Milanovic redid his sums and he found that he had underestimated the inequalities[3]. It really was a 20:80 split between rich and poor. Indeed, the top 10% of the world's population had 39 times more income than the bottom 10% — and it was getting worse.

But nothing beats this current financial crisis, except perhaps the Great Depression of the 1930s. This credit crisis has triggered off a major slump in capitalist production. There is a crisis of over-accumulation of capital relative to profit: the mass of profit in the US, Europe and Japan fell by the biggest margin ever in the last quarter of 2008. That has led to an 'overproduction' of goods and services globally on a scale not seen for over 60 years.

All the capitalist economists are agreed that the advanced capitalist economies are in slump, with annual output after inflation falling by up to 5-6% across the board in 2009. In the less advanced, so-called 'emerging economies', the situation is even worse, with falls in production in newly converted to capitalism Eastern Europe likely to be over 10%, in Singapore and other Asian exporting countries even more.

The question now is how much longer the slump will last. The Great Depression was called that because the slump did not end after a year or so. It started in summer 1929 and continued through to March 1933 (43 months). Then there was a recovery for a while, lasting until May 1937, before the slump resumed. Only preparations for the terrible world war of 1939-46 and the temporary ending of much of the capitalist system of production cut across the slump.

Since 1945, the average capitalist slump has lasted ten months, a much shorter period than before. The NBER says that this slump began at the end of 2007. So already this crisis has lasted 16 months and will continue for at least double the previous post-war average. But will it be longer than that even?

Most capitalist economists say no. They reckon that the huge bailouts of the banks and other financial institutions with taxpayer's money, plus the massive expansion of government spending and tax cuts to 'boost' demand in the economy will turn things around.

But this will not provide a turnaround in profitability. Banks and businesses may get government funding, but you can lead a horse to water, you cannot make it drink. Not until profitability improves will investment start again; job losses stop rising; and house prices bottom. And for that to happen, capitalism needs to destroy more of the weak.

There is an air of optimism in the ranks of capitalist investors on the stock exchange. After a reaching yet another new low in stock prices in March, the stock indexes have risen nearly 30% since as governments pump in public money and banks claim they are starting to make profits again; there is even talk of a 'bottoming' of the housing market in America and Britain; while China is supposedly about to renew its strong growth after a pause.

But this is more wishful thinking than judgement. I suspect that there are more shocks to come before we reach the bottom of this nightmare slump. The banks may be 'saved', but many businesses are set to go belly up this year and the jobless rate is nowhere near its peak yet. House prices still have further to fall and capitalist profits too.

And there is the payback afterwards. That's likely to be so large as to keep capitalism comatose like a zombie for years ahead. The bailouts, of course, are socialism for the rich, while working people get capitalism in the shape of job losses, wage cuts, repossession of their homes and soon reductions in public services and higher taxes.

HUMAN NATURE AND CAPITALIST CRISIS

Gordon Brown, Barack Obama, and most of the political leaders of capitalism tell us that they are putting in such huge amounts of money to stabilise the capitalist system. For the moment, governments are increasing their debt and borrowing to take on the rotten debt of the bankers. They are paying for this borrowing by printing money (sucking funds out of thin air).

But there is no free lunch (except for bankers). Eventually, all this public sector debt (likely to hit 100% of annual output in the UK, the US and others) will have to be paid back or serviced with interest in perpetuity. That means higher taxes and reduced public services. It means pensions and benefits for the old, the sick, the carers and the unemployed must be massacred. Capitalism cannot be revived without the help of the state and that means us.

1. Bob Woodward, Maestro, How Alan Greenspan conducted the economy, *2000*
2. C Reinhart and K Rogoff, This time is different, *2009*
3. B. Milanovic, Worlds Apart, *2007.*

Cycles and crisis

The Kondratiev prices cycle is about 64 years long and the Marxist profitability cycle is about 32 years long — trough to trough. So for example, the Kondratiev prices cycle peaked in 1920 and also in 1982 and troughed in 1884 and 1946. The Marxist profit cycle, being smaller in duration, peaked in 1964 and 1997 and troughed in 1946 (matching Kondratiev) and 1982 (when Kondratiev peaked).

By feeding in the profit cycle, you can break up the Kondratiev cycle into 'seasons': spring, summer, autumn, winter[1]. Thus, in a Kondratieff spring, prices are rising and so is profitability; conversely in a Kondariev winter; prices are falling and so is profitability (that's the stage we are in now).

If we link the environment of capitalist boom and slump and class struggle to these seasons, we come up with an interesting set of predictions. It seems that in Kondratiev springs, capitalism booms and the working class grows in strength, but without taking on the capitalist class in major struggle. That makes sense as profitability is only rising after a major period of depression or war that workers must still recover from.

In Kondratiev summers, profitability falls, capitalism goes into crisis and a stronger working class engages in heightened struggle. In Kondratiev autumns, profitability rises after a series of recessions and defeats that have weakened workers, allowing a capitalist boom and a more passive working class. In Kondratiev winters, profitability falls again and capitalism enters a period of depression and sometimes wars, with workers trying to defend their positions, but on the back foot. Then the cycle starts again as we enter a Kondratiev spring.

If this is right, then we are now in a Kondratiev winter with prices falling (disinflation turning to deflation) and profitability falling through a series of recessions/slumps to around 2014.

CYCLES AND CRISIS

Here is the bad news: the current phase is not necessarily an environment for major class struggle; instead it is one for workers to be on the defensive, facing reactionary warlike movements. From 2014, we would enter a Kondratiev spring where capitalism would boom on the back of capital destruction from previous recessions (and maybe war) and workers would gradually renew their strength.

From 2030, we would enter a new Kondratiev summer, when profitability would fall, capitalism would be in crisis again and class struggle would reach a peak. This would last until 2046. This is really what we call the long view!

1. See Michael Alexander, The Kondratiev cycle, *2002*

Marxist theories of crisis

Marx never fully developed a theory of economic crisis in one place in his writings. There are many thoughts and ideas spread through all his works. And his conception of capitalist crisis was fledged out over the years.

As a result, Marx's writings are sometimes ambiguous and open to significantly different interpretations. Many of his followers in the socialist movements immediately after his death in 1883 never read all the three volumes of *Capital*, with the latter two only put together from Marx's notes by Engels and later Kautsky. And most were unaware of the other notebooks that contained an analysis of capitalist crisis, like *Grundrisse* or the volumes of the *Theories of Surplus Value*.

As a result, this led to a distorted and unclear view of Marx's theory of crisis. The mainstream Marxist explanation that was taken up by the leadership of Marxist movements swung between two schools.

The first was that capitalist crisis was a crisis of overproduction. Capitalism was bound to go into crisis because capitalists accumulated and produced blindly without taking into account the demand for their production. They squeezed the workers' wages and employment and as a result could not sell all their goods to the workers. This problem of endemic overproduction was compounded by the existence of money capital. Money could be 'hoarded' or saved and not spent. Thus not every seller would have a buyer, opening up the possibility of a crisis of overproduction.

This overproduction or underconsumption view of Marx's theory of crisis has some validity. After all, Marx did say that '*The last cause of all real crises always remains the poverty and restricted consumption of the masses as compared to the tendency of capitalist production to develop the productive forces in such a way, that only the absolute power of consumption of the entire society would be their limit*'. [1]

MARXIST THEORIES OF CRISIS

But perhaps the phrase "the last cause" gives the game away. Marx is saying that once the crisis is under way it is the insufficient funds of the workers that makes it impossible for capitalism to avoid a slump. But the last cause is not the first. Moreover, to accept overproduction or underconsumption as the cause of crisis would be suggest that capitalism is not just prone to crisis but that it is impossible – because the working class can never buy all the goods that they have produced. That is because the value of those goods must by definition be greater than the value paid to the workers as variable capital.

Overproduction is what the slump is by description, but not the cause. As Marx made clear in another passage. *"It is a pure tautology to say that crises are provoked by a lack of effective demand or effective consumption ... The fact that commodities are unsaleable means no more than that no effective buyers have been found for them ... If the attempt is made to give this tautology the semblance of greater profundity, by the statement that the working class receives too small a portion of its own product, and that the evil would be remedied if it received a bigger share, i.e. if its wages rose, we need only note that crises are always prepared by a period in which wages generally rise, and the working class actually does receive a greater share in the part of the annual product destined for consumption. From the standpoint of these advocates of sound and 'simple' (!) common sense, such periods should rather avert the crisis. It thus appears that capitalist production involves certain conditions independent of people's good or bad intentions, which permit the relative prosperity of the working class only temporarily, and moreover always as a harbinger of crisis.'* .[2]

Engels also criticised this view of capitalist crisis. *"the underconsumption of the masses, the restriction of the consumption of the masses to what is necessary for their maintenance and reproduction, is not a new phenomenon. It has existed as long as there have been exploiting and exploited classes. The underconsumption of the masses is a necessary condition of all forms of society based on exploitation, consequently also of the capitalist form; but it is the capitalist form of production which first gives rise to crises. The underconsumption of the masses is therefore a prerequisite condition for crises, and plays in them a role which has long been recognised. But it tells us just as little why crises exist today as why they did not exist before'*.[3]

The other school of Marxist thought on capitalist crisis is that crises come about because of the anarchic and unplanned nature of capitalist production[4]. That leads to disproportionalities in various sectors of the economy, which eventually dislocate it. Under this theory, overproduction is not the cause. Capitalists compete viciously with each other for market share and in so doing produce blindly without care for the market.

The disproportion theorists have one thing in common with the underconsumptionists. They both ignore or dismiss what Marx called the most important law of motion of capitalism, the tendency of the rate of profit to fall. Apparently, all the writings that Marx makes about profitability plays no role in the boom and slumps of capitalist production.

But not only is it empirically wrong to deny the role of profitability in causing capitalist crisis, it is also not a true interpretation of Marx's own view. Profitability has a big advantage over the other interpretations of the Marx's theory of crisis. It is measurable and thus provides a scientific method of prediction. If profitability is measured as falling over a long period, that will be a very good indicator of an oncoming slump. Overproduction can only be measured when the crisis is upon us — because it is a description of the crisis not a cause. Similarly, disproportion is very difficult if not impossible to measure and thus does not provide much predictive power. Falling profitability does not cause crisis as such: it creates the conditions for the mass of profit to fall (or grow so slowly that capitalist consumption is affected) and this is what kicks off crisis[5].

The profit cycle is a relatively long term (16-18 year phases up or down) process. We are now in a down phase for profitability and even though the rate of profit rose from 2002 to 2005, this is still in a period where

Marx's law of the tendency of the rate of profit for fall is operating in a down phase and thus creating the conditions for more and deeper crises as in the period of 1965-82 (that downphase had the most and worst post-war slumps — until now).

The rate of profit rose from 2001 to 2005. So does that mean the Great Recession was not caused by declining profitability? The answer is that by 2005, the value rate of profit began to fall again. It had never surpassed the level reached in 1997. That is why the huge expansion of fictitious capital from 2001 with new forms of credit collapsed into the biggest crisis since the 1930s.

The way to think of it is the opposite of the underconsumptionists: the overaccumulation of capital relative to profitability leads to overproduction relative to effective demand — not the other way round. As Marx put it: *"Overproduction of capital, not of individual commodities (although over-production of capital always includes over-production of commodities) is therefore simply over-accumulation of capital...The purpose of capitalist production, however, is self-expansion of capital, i.e., appropriation of surplus-labour, production of surplus-value, of profit."* [6]

1. *Karl Marx,* Capital *Vol III, Chapter 30.*
2. *Karl Marx* Capital *Vol II,Chapter 20.*
3. *Friedrich Engels,Preface to first edition of* Capital *Vol II.*
4. *Leading Bolsheviks like Lenin and Bukharin saw capitalist crises as a product of disproportion and anarchy in production. See Bukharin,* Imperialism and the world economy. *Also see Simon Clarke,* Marx's theory of crisis, *1994. Clarke argues that Marx also held this view — I don't agree.*
5. *See Chapter 24.*
6. *Karl Marx,* Theories of Surplus Value, *Chapter XVII*

The Great Recession — is it over?

For the capitalists, this Great Recession is more or less over. The pace of decline in the major capitalist economies slowed in the second quarter of this year. Indeed, in some major economies like Germany and France, national output rose. And in some smaller ones like Australia and Norway, there was a small pick up in growth.

At the same time, the larger, less mature capitalist economies like India and Indonesia continued to grow, while China also maintained positive growth. Indeed, in Asia's less developed capitalist economies, which contribute about 10-15% of global output, industrial production is up sharply.

On many measures of capitalist economic activity, the worst appears to be over — at least for now. Measures of business confidence have turned up — they may not indicate much growth but they do indicate a bottom.

The stock markets of the major economies have experienced a massive rally in prices. From lows in March, there has been a 50% rise in stock prices across the board, led by the financial sector and bank shares. Share price indexes are still well below the peak at the start of the Great Recession in October 2007, but at least they are going in the right direction for capitalist investors.

The epicentre of the crisis that triggered it all was the housing market, particularly in the US, but also in Europe and other capitalist economies. Prices of the average home in the US have plummeted by 30% from their peak, and similar falls have been experienced in the UK. Sales transactions and mortgage applications have fallen over 75%. But in the last few months, there has been a stabilisation of sales and even a small increase in prices in certain countries. The bottom of the housing bust is nearly there, even though prices could fall further yet as unemployment rises and more people default on their mortgages.

GREAT RECESSION — IS IT OVER?

The OECD and other economic forecasters have now upgraded their estimates of growth in national output for the major economies. They now expect GDP to rise in the US and Europe in this third quarter of 2009, with the UK lagging behind and not recovering until Christmas. But recovery is now underway.

The OECD now forecasts that the Great Recession that officially started in 2008 will have fallen 3.7% in the top seven capitalist economies this year. That follows a 4% plus decline in 2008. So this recession will mean that the top seven economies will have lost 10% of their national output in less than 18 months. But it is even worse than that if you take into account the loss of potential output that should have been achieved by these capitalist economies of say 3% a year. In effect, 15% of output has been lost forever.

Also staggeringly, we have seen a fall in world trade of about 15% in real terms since the start of the Great Recession — the whole capitalist world has been involved and there has been no escape for even the less developed capitalist economies of Asia, Latin America and Eastern Europe (and of course Africa).

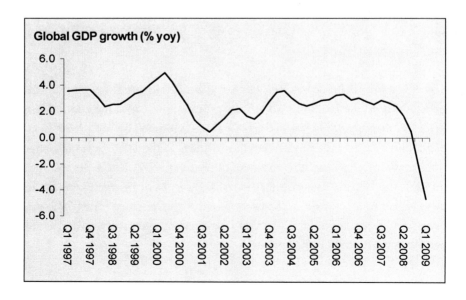

Indeed, the former planned economies under the Russian axis that became capitalist economies in the 1990s after suffering a massive decline in living standards have now suffered the most acute depression in their living memory with falls in national output of 10-25% in one year! So much for the freedom of the market!

It was the same story for profits. As a percentage of national output, US pretax profits had reached 21% in 2006 and then began to slip. During the recession of the last 18 months, profits fell to just 14% of GDP. But in the last two quarters, US profits have risen back to 16% of GDP.

As for the global financial system, the IMF now puts the total loss from the credit crunch at $3.4trn, or 6-7% of world GDP, lost forever. By region, the IMF reckons that half of the forecast losses for the banks of $2.8trn will be incurred by European banks (including the UK) while the US banks will suffer about $1trn in losses[1].

According to the latest data, global losses for all sectors of the financial sector have now reached $1.6trn and for the banks alone at $1.1trn[2] — way larger than the great and good said would happen. Back in November 2007, Bernanke said that the losses would be a maximum of $150bn!

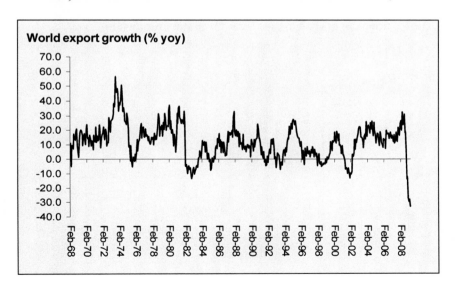

World export growth (% yoy)

GREAT RECESSION — IS IT OVER?

And both the IMF and the OECD have had to raise their loss forecasts at regular intervals.

Regionally, the admitted losses so far have fallen on the US overall at $1.1trn, Europe at $500bn and Asia at just $40bn. With the banks, it has been $660bn for the US banks, $470bn for Europe and just $40bn for Asia. So the US banks have suffered about 65% of their ultimate losses, while the European banks have admitted about only 40% of theirs. The ECB says Eurozone banks face another $300bn in further losses.

The key question now is whether the banks and other financial institutions (insurance, pension funds and hedge funds) have raised enough capital to cover future losses (assuming that these institutions can also make profits from hereon to help restock capital reserves).

The latest data show that globally financial institutions have raised $1.3trn in new capital (sourced both from state funds and private investors) compared to estimated losses of $1.6trn. US institutions have raised $750bn compared to losses of $1.1trn so far and European institutions have raised $460bn to nearly match losses of $500bn. For banks alone, $1.1trn in new

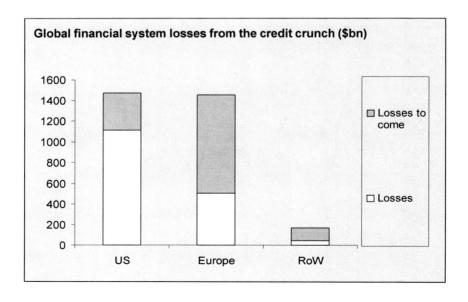

Global financial system losses from the credit crunch ($bn)

capital has been raised to cover losses of $1.2trn, with the US banks raising $500bn to cover $600bn in losses and European banks $450bn to cover $460bn in losses.

This suggests that, unless governments are prepared to come in with another bailout, banks globally will be unable to expand credit for some time ahead as they try to raise reserves and capital to meet capital adequacy levels. This is the real hit to future economic growth globally. The banks will not help economic growth for the next two years at least unless they can raise more capital.

Governments won't be abel to help much more because in developed countries they have already put up $11trn of taxpayer funds, or one-fifth of global output, to support the financial sector. This includes buying up toxic assets, recapitalising banks, providing liquidity support, deposit insurance and loan guarantees — the biggest input of taxpayer's money since the second world war.

The Great Recession has been hugely damaging to capitalism. Nevertheless, economic recovery is now ahead — there is light at the end of the tunnel for capitalism.

But for the working class, the Great Recession has a long way to go yet. Unemployment is rising sharply. In the US, it has hit 9.7%, the highest level for 26 years and is expected to rise above 10% by the end of the year. If you include all the people receiving some form of benefit, there are 15m Americans now looking for work. If you add in all those who have given up looking for work, the rate reaches 16%. The US economy has lost an unbelievable 3.47m goods-producing jobs since the recession began in December 2007.

About 4.3% of U.S. homes, or one in 25 properties, were in foreclosure in the second quarter, the Washington-based Mortgage Bankers Association said last month. That's the most in three decades of data, and loans overdue by at least 90 days, the point at which foreclosure proceedings typically begin, rose to 7.9%, the highest on record.

America's working class have taken a huge hit. There was an average $2000 decline after inflation in real household income in 2008, the largest annual drop in 40 years! Real incomes for average Americans are now back where they were 12 years ago. And such is the inequality of income and wealth in the US, for the bottom 20% of households, the fall has been even worse. In contrast, just 25 years ago, the top 20% of American households has 45% of all income; by 2008, that share had reached more than 50%.

Because of the loss of jobs and incomes, the number of Americans without any health insurance has risen even more during the Great Recession to reach 46m, or 15% of the population.

The burden of meeting debt repayments remains at record levels of around 18-19% of average income, even though interest rates have fallen and many of those in still in work are trying to pay down their debts. According to a recent survey by ACNielsen, Americans are "among the most cash-strapped people in the world", with 22% having no money left after having paid for essential living expenses. Out of 42 top capitalist nations, Americans saved the least.

The big disaster has been the loss of wealth tied in the value of the homes that Americans have bought and in the value of the shares they own through their retirement accounts. Since the start of the Great Recession, household wealth has plummeted by 20% with $14trn being lost in value; $5trn from the value of homes; $6trn in the stock market and another $3trn from other investments.

It is the same story in the UK, where the HBOS bank estimates that an average of £31,000 per household has been lost in wealth because of the Great Recession: £422bn from falling house prices and £393bn from lower share prices. This is the first fall since 2001. British workers have tried to reduce their debts accordingly and been forced to default on their mortgages. Even so, net wealth (after reduced debt) fell 10% in 2008.

So what sort of recovery can we expect now that the Great Recession has bottomed? The optimists of capitalism hope that it will be V-shaped. That means they expect that the sharp fall in global output and profits will be mirrored in reverse by a sharp recovery so that, by this time next year, the major capitalist economies will be growing at 3% or more in real terms. The losses suffered during the Great Recession will be quickly recovered and it will be business as usual for capitalism.

This is the 'natural' sort of recovery under capitalism and was experienced, for example, after the big slump of 1974-5, after which followed five years of strong economic growth before capitalism dropped into an even deeper slump in 1980. It was also the experience after the shallow recession of 2001, which was followed by the strong boom of 2002-07. But it may not happen this time.

In the natural recovery, the recession reduces the cost of production and devalues capital sufficiently to drive up profitability for those capitalist enterprises still standing. Unemployment drives down labour costs and bankruptcies and takeovers reduce capital costs. Businesses then gradually start to increase production again, and eventually begin to invest in new capital and rehire those in the 'reserve army of labour' without a job. This boosts demand for investment goods and eventually workers start buying more consumer goods and recovery get under way.

But such is the overhang of spare capacity in industry and construction this time and such is level still of debt owed by businesses, government and households alike that this recovery may be stunted. After all, every major capitalist economy now finds that it has more than 30% more capacity than it needs to meet demand. That is a record high of overcapacity in industry. Production is going to have to rise some way before new investment will be considered.

It could take the form of a U-shape: what is called a 'jobless recovery' as we saw after the recession of 1991-2. In the early 1990s, businesses renewed investment slowly and held back from rehiring workers for several years. So economic growth was slow in resuming.

It could even become W-shaped. There would be a double-dip. The weight of overcapacity and debt would be too much to allow the revival of consumer spending and investment, so the economic recovery would be short-lived and the major capitalist economies would slip back in recession. That is what happened in 1980-82. It took two recessions then to get things going again.

Even worse, the recovery could take an L-shape. As in Japan after the collapse of the great credit bubble there in 1989, the economy remained in the doldrums for a whole decade. Huge debt has piled up in the banks and rather than write these off and cause major bankruptcies and a banking crisis, the Japanese government used taxpayer's money to bail the banks

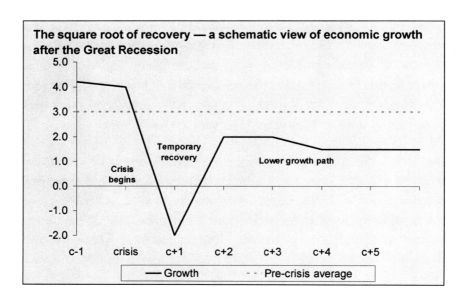

The square root of recovery — a schematic view of economic growth after the Great Recession

out with loans and guarantees. The banks in turn sat on their debts, but did not lend money for new investment. This sounds similar to current environment.

But probably, the recovery will be more like a square root sign. The big fall in output is over. Now there will be an upturn. But it will fall short of restoring the rate of economic growth achieved before the Great Recession. Instead of 3-4% a year, output in the major economies will be closer to 1-2% a year. That will not be good enough to restore profitability to previous levels. The capitalist system will thus face the risk of a new slump further down the road.

1. *IMF* Global Financial Stability *report, October 2009.*
2. *IMF op cit.*

The bankruptcy of economics

The Great Recession of 2008-9 may now be over and recovery is under way. But capitalism has not escaped. As night follows day, there will be another slump. And just as the first simultaneous global recession after the second world war in 1974-75 was followed by recovery, it was only five years before the capitalist world suffered an even deeper and long-lasting slump in 1980-2.

Of course, the great thinkers of capitalist economics have no idea what is going to happen. They were clueless in expecting or foreseeing the Great Recession; they have been unable to explain the causes of the slump; and they will be equally unable to forecast what will happen now.

As for an explanation of the causes; again there is confusion. It was due to lax monetary policy (cheap interest rates and lavish liquidity) promoted by central bankers; it was due to exotic and risky investments that were not controlled by the official regulators properly; it was due to bankers being paid ridiculous amounts of bonuses that encouraged them to take too many risk; it was due to people's greed (as homeowners took on too much debt that they could not afford and lenders encouraged and allowed them too to make profits).

All these causes are true, but they are also not the whole or even the main truth. Former US Fed Chairman Greenspan, when interviewed for BBC Two's *The Love of Money* series, explained the current economic crisis was a "once in a century type of event", and one that he did not expect to witness. But he had.

He now realised, that although capitalism was a great system, it could be damaged by human beings! *"It's human nature, unless somebody can find a way to change human nature, we will have more crises and none of them will look like this because no two crises have anything in common, except human nature."*

THE BANKRUPTCY OF ECONOMICS

Greenspan is a follower of the weird and reactionary American philosopher and novelist Ayn Rand[1] who propounded the view that the capitalist economic system was perfect if was not for human behaviour, which was crass and venal. So presumably what Greenspan means by his remark is that human behaviour causes crises — namely, that people are driven by greed and fear. They get too greedy and take excessive risks, bringing everything down and they get frightened and stop spending and investing to excessive levels in a climate of fear. There is nothing wrong with capitalism except people. Such is the level of understanding about the cause of the Great Recession from the 'great and good' sitting at the commanding heights of capitalist power.

Now that the worst seems to be over for the capitalist system, there is a bit of soul-searching going on among capitalist economists and strategists. How did they fail to forecast this disaster that nearly brought them down?

There is a crisis in capitalist economic theory. Whether a capitalist economist is a 'free marketer', a 'monetarist', a 'neoclassical' supporter, a 'Keynesian', or even a follower of the so-called 'Austrian school', hardly anyone predicted the Great Recession. That is because all these schools of economics do not think there is anything flawed in the capitalist mode of production.

The classical economists of the early 19th century were much more objective. Adam Smith, David Ricardo and Thomas Malthus were among the first economists and they quickly identified that capitalism was a troubled system for organising the production of things that human beings used. They had different explanations: but they recognised that capitalism could have crises of its own making.

Subsequent schools of economics afterwards were apologists. They denied that there was an inherent problem in the capitalist mode of production and its relations between the owners of the means of production (money, plant, machinery and raw materials) and the producers of new value in production (labour).

THE BANKRUPTCY OF ECONOMICS

The neoclassical school (after the classical) is the largest in capitalist economics. For this mainstream school, the capitalist system of production works perfectly to use up all resources efficiently and get prices for goods and labour just right. Thus capitalism can move forward in perfect equilibrium and without crises as long as the capitalist market of 'perfect competition' is not distorted in any way by outside agencies, namely governments with regulations and taxes; or trade union ruining the perfect market for labour; or monopolies distorting perfect competition in production and investment.

Over the 25 years from 1982 to the Great Recession, the government's role in capitalism was reduced, the trade unions were weakened and monopolies were reduced. This explains the great boom in profits and economic growth, say the neoclassical school. Crises were being eliminated and anyway would be less damaging. Booms and slumps were over. The Great Recession could not happen.

The extreme variant of the neoclassical school were the free marketers who believed in what they called 'efficient markets'. Capitalism worked best when there was a perfect market where every participant has the fullest amount of information about prices and demand and supply immediately to hand. Such a market would perfect and completely efficient in managing resources.

The best example of such a market was the market for stock and shares. The stock exchanges of the world were thus the best indicators of the health of capitalism. If stock market prices rose, capitalism did too. What could be a greater irony! The most volatile and unpredictable market in capitalism was now the standard bearer of successful, crisis-free capitalism — the stock market.

Not all agree with this Panglossian view of capitalism. A variant of the neoclassical school were a group of Austrian economists from the 1930s like Kurt Wicksell and Fred Hayek (much adored by the Thatcherite wing of the British Tories in the 1970s). The Austrian school accepted that capitalism could grow in equilibrium without slump. But crises were not because of 'imperfect' competition, but because of a problem in the monetary part of the capitalist system. There was a tendency to excessive credit that generated 'bubbles' in the capitalist economy that would eventually burst, leading to a crisis of production caused by a contraction of credit. Excessive credit was the product of governments and central banks being in control of money. Reduce the power of government and abolish central banks and let the market decide is the answer of the Austrian school.

Some in the Austrian school forecast the credit crunch that preceded the Great Recession, but they have forecast disaster every year in the same way that weather forecasters say there will be a hurricane in the Gulf of Mexico. It's going to happen but when and how damaging, the Austrian school could not say.

The other great school of capitalist economics that opposes the mainstream neoclassical school are the Keynesians. The Keynesians saw a problem in the circulation of money like the Austrians, but the problem was not too much credit, but too little! Again, there was nothing wrong with the capitalist mode of production for profit. The problem and cause of crisis was that the financial sector held the money. They would squeeze the profits of the industrial sector. Interest rates would rise too high. Once industrial capitalists were starved of cheap funds to invest, they would stop production and investment and the slump would begin.

The slump would not correct itself automatically, as the neoclassical school believed, without the state intervening to provide cheap credit or even to invest and spend directly using taxpayer's money. Contrary to the Austrians, the last thing you should do is cut credit even further and wait for the financial sector to recover.

But again, the Keynesians were absent from any forecast of the Great Recession. They saw no crisis coming — on the contrary, credit was accelerating, consumers were borrowing and spending up to 2007. Indeed all was well. Now the Great Recession has come, they call for more credit and more government spending like repetitious parrots.

Back in the 1980s, an American financial consultant and economist, Hyman Minsky[2] became convinced that capitalism did have a problem. Again Minsky did not see any problem with the production process of investing for a profit. Again what worried him was the monetary system. Minsky took Marx's idea of the possibility of crisis inherent in the circulation of money and argued financial markets were inherently unstable (the opposite of the efficient market proponents).

Because participants in the stock market and other financial markets did not have all the information they needed, they were unpredictable about their investment decisions. They may not invest; instead they may hoard money for a while. That unpredictability could lead to crisis in the circulation of credit; what came to be called a 'Minsky moment'. Thus the cause of the capitalist crisis was a virus that started in the financial sector and spread to the production sector of capitalism.

Minsky moments had long been denied by the mainstream of capitalist economics. Now they have made a comeback as an explanation for the Great Recession, an explanation adopted even by some Marxists[3]. And yet, insightful as Minksy's idea is, it is no more than Marx had explained more than 100 years earlier. And most important, it did not really forecast when such crises of instability would erupt. They may and they may not.

1. Ayn Rand was Russian/American novelist who developed a philosophical system she called objectivism, claiming that the reality of human competitive behaviour could not be denied and, on that basis, the laisser-faire capitalist economy and egoism should be accepted.
2. Hyman Minsky was an American economist of the post-Keynesian tradition, arguing that financial bubbles and instability is endogenous to capitalism.

3. Fred Moseley, Marx, Minsky and Crotty on crises in capitalism, *October 2007*

Will there be another slump?

The leading theorists of capitalism were unable to warn the commanders of the capitalist system of the disaster ahead. The leading spokesmen of capitalism, the central bank leaders like Ben Bernanke or Alan Greenspan before him at the US Fed, or Mervyn King at the Bank of England, saw no dangers in the huge rise in housing prices, the massive expansion of credit and development of all kinds of new and exotic financial instruments that the big bankers of the world were dabbling in.

For example, Bernanke propounded in March 2005 that *"increases in home values, together with rising stock market value have aided household wealth, through cashout refinancing and lines of credit. Higher home prices in turn have encouraged households to increase their consumption — all these are good things"*.

When the housing boom burst in 2007, Bernanke was quick to deny any fallout for capitalism. *"We have not seen any major spillovers onto other sectors of the economy"*, he claimed in June 2007. By November, when the losses for the banking system began to accrue, Bernanke told the US Congress that any losses for the financial system would be no more than $50-150bn. They have currently reached $1.6trn and are expected to be at least double that ultimately.

The 'free marketers' were equally unable to see ahead. Robert Lucas, the President of the American Economic Association, the body representing all capitalist economists, told his audience in 2003, that *"the central problem of depression-prevention has been solved"* — in other words, economies could avoid any recessions from now on.

Indeed, the economic theory of 'free marketers' was that the capitalist economy would avoid crises as long as all the economic agents has perfect information about prices. The stock market was the best example of an efficient, perfectly informed market and so if it went on upwards, it showed that all was well with the capitalist world. No wonder, the chief of the big corporations and investment banks spent their time trying to get their stock price up rather than worrying about profitability.

Indeed, free marketers argued that capitalism would always grow in a steady and balanced way without crises as long as workers accept the rate for the job depending on the rate of growth in value — in other words, if capitalists get less profit, then workers should immediately accept less wages. If they don't then, they will lose their jobs. It is their 'voluntary' decision.

Monetarists like Ben Bernanke and the late Milton Friedman reckoned that capitalism would always avoid crises as long as central banks provide the right amount of money for demand in the economy. Too high interest rates and too little 'liquidity' could cause a crisis in production. The policy of low interest rates and bounteous amounts of liquidity had created the boom of 2002-07 without any risk.

The Austrian school of capitalist economics argued that you can have too much of this good thing: the build-up in credit would mean a bust and a sharp contraction later. In that sense, the small number of Austrian econo-mists was more aware of a possible economic slump. But, of course, their solution was for government spending to be slashed and for workers to take big cuts in wages. That was politically unacceptable.

The Keynesian school of economics had been on the wane before the Great Recession. The Keynesians had been dismissed as out of date as there was no possibility of a slump as long as capitalist markets were free of government interference and regulation, government spending was kept down and monetary policy was just right.

Such was the mantra of most capitalist governments including those of so-called socialist persuasion like New Labour in the UK. Gordon Brown told all who would listen that the cycle of booms and slumps had been broken and that balanced budgets and an independent central bank with a prudent monetary policy would do the trick. The Bank of England was freed from democratic accountability as the first economic act of the New Labour government in 1997. Keynes was dead, theoretically as well as literally. Brown went on to argue that such policies had made the UK 'best-placed' to deal with any ensuing recession that might arise unexpectedly. However, reality has proved to be a cruel corrector.

Between 1980 and 2007, IMF researchers found that there had been nearly 50 financial crises around the world, a greater figure than in the previous 30 years and that many of these had led to a collapse in production or a slump[1]. On average, the loss of output was as high as 18% from peak to bottom and most lasted around one year. Many capitalist countries had repeated crises. Of course, only a few led to general global economic recession — the main ones being 1980-2, 1991-2, 2001-2 and now 2008-9. So there have been four major world capitalist slumps in the last 25 years.

Since the Great Recession began, many capitalist economists have suddenly refound Keynes as their mentor. This British economist is famous for proposing capitalist solutions to crises: namely, low interest rates, massive liquidity and if necessary huge public spending to boost economic growth if the capitalist sector will not, even if that means big government deficits and just printing money for a while. It is this solution that the G20 government have now adopted. Government deficits are heading well above 10% of annual output in many countries and government debt is mounting up towards 100% of GDP.

Ironically, Keynesian economists were no better at predicting a slump than the 'free marketers' or 'monetarists. None raised their voices when the great housing and credit boom was in full swing. That is because Keynesians like the other schools of capitalist economics do not understand the nature of capitalism and its inherent tendency for crisis.

What is a capitalist crisis? It appears as a crisis of overproduction. Too many goods and services are produced compared to the demand for them. In any sane world, we cannot understand how you could ever produce too much given the pretty and deprivation in the world and even in the advanced capitalist economies. But that's the insanity of capitalism.

Production is for profit under capitalism and 'overproduction' is when production does not produce sufficient profit for capitalists to continue producing. That happens when the cost of investing in machinery and plant and labour and the cost of maintaining it becomes greater than the extra income 'earned' from producing things and services with that investment. Or at least the profit is not enough to invest in new capital and finance the high living standards of the capitalist class and its hangers on.

Why or when does profit fall to such a level? It is Marx's great insight to show that, as capitalists accumulate capital and appropriate the new value created by the labour they employ using the machinery that they own, there is a tendency for profitability to fall. Despite many ways in which capitalists try to avoid this inexorable tendency, it will exert itself and begin to drive down profitability.

Eventually a point is reached when the mass of profits generated by assets (labour and machinery) that the capitalists own and employ is not enough. Then capitalists reduce production, close businesses down, lay off labour and write off assets to reduce costs. The rise in unemployment and the reduction in wages mean that workers cannot buy as many goods and services, while businesses no longer buy so many goods and services from other capitalists. In short, there is overproduction relative to demand.

A capitalist crisis will not go on forever. Eventually, the costs of production can be reduced enough to create better profitability for those capitalist businesses still left. And with many going out of business, it leaves more of the market for the survivors. In effect, there is a big depreciation of costs relative to revenue and profits start rising again.

That is what is beginning to happen now. Profitability has bottomed after a very large fall. Recovery is the order of the day. Will this recovery be sustainable? The answer lies in the amount of the depreciation in capital values that capitalists have been able to achieve to restore profitability.

This has been a Great Recession. But even so, it still has not really restored profitability to levels that could sustain a long boom in capitalist production. That's because the size of accumulated capital relative to profits remains very high. That can be measured in two ways: first the size of industrial capacity (machinery and plant) relative to output. At the bottom of this slump, capacity utilisation was as low as 70%. In other words 30% of industrial capital is permanently idle and needs to be written off.

Second, there is still a huge overhang of fictitious capital (debt and loans) pressing down on the profitability of capitalist production. A major cause of the Great Recession was the buildup of cheap credit (debt) by the financial sector of capitalism during the 2000s. Much of this cheap credit was invested not in the production of goods and services but property, the stock market and all sorts of exotic debt instruments. When the property market went bust, it brought down the credit market and the financial sector globally with it.

But even though much of the value of the property market has been reduced (by 30% or more), the debt that financed it has not been paid down much. Banks have written off about $2-3trn out of debt assets of around $60trn globally, so less than 5%. They still hold trillions of debt that represent worthless assets. Before profitability can really be restored, much more of this fake value needs to be destroyed.

However, the reverse is happening. Governments are raising huge amounts of debt by issuing government bonds and central banks are printing trillions of paper money to provide funds for banks and other financial institutions to restore their balance sheets — at our expense. The result is that most of the debt that triggered the credit crisis remains — but now much is on the books of governments, not banks.

WILL THERE BE ANOTHER SLUMP?

Down the road this debt must be serviced. And it must be paid down if the cost of capital is not to rise too much to squeeze profitability. So profitability may recover a little now that economic recovery has started, but soon it will start to fall again. It will take another slump to reduce the cost of capital and reverse the squeeze on profits. That may be few years away — probably around 2014. And this slump may be so severe that it would make the Great Recession of 2008-09 look not so great after all.

1. *IMF,* The anatomy of banking crises *April 2008,*

A nasty Turner for the worse

Lord Adair Turner is head of the UK's Financial Services Authority, the body in charge of regulating the banks and other financial institutions. He is member of the 'great and good' of the British ruling class. He went to Cambridge and got a double first-class degree. He worked his way through the oil giant BP, the management consultants McKinsey, into Chase Manhattan Bank and then to the head of the bosses organisation, the Confederation of British Industry (CBI), before he became a director of the now taken-over mega investment bank, Merrill Lynch.

So he knows a thing or two about the global financial sector and the workings of the banking industry. He certainly partook of the grotesque megabonuses that bankers and financiers 'earned' during the Great Credit Boom of 2002-07.

Some weeks ago, he was interviewed by *Prospect* magazine, a small mouthpiece of the Blairite wing of New Labour. In that interview, Adair blurted out a telling truth about finance capital that its proponents did not want to hear. Adair said that *"many financial activities which had proliferated over the last ten years were 'socially useless'"*.

In this, he was ironically echoing the words of Stephen Green, the Chairman of the British Bankers Association, who had said more or less the same thing, that *"in recent years, banks have pursued short-term profit by introducing complex products of no real use to humanity"*!

The reaction to these comments from financiers has been apoplectic. As one guest at the Lord Mayor's Banquet remarked, when Turner reiterated his comments to the massed ranks of the City of London, "probably 60% of the people in this room would willingly shoot Turner over that speech".

One City leader commented on the *Prospect* interview that he was "appalled, disgusted, ashamed and hugely embarrassed that I should have lived to see someone who commands a senior and important position as head of the UK regulatory regime making such damaging and damning remarks".

And Turner went further in his populist attack on his own industry. He said the current credit crisis was *"cooked up in trading rooms, where not just a few, but many, people earned annual bonuses equal to a lifetime's earnings of some of those now suffering the consequences"*.

Adair defended his position by pointing out that financial services do not deliver anything that people can consume, they are just lubricants of a capitalist economy — the plumbing of a house if you like. In that sense, they add no value. But if the plumbing goes wrong, it is very damaging in its impact.

Turner described the damage: *"this was the worst crisis in 70 years — indeed it could have been the worst in the history of market capitalism. Real disaster – new Great Depression — was only averted by quite exceptional policy measures. Even so, major economic harm has occurred. Hundreds of thousands of British people are newly unemployed; tens of thousands have lost their houses to repossession; and British citizens will be burdened for many years with either higher taxes or cuts in public services because of an economic crisis"*.

Turner warned the bankers: *"We cannot go back to business as usual and accept the risk that a similar crisis occurs again in 10 or 20 years time. We need radical change"*.

Hold your horses! What did Turner mean? Is he advocating the end of the capitalist system or at least the full and democratic public ownership of the banks? No, the bankers could breathe a little. That was not what ex-banker Turner had in mind.

A NASTY TURNER FOR THE WORSE

He wants to increase the amounts of back-up capital that banks must have before they can lend or invest (although he did not say by how much); he wants banks to issue only 'socially useful' products (whatever they might be); and he wants bonuses to be controlled. So his radical change is no turner at all.

The irony is that many of the bankers' weird and exotic financial instruments that went wrong in the great credit crisis were regarded as very socially useful because they supposedly 'reduced risk' or 'hedged risk'. Bonuses, from which Turner himself benefited at Merrill Lynch, were designed to ensure better performance — and who is to say otherwise? As for bank capital, the best way to ensure that banks do the right things with our money is for us to own them outright and make them accountable to society.

Turner does not reject capitalism. He told the City bankers that *"Adam Smith's insight that good economic results can flow from the private pursuit of profit remains valid and vital."* But he cannot help blurting out that capitalism is inherently unstable: *"it involves rejecting an intellectually elegant, but also profoundly mistaken faith in ever perfect and self-equilibrating markets, ever rational human behaviours"*.

So there it is. Capitalism is a system for profit. But it does not work because it is not planned and it is not rational. Indeed, it is positively damaging to the majority of people. But there is no alternative, so let's see if we can regulate it better. Some hope!

Business as usual

So, it's business as usual, then, regardless of whether it makes most people howl at the moon with rage? Goldman Sachs, this pillar of the free market, breeder of super-citizens, object of envy and awe will go on raking it in, getting richer than God? An impish grin spreads across Blankfein's face. Call him a fat cat who mocks the public. Call him wicked. Call him what you will. He is, he says, just a banker "doing God's work." Interview with Lloyd Blankfein, CEO of Goldman Sachs, Sunday Times, 8 November 2009

October 2009

The big banks in the US and Europe have been announcing mega results for the third quarter of this year. The banks are once again making money. Sure, they are still having to write off losses on the so-called 'toxic' assets they held, namely the mortgage-backed securities that have defaulting mortgages behind them, or the increasing amounts of defaulting commercial and residential real estate and consumer loans that they face as the Great Recession bites on households and small businesses. But now they are able once again to make profits to cover these losses.

This is not because the banks are making money on loans to industry or individuals. On the contrary, banks are continuing to cut back on lending there. Anyway, most large companies do not want to borrow and run up more debt. Instead, they have stopped investing in new plant and technology and have cut back staff to build up cash balances and pay down existing debt. It's only the minnows of industry, the small wholesalers and shopkeepers, the tiny engineering and other service companies that need to borrow to survive and are finding it impossible to get loans from the big banks on reasonable terms.

So how are the banks making money? It's a combination of two things. First, they are able to obtain very cheap money. The central banks of the world: the Federal Reserve, the European Central Bank, the Bank of

BUSINESS AS USUAL

England, the Bank of Japan and others have cut the interest rates they charge the banks for borrowing to virtually zero.

At the same time, they have launched massive programmes by purchasing the 'toxic' assets of the banks in return for cash. These programmes of what is called 'quantitative easing' have stuffed the bank's balance sheets with cash. This cash is just printed up by the central banks.

So the big banks have become flush with free money. What have they done with it? They have bought government bonds first — something for which governments are grateful as they are running huge budget deficits that are financed by new borrowing, mainly in the form of new bonds. These bonds yield 3-4% a year and have been paid for by the free cash given to the banks for their 'dud' assets by the central banks and their governments (ie the taxpayers). This is a perfect circle of financial trickery.

But the banks have also started to buy stocks and shares everywhere, as well as other so-called 'risk assets' like various commodities (oil, copper, wheat, gold etc) and emerging market debt. The prices of these have rocketed upwards — the equity rally that began last March has now driven up stock market indexes by 60%! This adds to the wealth of the banks in their balance sheets.

So the banks have not returned to their traditional role of taking in deposits from workers and businesses, borrowing a bit from each other, and then lending the money, as a multiple, back to businesses and households who need the loans. Instead, they have become giant hedge funds, betting taxpayers money on a rise in the stock market, government debt and commodity markets.

In that sense, it is 'business as usual'. The banks have resumed the role that they had adopted at the start of the credit crisis in 2007 — betting on the prices of financial assets financed through borrowing. So far, it's working because governments are financing it all for virtually nothing.

Governments have done this for two reasons. First, if they had not 'bailed out' the banks, then the banking systems of the US, the UK and Europe would have collapsed and credit would have dried up. It is debatable whether that would have meant the end of the world 'as we know it' and engendered a new Great Depression, but certainly that was the fear.

Consequently, the big banks were given billions, either in the form of the purchase of equity capital (shares in the bank), or through the purchase of the bad assets on the banks' books or through guaranteeing the debt that the banks issued to raise money. Overall, governments and central banks provided the equivalent of $11trn to the banks through these methods, or 20% of the world's annual output.

The other reason that governments gave the banks this financial support is that, above all, they did not want to take them into public ownership. Sure, even the US government has had to take a share of ownership in several banks. But it was very reluctant to do so and tried to avoid it up until the last moment. The sheer anger of the electorate made them realise that they had to do it. However, at the first possible opportunity, these pro-capitalist governments, especially the 'centre-left' governments of Britain and America, want to return the taxpayers' shares to the private sector. They are very happy to go on lending huge amounts to the banks, but they don't want to own them.

This approach matches their previous policy of 'light touch' regulation during the great credit boom before it went bust. Governments of centre-left or centre-right hues were very keen to let the likes of Goldman Sachs, Merrill Lynch, Morgan Stanley, Bear Stearns, Lehman's, HBoS and RBS take huge risks on betting on the housing market and buying up trillions of dollars of so-called asset-backed-securities with no little or no attempt to 'regulate' the risk. It was 'light touch' before the crisis and now the financial crisis has subsided, it will be business as usual.

It's certainly business as usual for the top bankers' bonuses. With several top banks gone bust or taken over, the survivors have now increased their market share and are able to rack up bigger profits. Goldman Sachs is the world's top investment bank, namely it does not lend money to the likes of you or me; it uses its funds and the funds of other institutions to invest in stocks and shares, bonds and other financial assets and make bets on these markets going up or down.

In the just reported third quarter of 2009, GS made $3bn profit out of $12bn in revenues collected. It has repaid the money it borrowed directly from the government ($10bn), with interest. But it used that money and more to take advantage of financial markets where others had gone bust.

What is not realised is that GS, just like the other banks, did this with taxpayer help. They were able to borrow $28bn guaranteed for any losses by the government. Also, when the world's largest insurance company, AIG, went bankrupt, they owed, among others, Goldman Sachs about $13trn. Normally, creditors are lucky to get any money back if a company goes back. But GS got paid back in full with government funds. The US government was so worried that AIG's collapse would bring down the whole pack of cards; it bailed out all the creditors to the tune of $120bn.

But the US government was not worried about 'systemic risk' with the smaller banks. Apart from Lehman's Brothers, none of the big banks were allowed to fail: they were taken over, sometimes in 'forced mergers' as with Bank America and Merrill Lynch or Lloyds Bank and HBoS in the UK. In contrast, hundreds of small banks, often financing the business of local communities have been liquidated. To date, 106 such banks in the US have gone to the wall. There's one law for the big and one for the small.

And that is not so surprising when you notice that the heads of the big banks are so closely connected to the heads of the government. In the US, the Treasury Secretary Timothy Geithner used to work for Goldmans and so did White House economics supremo, Larry Summers. Under Bush, former Treasury Secretary Hank Paulson, who arranged the AIG bailout for GS and the decision to buy $700bn of 'toxic' assets from the banks, used to be the head of Goldman Sachs.

Overall, GS has got free money worth around $70bn in the last year. It has paid back about $20bn of that. But in the meantime, it has been able to make over $30bn in profit! What is GS doing with those profits? It is paying its bankers and directors around 50% in straight bonuses. This year, GS employees will get about $16bn in bonuses on top of their salaries — at a time when a record number of Americans (32m) are on food stamps, unemployment of various sorts has reached 16% of the workforce and people are losing their homes.

Of course, the bonuses won't be shared out equally: some will get more than others — indeed, some traders will pocket over $25m in one swoop. But that is the essence of Goldman's philosophy, at least according to its vice chairman of the international board, Lord Brian Griffiths of Fforestfach. As the good life peer of the British House of Lords and a practising evangelical Christian, recently put it: "we have to tolerate inequality as a way to achieve greater prosperity and opportunity for all".

Inequality is apparently necessary during this crisis to restore prosperity across the board. It is not just the bankers who need more to make capitalism work. The heads of the top 100 British companies saw their bonuses cut by one-third in 2009 to an average of just £502,000. But they still got an inflation-busting 7.4% hike in their basic pay to an average of £820,000. Even though their efforts saw their companies produce 20% less profit, these chief executives managed to increase their salaries twice as fast as their shop floor employees in this Great Recession.

The Christian Lord , who is also author of a book entitled *Morality and the Marketplace*, did recognise the moral obligation that taxpayer-financed GS directors had to the world: "To whom much is given, much is expected and there is a sense that if you make money, you are expected to give". This call for charitable works by GS has been well expressed in GS funding of top private schools in America and in purchasing VIP tables at $22,000 each for the Formula One motor racing after-race parties. Truly a wonderful philanthropic gesture.

The good Lord was backed up by British Royalty. The grand old Duke of York, Prince Andrew, the Queen of England's younger son, complained in an interview that he did "not want to demonise the banking and financial sector. After all, bonuses, in the scheme of things, are minute. They are easy to target. A number will have abused their privilege of a bonus, so get rid of the excesses, but don't throw the baby out with the bath water."

The good prince will be pleased to hear that there is no intention on the part of politicians of any bankers' babies being thrown out. There is much blather about ending the 'bonus culture' and 'reining in the banks'. But it will come to nothing. The British New Labour government is sitting on its hands. It does not want to nationalise banks that have all this taxpayer largesse and it does not want to 'damage' the great contributions that the City of London makes to budget revenues and to exports with too 'heavy regulation'. After all, the UK is now a *rentier* capitalist economy that makes more or less nothing useful and increasingly lives parasitically off the investment and accumulation of funds deposited it with it by other capitalist producer economies.

The British Conservative opposition party, which is likely to gain power after next May's general election, and then introduce swingeing cuts in public services to pay for the bankers' bonuses, has proposed that the bonuses of high street banks that are supposed to lend to ordinary people should pay most of the bonus in shares, not cash. This measure would not apply to Goldman Sachs and those who have made the most profit, because they don't lend money for business or homes; they just invest and speculate.

The Obama administration is proposing to 'regulate' those banks like GS that are "too big to fail" — namely a bank that if it went bust would bring down the others. The White House plan is to get these banks to hold more cash in reserve and reduce the amount of leverage (borrowing) they can do in order to speculate. But that's it.

Some have proposed, like Mervyn King at the Bank of England, that some banks should be broken up between those that just make investments (like Goldman Sachs) and those that lend money (like Citicorp or Barclays) — you cannot do both, he argues. But that will just make the former richer at the expense of the latter. And anyway, governments have no intention of stopping the banks doing what they want.

There is an obvious solution. Bring them all into public ownership and make them democratically accountable to the elected institutions with a measure of control for the workers in them. Then the top bankers and their bonuses can be reined in; then the risk of excessive borrowing and speculation can be stopped; then banks can be made to lend money to the small businesses and individuals who desperately need it. It seems an obvious solution — does it not? But that would not be business as usual.

What next?

As I write, the Great Recession seems to have bottomed and economic recovery is under way. Several of the mature capitalist economies have recorded rises in national output in the third quarter of 2009, while most the largest less-developed capitalist economies, like China, India or Brazil are already increasing their growth rates.

The Great Recession was aptly called because the contraction in world output had never been as much since the Great Depression years of 1930-2. But the Great Recession is closer to the simultaneous economic slump of 1974-5, which was also steep and confirmed the downward trajectory of profitability in the advanced capitalist economies that had begun in 1965 and had already bred a mild economic recession in 1969-70, just as the downward phase of the profit cycle that began in 1997 led to the mild recession of 2001.

We are now in a downward phase of the profit cycle that should last at least until around 2014. The latest figures for the US rate of profit confirm that process. After the peak of 1997, the rate of profit fell to 2001, before recovering as a result of the recession then to rise up to 2005, although still below the peak of 1997. After 2005, US profitability began to fall, culminating in the fall in the mass of profit itself and a drop in the available surplus-value going to the capitalist class for consumption. That provoked a strike of capital in investment and the start of the Great Recession at the beginning of 2008.

The depth and length of the Great Recession was also the result of the massive expansion of fictitious capital in the form of credit (bank loans, corporate debt and above all, new forms of credit in derivatives, or options to bet on debt prices)[1]. As soon as the rate of profit peaked in 1997 and began to fall, the growth in these new forms of credit accelerated. As Marx has explained, once capitalists feel the pressure of falling profitability, they look to delay the impact on profits by extending credit. As the return on investment in production of things and the creation of real values begins to slide, capitalists turn to other investments outside of the accumulation process — in this case, speculation in asset-backed debt securities, the real estate market and of course, the stock market.

From 2002 to 2007, the stock market rocketed upwards, trying to get back to its peak in 2000, after the bursting of the internet bubble had led to a huge fall. At the same time, real estate prices shot up at unheard of rates, driven by the cheap credit made available by finance capital hungry for high returns. These returns were spread around the financial sector through the new forms of credit. The capitalists, particularly finance capital, appeared to have never had it so good. They all danced to the party that seemed to go on forever.

But of course, nothing lasts forever and this profit boom was an illusion because profitability began to fall again from 2005. As it did, the boost to fictitious capital became even more frenzied, until the whole Ponzi scheme

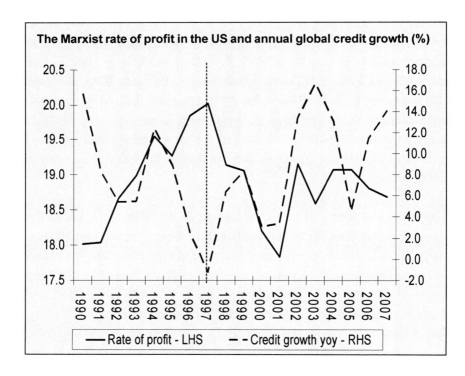

The Marxist rate of profit in the US and annual global credit growth (%)

burst in mid-2007. We know the story from there, as this book has tried to describe.

The downward phase of profitability will continue to determine the health of the capitalist system. It is not over. As we have argued in this book, phases of the profit cycle (and the closely connected stock cycle) last around 16-18 years. So the bottom of profitability will not be reached until about 2014-15 and the bear market in stocks a little later.

There is still some way to go before the bottom is reached, even if there is a short recovery in profitability over the next few years. This period is the 'winter' phase of the Kondratiev cycle of capitalist production, which is where the rate of profit falls and the prices of production do not rise very much or even fall. Such an era spells depression, weak economic growth, low or falling prices and high unemployment.

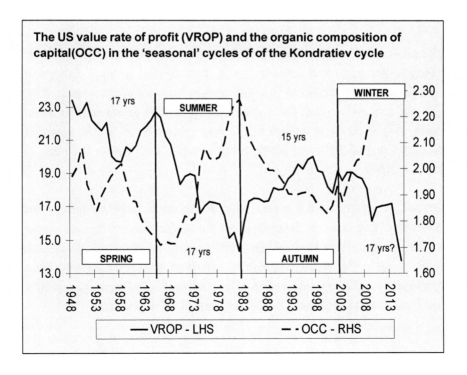

The US value rate of profit (VROP) and the organic composition of capital(OCC) in the 'seasonal' cycles of of the Kondratiev cycle

WHAT NEXT?

The last winter phase was in the Great Depression years of 1929-46. Then it took two large and deep recessions in 1930-2 and 1937-8 and finally a world war to drive down the costs of capital (both constant and variable) to create a more sustainable rising phase for profitability.

The previous winter phase before that was in the period 1866-84, which culminated in a deep slump in the mid-1980s and almost a decade of depression afterwards, before profitability and economic growth could be sustained and capitalism and the Kondratiev cycle moved into its spring 'recovery' period.

If the period we are now going through has been correctly identified, it tells you that capitalism has another large recession ahead, probably in 2014 or so, and unless that does the job in restoring profitability by the sufficient write-off of 'excess capital', both fictitious and real, then capitalism will stay in depression. Of course, a world war would do the job more quickly and more effectively, as in 1940-46, but that is just too terrible to contemplate!

The pro-capitalist governments of the major economies are desperately trying to get economic recovery going by pumping in huge dollops of credit and taxpayer cash to help the banks and restart investment. This will not succeed, except for a very short period of no more than a few years, if that. Excess capital in the major economies is still hovering around a record 30% and profitability remains well below the peak of 1997 or 2005.

Instead, governments are engendering a new credit bubble based on the issuance of public sector debt to replace the contraction in fictitious capital in the private sector through the fall in house prices, bank assets and stock prices. The result will not be sustained economic growth, but a brief burst in inflation, rising costs of borrowing that will squeeze capitalist investment and then a new bout of stagnation of depression.

The ultimate truth of capitalism is that profits are its life blood. If profits from the accumulation of capital do not return, capitalists will not invest and will not produce. Profits can only come from the activity of a labour force, using technology to produce things and services. Speculation on the stock market and government handouts cannot replace that. Production is not for need and is not planned. It depends on profit appropriated by capitalists from labour's efforts and realised in a competitive, anarchic struggle in markets. Without sustained and rising profitability, there will be no new prosperity.

1. See David Roche and Bob McKee, New Monetarism, *2007*

Measuring the rate of profit

The Marxist definition of total value is constant capital (c) consumed in production in, say one year, plus new value created, divided between variable capital (v) and surplus value (s). That's c+v+s.

In bourgeois economic accounting, gross domestic product (GDP) is the gross value added by each industry in the economy. Raw materials are included in the raw materials industries. The statisticians measure gross sales in the various sectors of the economy and deduct inputs (raw materials) to reach GDP. So, when aggregated, only the final output net of inputs is recorded as GDP. If GDP were to include all the inputs at each stage of production, it would be many times larger.

So total output, or total value added, can be measured as final output from all businesses less intermediate inputs going into the production process. This is achieved by considering how each business or enterprise adds value to the inputs it receives, so that the output of the business is measured in terms of the value added by means of its production activities.

For a single enterprise, value added by production activity is measured as gross output less inputs from other businesses less inputs from abroad. Summing up the value added by all enterprises, the domestic intermediate transactions between businesses cancel out. For the total economy, value added from the production side is measured as gross output less inputs from abroad (imports).

One firm's input is another's output, so the input-output matrix solves the problem of double-counting. Of course, there are stocks of raw materials built up before and after the production process. The statisticians cover these changes in inventories in their measure of GDP. But these are relatively small. So the problem of deducting circulating capital or raw materials does not really arise.

MEASURING THE RATE OF PROFIT

Net value added then accounts for the consumption of fixed capital in the production process. Net value added gives us new value created in Marxist terms, or v+s. We can then find surplus value by deducting employee compensation (v) from net value added.

In my view, it is correct in calculating the overall rate of profit in the economy to include all employee compensation including that of unproductive workers. Unproductive sectors may not add to new value, but they do enter into the average rate of profit for the economy and so must be included.

The productive sectors create the new value which gets transferred to the unproductive sectors, so the rate of profit for the economy as a whole is thus averaged. So employee compensation for public sector and other unproductive layers should be included in variable capital.

We can get constant capital (c) from net fixed assets (fixed assets net of depreciation). If we deduct circulating capital consumed from GDP, we must deduct the value of wear and tear and obsolesence (depreciation) of fixed assets too.

I think it is correct to use replacement cost to value fixed assets. The rate of profit should be based on the cost of constant capital facing the capitalist at every new moment of production. Using historic cost would offer a lower cost that would not be realistic at each production moment. Yes, that means prices would have boosted the fixed asset figure each year, but that applies to GDP and employee compensation as well. I think Marx would agree.

The fixed asset figure must exclude non-capitalist sectors, because the rate of profit is only relevant to capitalists engaged in production and accumulation of capital. It is not relevant to include the fixed assets owned by government or to include residential assets (houses and flats) in any figure for capitalist accumulation. Government employee compensation should be in varibale capital, but government fixed assets are not in constant capital. Similarly, the real estate sector enters into the distribution of overall profit and the profit rate in the economy, but people's homes are not part of constant capital for capitalist accumulation.

I would, however, include financial sector fixed assets as part of constant capital (some don't) as the sector does add to the process of capitalist production, unlike residential real estate investment. As Marx says, the circulation part of capital is part of the reproduction and accumulation of capital. Within the capitalist sector, however, there are unproductive workers or sectors. But I don't think you should exclude these as part of the cost of variable and constant capital.

In conclusion, constant capital is net private non-residential fixed assets in replacement cost; variable capital is all-economy employee compensation. Total value is the net domestic product (GDP less depreciation). Surplus-value is the difference between net domestic product and employee compensation. Using these concepts, we can get data for the US economy for these categories. The US Bureau of Economic Analysis provides time series going back to 1929 as follows. Net value added: Table 1.9.5 Net value added by sector; Employee compensation: Table 6.2 A-D; Net fixed assets, private non-residential: Fixed asset table 4.1. (This series deduct depreciation but probably not as capitalists actually do, namely with 'moral depreciation' (writing off plant and equipment before their physical life is exhausted, but I don't think this is decisive for the overall trend results).

In a paper released just as this draft was being completed, Andrew Kliman[1,] made a thorough analysis of the US rate of profit from 1929 up to 2005. In it he argued that there has not been any significant rise in the rate of profit from 1982 and it would be more accurate to describe the whole post-war period as one where there has been a 'persistent' fall in the rate.

His measures differ from mine. First, he uses only the corporate sector for his rate of profit and so excludes the government sector and the non-corporate sector. This removes the bulk of variable capital that the whole capitalist system must pay for. I cannot see that this will provide an aggregated measure of the rate of profit in a capitalist economy. But then Kliman reckons it is foolish to try and develop 'a Marxist rate of profit' because there is no one agreed way of doing so. So he uses different measures for the rate of profit according to different purposes.

Second, he uses historic cost measures for the net stock of fixed assets and not replacement costs. Kliman argues that using replacement costs would be wrong as it only accounts for inflation of fixed assets and not for the whole economy and thus exaggerates the rise in the rate of profit when inflation is low and falling by reducing the rise in fixed assets and vice versa. If you want to build in the impact of rising prices at each stage of production, you need a monetary measure of labour values, not capitalist market price measures, says Kliman. He prefers to use historic costs as a result. Kliman does develop a such monetary expression of fixed assets, but shows that the results are little different from historic cost measures.

In contrast, in a recent paper[2] Alan Freeman measures the rate of profit in a similar way to me. He uses current prices measures of the net stock of private fixed assets, as I do, rather than historic prices, to show how the rate of profit moves. Fred Moseley has argued that Marx would have used replacement costs to measure constant capital[3]. In a careful reading of Marx's comments on the issue, he shows that Marx assumed constant capital was determined by the 'current reproduction costs' of the means of production. Moreover, this does not mean that there is a simultaneous determination of input and output prices as the neo-Ricardian theory claims. Constant capital is still a given monetary amount in the process of accumulation: it is just that its value will have changed from the previous period of accumulation.

But does using historic costs make much difference to the trends in a Marxist measure of the US rate of profit? See the graph below. It shows pretty much the same trend in either measure. The golden age period peaks in 1965 in both cases and troughs in 1982 in both cases. Again both measures peak in 1997 and then recover before peaking again in 2005 at a lower level than in 1997. And both show a secular fall in the rate since 1944. It's true that the replacement cost measure does exaggerate both the decline after 1965 and the rise after 1982. But in my view, it does not make a decisive difference to the conclusions.

Kliman also argues that the BEA NIPA figures for depreciation do not properly account for moral depreciation. He makes an adjustment to the NIPA data for the period after 1982 when the great hi-tech computer software revolution began. In adding in more depreciation due to the moral force of competition, Kliman argues that this will reduce the rise in the rate of profit after 1982. But this argument depends on accepting that moral depreciation first cuts profits and only later raises the rate of profit when firms write off assets. So I'm not sure it makes much difference to the overall results after 1982 and certainly becomes less relevant over several cycles of profitability.

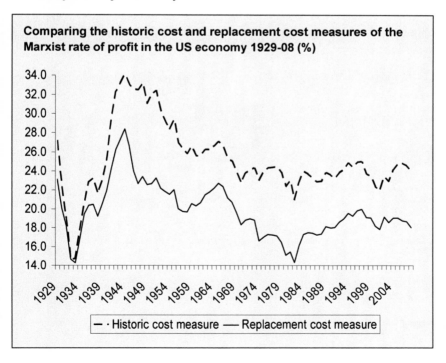

Comparing the historic cost and replacement cost measures of the Marxist rate of profit in the US economy 1929-08 (%)

MEASURING THE RATE OF PROFIT

Sticking to my methodology, the very latest data confirm my conclusions made over three years ago, namely that the rate of profit has moved in a 'cycle' of about 32-34 years from trough to trough, with an upward and downward phase. We are currently in a downward phase that began in 1997.

The main driver of the rate of profit is the organic composition of capital (OCC), vindicating Marx. This is inversely correlated with the rate of profit at about two-thirds for the period 1948-07. There is also a clear downward trend line in the rate of profit since 1948. This secular decline over and above the cyclical movement is probably due to the growth of unproductive sectors in the capitalist economy.

1. Andrew Kliman, The persistent fall in the rate of profit underlying the current crisis, *October 2009.*
2. Alan Freeman, What makes the US rate of profit fall, *MRPA paper 14147, March 2009.*
3. Fred Moseley, The determination of constant capital in the case of a change in the value of the means of production, *October 2005.*

Accumulation, the mass of profit and capitalist consumption

The Marxist definition of total value is constant capital (c) consumed in production in, say one year, plus new value created, divided between variable capital (v) and surplus value (s). That's c+v+s.

In bourgeois economic accounting, gross domestic product (GDP) is the gross value added by each industry in the economy, so raw materials are included in the raw materials industries. The GDP statisticians take firms and industries, calculate their gross sales and deduct inputs (raw materials). When aggregated, only the final output net of inputs is recorded as GDP. If gross output were to include all the inputs at each stage of production, it would be many times larger.

Total value is thus the gross domestic product less the loss of value from wear and tear and obsolesence in the means of production over the period of production (depreciation). Thus total value will be net domestic product. Deducting the cost of employing the labour force (employee compensation) from net product gives you the surplus value created in production by labour and appropriated by the owners of the means of prioduction, the capitalists.

Marx's law of profitability reveals that, as capital is accumulated and new value is created by the labour force, the return on capital invested will start to decline over time. But the mass of profit can still rise even though the rate of profit is falling. Indeed, that will be the case for a long period of time, until finally, the inexorable downward pressure on profitability drives down the mass of profit. That is the signal for capitalist crisis.

Such a crisis could come even earlier if the pressure on the mass of profit is such that it starts to squeeze the share of surplus value that is siphoned off for capitalist consumption[1]. Capitalists cannot live on air — on the contrary, they wish to improve their living standards. But if the mass of profit does not grow sufficiently to provide enough both to sustain the existing level of investment in new production and enough for improving prosperity for capitalists, a crisis can be triggered. Capitalists will reduce investment to sustain living standards and thus cause a reduction in economic growth.

In the example below, the capitalist economy starts off with constant capital (C) of 200, variable capital (V) of 100. We assume that the rate of surplus value on the capitalist investment in variable capital of 50%, or 50. So the total value (TV) created in the first year of production would be 350.

Assuming that the rate of accumulation of constant capital (ac) is 8% a year and for variable capital (av), it is half that rate at 4% a year; then constant capital will rise 16 in Y-2 to reach 216; variable capital will rise 4 to reach 104, generating 52 in surplus value to take total value to 372. Out of the 52 in surplus value, given our accumulation assumptions, capitalists can take out 31 for consumption in Y-2.

Surplus value can thus be broken down into k+ac+av. The rate of profit (ROP) is thus k+ac+av divided by C+V. The rate of profit falls from 16.7 in Y-1 to 16.3 in Y-2. But the the mass of profit or surplus value has risen from 50 in Y-1 to 52 in Y-2 and capitalist consumption has also risen from 26 in Y-1 to 31 in Y-2.

But as the process of accumulation proceeds over several years, the rate of profit continues to fall because the organic composition of capital (C/V) rises. Eventually, capitalist consumption (k) stops rising in Y-12. That is the moment of crisis. If capitalist living standards are to be preserved, the rate of accumulation must be reduced and investment must be cut back and workers sacked. If accumulation were to continue, eventually capitalists would have to live on air by Y-29!

In chapter X on the mass of profit, this process is applied to the US economy using the actual data for the economy and projected to 2016. It

ACCUMULATION AND CAPITALIST CONSUMPTION

Accumulation, mass of profit and capitalist consumption

	C	V	k	ac	av	TV	ROP
Y-1	200	100	26	20	4	350	16.7
Y-2	216	104	31	17	4	372	16.3
Y-3	233	108	31	19	4	396	15.8
Y-4	252	112	32	20	4	421	15.4
Y-5	272	117	32	22	5	448	15.0
Y-6	294	122	32	24	5	476	14.6
Y-7	317	127	33	25	5	507	14.3
Y-8	343	132	33	27	5	540	13.9
Y-9	370	137	33	30	5	575	13.5
Y-10	400	142	33	32	6	613	13.1
Y-11	432	148	34	35	6	654	12.8
Y-12	**466**	**154**	**34**	**37**	**6**	**697**	**12.4**
Y-13	504	160	33	40	6	744	12.1
Y-14	544	167	33	44	7	794	11.7
Y-15	587	173	33	47	7	847	11.4
Y-16	634	180	32	51	7	905	11.1
Y-17	685	187	31	55	7	966	10.7
Y-18	740	195	30	59	8	1032	10.4
Y-19	799	203	29	64	8	1103	10.1
Y-20	863	211	28	69	8	1179	9.8
Y-21	932	219	26	75	9	1261	9.5
Y-22	1007	228	24	81	9	1349	9.2
Y-23	1087	237	22	87	9	1443	8.9
Y-24	1174	246	19	94	10	1544	8.7
Y-25	1268	256	16	101	10	1653	8.4
Y-26	1370	267	13	110	11	1770	8.1
Y-27	1479	277	9	118	11	1895	7.9
Y-28	1598	288	5	128	12	2030	7.6
Y-29	1725	300	0	138	12	2175	7.4

shows how capitalist consumption slumped in 2009 and will do so again in 2014 or so.

1. The whole of the following argument was first developed by Henryk Grossman in his book, The law of accumulation and the breakdown of the capitalist system, being also a theory of crises, *1929. Grossman seems to develop this argument to try and prove that there will be a final breakdown of the capitalist system, although once he has included the 'countervailing influences' on the rate of profit, he comes up with a more cyclical interpretation of the accumulation process.*

Bibliography

AEA readings in business cycles, 1965

George Akerloff and Robert Shiller, *Animal spirits*, 2009

Michael Alexander, *Stock cycles,* 2000.

Michael Alexander, *The Kondratiev cycle*, 2002

Robert C Allen, *The British industrial revolution in global perspective*, 2009

Philip Ball, *Critical mass*, 2004

Brian Berry, *Long-wave rhythms is economic development abd political behavior*, 1991

Roger Bootle, *The death of inflation*, 1996

Mick Brooks, *The Marxist theory of crisis*, 2007, www.socialist.net
          What is financialisation?, 2009, www.socialist.net

Mark Buchanan, *Ubiquity*, 2000

Nicolai Bukharin, *Imperialism and the accumulation of capital,* 1972

Alex Callinicos, *Imperialism and global political economy*, 2009

George Cooper, *The origin of financial crises*, 2008

Stephen Cullenberg, *The falling rate of profit*, 1994

Richard Day, *Crisis and crash*: Soviet Studies of the West, 1917-39, 1986

Ben Fine, *The value dimension*, 1986

Alan Freeman and Ernest Mandel, *Ricardo, Marx, Sraffa*, 1984

Jeffrey Frieden, *Global capitalism*, 2006

JK Galbraith, *A short history of financial euphoria*, 1993

Dan Gardner, *Risk*, 2008

Andrew Glyn, *Capitalism unleashed*, 2006

Henryk Grossman, *The law of accumulation and breakdown of the capitalist system*, 1929

David Hackett-Fisher, *The Great Wave*, 1996.

Chris Harman, *Zombie Capitalism*, July 2009

John Harris, *The big slump*, 1967

Historical Materialism, No 4, Summer 1999

David Horowitz, *Marx and Modern economics*, 1968

John Maynard Keynes, *The general theory of employment, interest and money*, 1936

Charles Kindleberger, *Manias, panics and crashes — a history of financial crashes*, 2000

Andrew Kliman, *Reclaiming Marx's Capital*, 2007

Rick Kuhn, *Henryk Grossman and the recovery of Marxism*, 2007

Rosa Luxembourg, *The accumulation of capital*, 1972

Charles Mackay, *Extraordinary popular delusions and the madness of crowds*, 1995

Angus Maddison, *Dynamic forces in capitalist development*, 1991

Ernest Mandel, *Late capitalism*, 1972

Ernest Mandel, *Long waves of capitalist development*, 1980

Michael Mandel, *The coming internet depression*, 2000

Michael Marshall, *Long waves of regional development*, 1987

Paul Mattick, *The economics and politics and the age of inflation*, 1978

Paul Mattick, *Economic crisis and crisis theory*, 1981

K Marx and F Engels, *Letters on Capital*, 1983

K Marx, *Capital: Volumes I, II,III*, 1967

Marx and Engels, *Selected Correspondence*

K Marx, *Theories of Surplus Value, I,II,III*

K Marx, *Grundrisse*

Thomas McCraw, *Prophet of innovation*, 2007

David McNally, *Against the market*, 1993

Ronald Meek, *Studies in the labour theory of value*, 1956
Economics and Ideology, 1967

Branko Milanovic, *Worlds apart*, 2005

Hyman Minsky, in Kindleberger and Laffargue, editors: <u>Financial Crises:</u> *The financial-instability hypothesis: capitalist processes and the behaviour of the economy, 1982*
    Stabilizing and unstable economy, 1986

J Michie and J Grieve Smith, *Global instability,* 1999

Charles Morris, *The trillion dollar meltdown*, 2008

Randall E Parker, *The economics of the Great Depression*, 2007

Michael Perelman, *The natural instability of markets*, 1999

C Reinhart and KS Rogoff, *This time is different*, 2009

Barry Ritholtz, *Bailout nation*, 2009

David Roche and Bob McKee, *New Monetarism*, 2007

Robert Shiller, *Irrational exuberance*, 2000
        The subprime solution, 2008

Robert Skidelsky, *John Maynard Keynes*, 2004

Andrew Smithers and Stephen Wright, *Valuing Wall street: protecting wealth in turbulent markets* McGraw-Hill, 2000

George Soros, *The credit crisis of 2008*, 2008

Hernando de Soto, *The mystery of capital,* Bantam Press, 2000

Stuart Sutherland, *Irrationality*, 1992

Nassim Taleb, *The Black Swan*, 2007

James Tobin, <u>Journal of Money Credit and Banking</u>, Vol 1No 1 pp 15-29. (1969) *A general equilibrium approach to monetary theory*

Graham Turner, *The credit crunch*, 2009
    No way to run an economy, 2009

Andrew Tylecote, *The long wave in the world economy*, 1993

<u>Verso</u>, *The Value controversy*, 1981

John Weeks, *Capital and exploitation*, 1981

David Yaffe, *The Marxian theory of crisis, capital and the state*, <u>Economics and Society</u>, 1972

INDEX

Lightning Source UK Ltd.
Milton Keynes UK
UKOW05f0720170614

233572UK00001B/95/P